The American Minority Community

The American Minority Community

Judith R. Kramer

BROOKLYN COLLEGE

Thomas Y. Crowell Company

NEW YORK / Established 1834

Acknowledgment is gratefully made to The Macmillan Company for use of selections from Herbert J. Gans, *The Urban Villagers* (New York: Free Press, 1962). © The Free Press of Glencoe, A Division of The Macmillan Company. Reprinted with permission of The Macmillan Company.

L. C. Card 76–101948

Manufactured in the United States of America

IN MEMORY OF MY MOTHER

Keeper of the Dream

Preface

Many books have been written about minorities in American society. Most of them incorporate the perspective of the dominant group, dwelling upon its prejudice and discrimination as if the source of the minority problem were somehow more significant than its consequence. Such analyses implicitly, if unwittingly, enhance the power of the dominant group by rendering the minority group almost as irrelevant sociologically as it is treated socially. If there is any justification for still another work on the subject, it lies in the espousal of the point of view of the minorities themselves.

This book purports to explore the social and psychological consequences of the minority situation, a situation that is premised on coercion. In so doing, it starts where others leave off, concentrating on the meaning of minority membership. Members of minority groups have no choice about the status that is imposed upon them. How they cope (or fail to cope) with their categorization in the larger society is the focus of our attention here. Their structural adaptations will be examined in the context of their respective communities.

Excluded from full participation in dominant institutions, minorities are always at a disadvantage. And there is always the potential for conflict inherent in their relative powerlessness. They accept the rules of the game —and the goals—but they are rarely given a chance to play, let alone to win. Yet they continue to live, and perhaps to hope, while lacking many of the opportunities most members of the dominant group take for granted. Within their own communities, minorities, more or less effectively, come to terms with the deprivation and derogation they must endure.

Their accommodation is perforce a costly one, but one that permits them to retain the sense of humanity denied them in the larger society. We will explore the conditions of community for the major minority groups in the United States, the nature of their social organization and institutional resources, and the changing consequences for their communal structure. In effect, our interest will be in how minorities live with their situation—and what they do about it.

As is surely fitting for a book on the minority community, it became at some point a project of the primary group. Like the medical student who manifests the symptoms of all the diseases he studies, I experienced, in writing of minorities, everything each group endured. When I grew tired and discouraged, family and friends pitched in to expedite the process with moral support and material assistance. Without their help, there might not have been a manuscript. My thanks to them is no matter of mere sentiment.

My father, Stanley J. Kramer, called at regular intervals to check on my progress, not quite certain of what I was writing, but always certain that, whatever it was, I could do it. And perhaps for that reason, I could. Still, the time came when I couldn't stand the sight of another page. Then one sister, Barbara K. August, would grant long-distance permission to take time off from writing, while regaling me with tales of her growing children.

The other sister, Bernice K. Leader, took over the typing, reading the fine print for the intelligibility of its points. I am as indebted to her keen eye as to her quick hand, for it was her insistence on clarification that prodded me to restate when necessary. There was also that thankless task of telling me what only a best friend can—if only she will. I was fortunate to have Suzanne F. Fogelson tell me in no uncertain terms when a chapter wouldn't pass muster, risking my wrath, but not my ingratitude.

In addition I would like to thank my sociological friends for their consistently sympathetic encouragement. Mirra Komarovsky explained hopefully that some writing was necessarily a misery. And when sometimes it was more a misery than others, Celia S. Heller struggled valiantly to cheer me. On occasion I was able to discuss an idea with Lawrence A. Gooberman, who offered unfailingly constructive response—and equally effective conversational distraction.

Melvin M. Tumin has unknowingly served as a sociological sounding board. He has written much about minorities, all of which I have respected and with some of which I have disagreed. Here and there I have tried to answer his arguments as my appreciation of his work. My thanks also go to Thomas Simpson for his editorial services.

Needless to say, no one is responsible for the shortcomings of this book but myself. I was not always capable of fulfilling the aspirations of my family and friends, but I hope their efforts were not entirely in vain.

J. R. K.

Contents

PART IV

THE RACIAL VARIATIONS ON THE
MINORITY THEME

PART I

THE NATURE OF THE MINORITY SITUATION

Chapter 1

Consequences of Categorical Treatment

"IT is the essence of race relations that they are the relations of strangers,"[1] and hence the quality of the person is irrelevant to his minority situation. Foremost of the Chicago school of sociologists to follow Park's formulation, Louis Wirth conceptualized the minority group in terms of its treatment. Significantly, the minority, although not necessarily an alien group, is regarded by others, and hence by itself, as a people apart. Distinguished from the dominant group by physical or cultural characteristics, or both, it is excluded from full participation in the institutions of society.[2] Further marked by its lack of access to dominant values, the minority remains visible by virtue of its disadvantageous position, even after other distinctive characteristics have disappeared; this categorical status is in turn perpetuated by its own visibility.

Much has been said about what it means to be deprived of opportunity, yet little of it suggests the salience, and the significance, of categorical treatment for the minority group. "To the individual members of such a group the most onerous circumstance under which they have to labor is that they are treated as members of a category, irrespective of their individual merits."[3] Finally, the consequences of such treatment are characteristics that further set the minority apart and debar it from participation. The social and psychological consequences of categorical

[1] Robert E. Park, "The Nature of Race Relations," in *Race and Culture* (New York: Free Press, 1950), p. 114.
[2] Louis Wirth, "The Problem of Minority Groups," in Albert J. Reiss, Jr., ed., *On Cities and Social Life* (Chicago: University of Chicago Press, Phoenix Books, 1964), p. 245.
[3] *Ibid.*, p. 246.

treatment constitute the minority situation; its nature is determined by the power of the dominant group rather than by any characteristic of the minority group.

The importance of the physical and cultural characteristics of the minority lies in their visibility; these characteristics lend the group social identifiability. It is, however, the categorical treatment of the group that gives it a separate social identity. That differential response, otherwise known as discrimination,[4] may be part of the reason that a social category becomes an interacting group. Eventually, as we shall see, a community emerges out of the common life experiences of the minority group and its shared fate of restricted social rewards; a way of life is institutionalized, which affords some sense of autonomy. Nevertheless, the destiny of the minority is ultimately still controlled by the dominant group.

The Nature of Intergroup Relations

The dominant group by definition embodies the prevailing way of life; it controls access to values that are now desired by others, but still too scarce to be shared, by defining criteria of social eligibility. By declaring ineligible those with differing characteristics, the dominant group limits their life chances and thereby creates a minority situation. The exercise of such categorical exclusion permits the dominant group to maintain a monopoly of its way of life. The choice of disqualifying characteristics may well be arbitrary; groups are frequently singled out and denied participation as a result of historical circumstance. The minority situation is thus more a matter of social definition than of social difference. Some of the characteristics of the minority then develop as a consequence of its disadvantaged situation.

Minority groups are thus the product of the dominant group's power to establish its way of life as normative and to pass on the eligibility of its participants. Those who are defined as ineligible become as unequal as they are treated. Minority status becomes self-perpetuating as exclusion extends itself over time; deprivation of access to dominant values leads

[4] See Gordon W. Allport, *The Nature of Prejudice,* abridged ed. (Garden City, N.Y.: Doubleday Anchor Books, 1958) for a discussion of the dynamics of prejudice and its relationship to discrimination.

to lack of qualification for them. The involuntarily ascribed and negatively evaluated categorical status that emerges out of the minority situation not only takes precedence over any achieved status, it reduces the probability of such achievement, thereby lowering all life chances.

This sometimes self-limiting status is embodied in custom and enforced by coercion in periods of conflict; and conflict over its categorical ceiling is inevitable because the legitimacy of minority status is always more questionable than that of class or caste. The social subordination imposed by the minority situation is unstable since the grounds for its acceptance are so tenuous. Lacking any ideological justification, the minority situation is characterized by a perennial potential for conflict; conflict is indeed the underlying social process. Whatever the pattern of accommodation, it is periodically disrupted by conflict, which sometimes erupts explosively, because the relationship between the minority group and the dominant group is based on power and is therefore without legitimacy. The unequal, and inequitable, distribution of power that permits the dominant group to determine the life chances of the minority group rests on no socially shared rationalizations. Thus, part of the problem is that there is no way of mediating between groups that exist in different universes of discourse.

The minority situation inheres not in any intrinsic characteristic of the group, but in the combination of the desire for and the deprivation of values which is produced by the particular relationship of power between the dominant and the minority group. Implicit in this definition is the assumption that the minority group aspires to the achievement of dominant values, whether or not it is yet qualified. Members of the minority want to succeed in terms of the institutions of the larger society, and therefore they strive for inclusion. The problems of minority status increase with acculturation; as members of the group accept the desirability of dominant values, they want acceptance in return, at least enough to permit participation in the society. Hence, the greater the qualification for desired opportunities, the greater the frustration at the deprivation of values. Such frustration, compounded by a sense of injustice, is inherent in the American dilemma.[5]

The response to the minority situation requires an awareness of its relative, as well as real, deprivation. If the members of a group do not

[5] It is still Gunnar Myrdal in *An American Dilemma* (New York: Harper & Bros., 1944) who offers the fullest analysis of the role of values in rationalizing, if not justifying, race relations. When a given pattern of accommodation loses its (pseudo-) legitimacy, it begins to break down.

desire the dominant values, or if they are not yet qualified individually to gain access to those values, they are not in a minority situation, but rather in some form of class situation. A minority situation comes about when two social systems are no longer external to each other. The minority group begins to compete for status within the dominant stratification system and is debarred categorically. The minority situation is thus truly a matter of "when peoples meet" and not of mere coexistence, peaceful or otherwise.[6]

The relationship between dominant and minority group obviously implies contact. Insofar as there is competition for values, this contact eventually leads to conflict; the resolution of such conflict is some form of accommodation that imposes upon the minority an acceptance of its subordination.[7] The power of the dominant group rests, in the final analysis, on force. It maintains a monopoly of the means of physical coercion that underlie its potential for repressing protest and reinforcing acceptance. The dominant group by definition exercises control of the political and economic institutions and thereby establishes the limits of the minority situation.[8] Such institutional control is usually sufficient to enforce accommodation.

In his recent work, Michael Banton reviews the kinds of contact that are possible between groups and the nature of the intergroup relations that emerge. Not all contact results in a minority situation. He is at pains to point out that when two different groups first have dealings with one another, their transactions may be peripheral (as in trade relations), having no influence on the relations within either group; no change is brought about by such contact. As long as there is no serious competition for resources, peripheral contact may become institutionalized. Members of each group remain committed to their values, and no integral social system develops, not even a common political order. Only when one group suc-

[6] It is, of course, difficult to distinguish between the consequences of the minority situation and the consequences of a class situation in any given empirical context. See Everett C. Hughes and Helen M. Hughes, *Where Peoples Meet* (New York: Free Press, 1952), especially pp. 100–15, for a discussion of systems of social classification and their categorical consequences.

[7] When there is a sacred ideology justifying the consequent social deprivation, there is likely to be a caste situation.

[8] See Stanley Lieberson, "A Societal Theory of Race and Ethnic Relations," *American Sociological Review,* Vol. 26, No. 6 (December 1961), pp. 902–10 for an analysis of the types of intergroup contact and their respective consequences.

ceeds in subordinating the other does the political balance determine the intergroup relationship.[9] Such subordination may be the consequence of contact that is not itself coercive.

One of the ways in which critical social contact comes about is through voluntary migration, which is characteristic of the United States. Its ethnic history has been written many times, but its sociological depiction may perhaps be more clearly seen at some distance. In analyzing the structure of power in Canada, John Porter examines the processes by which immigrants fit into the social class system. In an economic structure reflecting the position of many ethnic groups, the "charter" members are empowered to evaluate the new arrivals.

> In this process of evaluation the first ethnic group to come into previously unpopulated territory, as the effective possessor, has the most to say. This group becomes the charter group of the society, and among the many privileges and prerogatives which it retains are decisions about what other groups are to be let in and what they will be permitted to do.[10]

The ethnic structure of a community, shaped early in its history, tends to be self-perpetuating, as is the "entrance status" of its constituent groups. The charter group appropriates for itself the socially preferred roles, assigning the remaining roles to other groups. The relative status is reinforced by stereotypes, and the cultural barriers at time of entry may harden into a set of historical relations perpetuating the entrance status of the respective groups. The disadvantaged position of newer groups means not only lower occupational status, but subjection to processes laid down and judged by the charter group. With acculturation, the entrance status of ethnic groups may improve in later generations.[11]

In this context, race is "an extreme case of status ascription making for rigid group membership."[12] It may operate simultaneously with other criteria of invidious status, but it is itself the harshest form of differentiation. Unlike ethnicity, which may diminish over time, race is never irrelevant under any circumstance; members of different racial groups always respond to each other as representatives of their respective categories rather than as individuals. "Whatever their personal qualities, individuals are ascribed

[9] Michael Banton, *Race Relations* (New York: Basic Books, 1967), pp. 68–70.
[10] John Porter, *The Vertical Mosaic* (Toronto: University of Toronto Press, 1965), p. 60.
[11] *Ibid.,* pp. 61, 63–64, 69.
[12] Pierre L. van den Berghe, *Race and Racism* (New York: Wiley, 1967), p. 24.

to one or the other category, and those in the lower are prevented from claiming the privileges of those in the upper category."[13]

Van den Berghe defines race sociologically as a group that is defined socially as different from other groups because of innate and immutable physical characteristics; these characteristics are believed to be intrinsically related to nonphysical attributes and abilities.[14] He goes on to explain,

> When cultural criteria of group differentiation are exclusively or predominantly resorted to, there results a more flexible system of stratification than one based on race, for culture can be learned and movement from one ethnic group to another is thus possible. Racial stratification, on the other hand, results in a nearly impermeable caste system more easily than ethnic stratification; race thus represents an extreme case of ascribed status and lack of social mobility.[15]

A society that is divided into segregated racial groups manifests the most rigid form of social pluralism. Intergroup contact is minimal, resulting in highly circumscribed and stereotyped relationships. Such social pluralism does not necessarily imply cultural pluralism. Prolonged, if partial or peripheral, contact may modify ethnic differences, eventually eliminating cultural heterogeneity. Even after acculturation, however, racial groups remain separate, with one still subordinate to the other. Social pluralism may thus persist in the absence of cultural pluralism, although the converse is not true.[16] This is why racial divisions continue over time to constitute a special instance of structural pluralism, while ethnic divisions are an instance of cultural pluralism that may pass after a period of contact.

The selective association among racial groups may give rise to subcultural differences, even when there is relative cultural homogeneity; there are then racial variations on the dominant theme of values. Social pluralism may thus be accompanied by a less than complete consensus of values. Cultural pluralism, by contrast, is characterized by the coexistence of several value systems, convergent on some points, or at least complementary, but more often incompatible, and therefore subject to some degree of conflict.[17] We will observe the extent to which cultural plural-

---

[13] Banton, *op. cit.*, p. 71.
[14] Van den Berghe, *op. cit.*, p. 9.
[15] *Ibid.*, p. 22.
[16] *Ibid.*, pp. 133–35.
[17] *Ibid.*, pp. 135–36, 138.

ism has diminished, if not yet disappeared, in American society, while social pluralism survives as a source of structural segmentation. Religious as well as racial groups have lost their original national identities. Although they continue to lead separate social lives, their way of life has grown so much alike that there is little left to distinguish them as ethnic groups.

Pluralistic societies of one kind or the other are likely to be held together by a mixture of political coercion and economic interdependence. Because the distribution of power follows the lines of social cleavage, it is concentrated entirely in the dominant group; this concentration is maintained by the extensive use of coercive means. Combined with economic interdependence, such power becomes an effective source of social integration. This is no status quo governed by a consensus in which the minority group accedes to its situation. There is no shared agreement, but an imposed acceptance of categorical status; the minority group submits perforce to its subordination. Dominant control of key economic resources further reduces even the potential self-sufficiency of subordinate groups. With the deliberate use of discrimination, the dominant group enforces a social pluralism that protects its privileged position, thereby countering the assimilative pressures of acculturation.[18]

It is perhaps for this reason that the minority situation has not been much explored by contemporary theorists; their characteristic functional approach does not explain a situation in which social patterns are maintained by force rather than by agreement. Where there is conflict, society is held together by coercion and constraint. People then do what they do because they have no real alternative. "They may be unaware of the alternatives or they may be coerced into submission."[19] In the case of the minority situation, it is not even a matter of learning to want what one can have, as functionalists would lead us to believe in other instances. One accepts the situation because one has no choice, but there is no socialization that prepares one to settle for so little in life, only the resignation that comes with its experience.

The empirical variations in the nature of intergroup contact and the degree of consensus in American society will be examined in the latter part of this volume. At this point we need only observe that it is shared values that lead to social conflict and exclusion; value differences are more likely to result in cultural conflict and marginality. A conflict of values

[18] *Ibid.*, pp. 139, 145.
[19] Banton, *op. cit.*, pp. 63, 67.

does not imply social conflict as long as *meaningful* contact is minimized. Indeed, contact first leads to psychological conflict, the marginality of mutually exclusive values. Increased intergroup contact leads to acculturation as the resolution of that conflict, and it is the dominant values that are accepted as normative. It is, however, the competition for these values, now shared, that leads to social conflict.

> When two societies are brought into contact, influences spread from each to the other. The stronger of the two societies is influenced less than the weaker in this way, and usually has less difficulty in containing any changes that may be initiated. The weaker society is at a disadvantage. Apart from any overt struggles between members of the two societies, contact usually creates a conflict of values within the weaker society. The process of change in the culture of a group of people adjusting to continuing contact with some other group is known as "acculturation." Conflict within such a society is a sign that acculturation is taking place.[20]

The dominant norms attract members of a minority group in part because of the strength and the status of their institutional support in the larger society. The very process of acculturation engenders social conflict because the dominant group wants to maintain a monopoly on its values. The minority group not only strives to gain access to those values, but it also seeks the appropriate status accorded such achievement. The dominant group counters such aspirations with continued exclusion of those whom they do not consider their equal, if only to enhance the scarcity value of a way of life that grows less distinctive with the acculturation of the minority. The initial issue in the minority situation is therefore a conflict of values versus a consensus of values. It is only when cultural marginality is resolved, as it eventually is with acculturation, that social conflict emerges.

The Psychology of the Minority Situation

The tensions of the minority situation derive not just from the lack of privilege, but even more from the lack of power to correct it. Members of the minority are unable to choose or to control the conditions under which they live; somehow they must learn to live with their situation

[20] *Ibid.,* p. 77.

nonetheless. Since the values and attitudes of the dominant group prevail by social definition, the minority group must come to terms with them. It does so at considerable social and psychic cost. Members of a minority group may perforce accept their situation, but they cope with some of its consequences with difficulty, if at all; not all of them can pay the high price that respectable (but not always self-respecting) accommodation exacts from them.

The uncertainties of minority status, both in the expectations for the self and in the responses of others, lead to a certain self-consciousness. It is in fact this self-consciousness that characterizes the member of the minority group; this may be the one remaining telltale trace that reveals his status when other more visible marks have faded. He is always uncertain whether the exclusion he experiences is personal or categorical. In 1922, Jessie Fauset, a Negro woman novelist, wrote:

> I think the thing that irks us most is the teasing uncertainty of it all. Did the man at the box office give us the seat behind the post on purpose? Is the shopgirl impudent or merely nervous? Had the position really been filled before we applied for it?[21]

The shared experience of the minority group thus includes not only its categorical status, but the uncertainty about when it is operating in institutionalized patterns and how it operates in interpersonal relations. The status is involuntary and usually inescapable (at least not without enormous guilt and anxiety), and so are its consequences. The uncertainty is compounded by an intensity that comes from having to prove oneself repeatedly, often without validation.

The inexorable essence of the minority experience is disjuncture. The normal procedures of others are not reasonable expectations for minorities. Dominance is expressed at all levels with practices of "interruption" in what would otherwise be considered a single action or process. The relationship between means and ends is so tenuous for members of minority groups that one does not necessarily follow from the other; going to school, for example, does not guarantee getting a job. Such a breakdown in instrumental relationships and normative expectations disorders the reality that others take for granted, and psychic disruption results from this disconnection between means and ends. A sense of inner chaos may accompany social deprivation and derogation; there is then confusion about the self and its situation.

[21] Quoted in Maurice R. Davie, *Negroes in American Society* (New York: McGraw-Hill, 1949), p. 439.

The stability of the self is further undermined when categorical treatment deprives the individual not only of access to the values he desires, but also finally of motivation to aspire to them. Inevitably there results ambivalence about both his self-image and his group identification. The negative self-image is not always unjustified since exclusion obviates the opportunity to establish a personal identity independent of the categorical status. Living with lowered life chances, the member of the minority group begins to incorporate the inferior social images attributed to him and may eventually become like the image.[22]

> The prejudging not only concerns the victim's external fate at the hands of his oppressor, but also his consciousness as it is shaped by their expectations. The most terrible thing that prejudice can do to a human being is to make him tend to become what the prejudiced image of him says that he is.[23]

As long as prejudice remains (and it is by definition resistant to change) its stereotypes impede the self-esteem of the member of a minority group. He is all the more likely to accept the negative evaluation of himself when he is allowed no way of achieving a sense of worth. His difficulties are compounded by the germ of truth in the stereotype supported by the self-perpetuating conditions of his situation. His diminished self-esteem heightens his anxiety to prove himself. This anxiety is exacerbated by his uncertainty about whether or not he can do so, even if he is given an opportunity to try. For the member of a minority it is not so much a neurotic manner of winning personal approval as it is a necessary matter of earning the social acceptance that has critical consequences for life chances. The function of tolerance, in so far as it does and should exist, is to grant time to the minority group to qualify itself to gain access to dominant values.

Some minority members may be sufficiently protected from the deleterious consequences of their situation to have positive self-images. Even so categorical status is incorporated and its stereotypes, albeit affirmative ones, threaten the potential development of individual identity.

> Those on the receiving end of negative identity assignments are very prone to accept the categories invented by their oppressors with the simple

[22] This may take the form of a self-fulfilling prophecy the operation of which has been conceptualized by Robert K. Merton in "The Self-Fulfilling Prophecy," in *Social Theory and Social Structure,* rev. ed. (New York: Free Press, 1957), pp. 421–36.
[23] Peter L. Berger, *Invitation to Sociology* (Garden City, N.Y.: Doubleday, Anchor Books, 1963), p. 102.

alteration of replacing the minus sign originally attached to the identity in question with a plus sign.[24]

The social and psychological frustrations of the minority situation engender tensions that require resolution; the patterns of response vary with all the possible forms of anger and apathy.[25] The dominance over the minority group results in some kind of aggressive response. When the situation is experienced as destructive, there is aggression toward the self or others, the expression of which may be active or passive. Many members of minority groups, as we will see, manifest an apathetic acceptance of their subordination to the dominant group. The question here is not why the dominant group subordinates; its vested interest in maintaining its position is self-evident. The question is rather why the minority group accepts its situation.

The obvious reason is, of course, that the effective coercion of the dominant group, even to the point of physical force, leaves the minority group no choice. It is also true that once the minority situation is embodied in custom, it does not require much reinforcement by coercion; the self-perpetuating responses lend an otherwise spurious stability, if not legitimacy, to a situation of underlying conflict. Properly fearful of dominant power, members of a minority group also grow anxious about their ability to determine their own destinies. Since they cannot control their life chances, they are anxious about their adequacy—at all levels, from the social to the sexual. There may be some gratifications of dependency, when there is sufficient paternalistic protection that people do not have to assume responsibility for their own lives. More often than not, however, there is no compensation to counteract the constraints of the minority situation.

With apathy, whether or not there is acceptance, aggression is turned inward, and the responses become self-destructive. The sense of inadequacy leads to lowered motivation, and then to avoid an intolerable reality there may be an escape into some addiction. The social irrelevance reverberates in personal impotence and its alternating rage and despair. Finally the situation perpetuates itself as much by its apparent lack of alternatives as its actual lack. Members of a minority group no longer know any other way to live, and they do not try to find one; they cannot become aware of values that remain concealed from them, and they cannot conceive of others. The absence of knowledge reinforces the absence of opportunity,

---

[24] *Ibid.,* p. 157.

[25] For an extended discussion of the types of responses of minority group members, see George E. Simpson and J. Milton Yinger, *Racial and Cultural Minorities,* 3rd ed. (New York: Harper & Row, 1965), pp. 130–78.

and social ignorance supports the status quo. When self-hatred sets in, minority members may be unable to avail themselves of what opportunities there are. If they are afraid to test the limits of reality, they will be unable to take advantage of any changes that may occur.

Few minority members are spared some self-hatred; it is perhaps the most painful psychological consequence of their situation. As Kurt Lewin has explained its sources, some element of self-hatred would seem all but inevitable.[26] Once members of the minority group are sufficiently acculturated to have adopted dominant values and attitudes, they cannot help but be influenced in their opinions about themselves by the low esteem in which they are held. Since the status that restricts their possibilities is inescapable, they cannot avoid its psychic cost in self-hatred. Recent research suggests that ideal group loyalty does not exist; there is always some claim to superiority or some display of defensiveness. Nevertheless, widespread negative identification seems to be unique among minority groups.[27]

Albert Memmi, the Algerian Jewish novelist, recorded in his diary his reaction to living in a ghetto as an adolescent. He debated the dilemmas of the resulting self-hatred as follows:

> In short, self-rejection, far from being the best response to the oppression, rapidly appeared to me one of the most characteristic traits of the oppressed. Far from being a free and courageous act, it was the expression of his nonliberty, of his barely disguised submission to the accusation and the aggression.
>
> But my real problem was that I had to cut myself off once and for all from the image of myself which had been imposed on me from birth by others and by my own people, and which had become second nature, without at the same time rejecting myself or my people, or scorning their universe, which was so largely my own.
>
> . . . I wanted to accept myself as a Jew while rejecting conditions made by the others and imposed on my existence.[28]

Although the Algerian ghetto of another generation may seem remote, some of the psychological consequences remain remarkably similar, if less dramatic, today. In a study of adolescents, Morris Rosenberg found that those who live in a "dissonant religious context" (i.e., in a neighbor-

---

[26] Kurt Lewin, "Self-Hatred Among Jews," in Arnold M. Rose, ed., *Race Prejudice and Discrimination* (New York: Alfred A. Knopf, 1953), pp. 321–32.

[27] Donald L. Noel, "Group Identification Among Negroes: An Empirical Analysis," *The Journal of Social Issues*, Vol. 20, No. 2 (April 1964), p. 72.

[28] Albert Memmi, "Does the Jew Exist?" *Commentary*, Vol. 42, No. 5 (November 1966), p. 76.

hood in which fewer than one fourth of the residents are of their religion) manifest lower self-esteem, depression, and psychosomatic symptoms. In other words, they experience the full impact of their minority status. The young member of a minority group who is without group support is likely to develop feelings of fear, anxiety, and insecurity when subjected to taunts and excluded from participation. By contrast, youngsters who live in neighborhoods in which half or more of the residents are of the same religion have a feeling of belonging and acceptance; there is enough social support to provide them with some positive group identification.[29]

The above differences are not strong ones, but they are consistently significant. When the qualities accepted by one's own group are rejected by the group with which one is living, one's self-esteem is affected, sometimes severely. Interestingly enough, the effect of such dissonance is heightened when a member of the dominant group lives in a minority neighborhood.[30] It is reminiscent of an old Yiddish proverb, "Gentiles aren't used to Jewish troubles."[31] The white Anglo-Saxon Protestant is less equipped for the experience of exclusion and suffers more emotional disturbance when he encounters it. Jewish high school students show the least effect, perhaps because they are prepared to expect prejudice. It is part of their socialization to attribute the problem to those who discriminate against them rather than to regard it as a reflection on themselves. To some extent such socialization succeeds in protecting them from the psychological effects of prejudice.

Still another study suggests that any disparity in status ranking is stressful. The inconsistency leads both to unstable self-images and to unsatisfactory social relationships because of the frustration inherent in the contradictory expectations of others and the uncertainty about what the individual is entitled to expect from them. This results not only in the psychophysiological symptoms of stress that reflect self-blame, but also in patterns of social isolation and political liberalism.[32] Again the same interesting twist—those with high racial and ethnic status tend to react physiologically, while minority members with high achievement respond politically. The former feel a sense of personal failure since they have no ascribed handicap to blame. If the latter, who are successful in spite

[29] Morris Rosenberg, "The Dissonant Religious Context and Emotional Disturbance," *American Journal of Sociology*, Vol. 68, No. 1 (July 1962), pp. 2–5.
[30] *Ibid.*, pp. 9–10.
[31] Hanan J. Ayalti, *Yiddish Proverbs* (New York: Schocken, 1963), p. 57.
[32] Elton F. Jackson, "Status Consistency and Symptoms of Stress," *American Sociological Review*, Vol. 27, No. 4 (August 1962), pp. 469–70.

of their social disadvantage, feel stress, they are more likely to blame it on the unjust actions of others.[33]

This brings us to a consideration, in passing, of aggression turned outward, of the angry response to minority frustrations that is not directed at the self, but is actively oriented toward others.[34] The rationality of such hostility varies with how realistic the chosen target is. The aggression may be directed at the dominant group in the form of militant protest, or it may be displaced from the source of the frustration on to another group. It may be expressed as deviant behavior that defies society at large or as revolutionary reaction aimed at the entire social structure. What form aggression takes, whether organized militancy or disorganized deviance, is in part a function of the nature of the minority community. In succeeding chapters we shall explore the functions of community as a source of social support for its members; the shared status of peers does temper their minority situation and channel their response. At this point, let us look at what is happening to that situation. What are the shifts in minority status that now shape the response?

[33] *Ibid.*, pp. 476–77.

[34] We will treat these responses in detail when we discuss the organized resources of the various minority communities.

Chapter 2

The Changing Nature of
the Minority Situation

THE prototype of minority status is no longer the wandering Jew, but the invisible man. The implicit shift in the source of categorical status has not been followed by any explicit change in sociological conceptualization. The traditional literature has focused on the marginality of ethnic groups, characterized by the cultural differences of their national origins.[1] As these groups merged into the religious divisions of the "triple melting pot,"[2] there was considerable discussion of the problems and processes of acculturation. The only sociological suggestion, however, that the minority problem is increasingly a racial one is the burgeoning empirical study of Negro identity; such studies are rarely accompanied by any appropriate theoretical treatment.

The Difference Between Marginality and Invisibility

Inherent in the concept of marginality is culture conflict. At that point when the minority individual has meaningful contact with the dominant culture, he begins to live on the margin of two social worlds whose norms and values are not only different, but often mutually exclusive. (For some

[1] See Everett V. Stonequist, *The Marginal Man* (New York: Scribner's, 1937) for an elaboration of the concept of marginality.

[2] For a discussion of the three major religious groups in the United States, see Will Herberg, *Protestant–Catholic–Jew* (Garden City, N.Y.: Doubleday, 1956).

groups, like the Jews, such contact occurs in the second generation, but in other groups acculturation and its concomitant marginality may be delayed for another generation or two by physical isolation and social insulation.) The marginal man, who may reject the group of his origins, is not accepted by the group of his aspirations. Belonging to neither group, yet subject to the contradictory cultural patterns and social judgments of both, he suffers psychological conflict, which is manifested in heightened ambivalence and self-consciousness. Sometimes this results in personal disorganization;[3] always there is role strain.

No matter how the marginal man behaves, he will violate the norms of one or the other group, for each is likely to define the same situation in a very different way. In so doing, the marginal man incurs not only the sanctions of one group, but also his own feelings of guilt. Though he may remain a stranger in each of the worlds in which he lives, he is also capable of cosmopolitanism and thus of rational resolution of the psychological conflicts engendered by their cultural differences. If he must somehow come to terms with the contrasts presented by both worlds, he also has the detachment prerequisite to the attainment of a less parochial perspective. Lacking the solid substance of cultural conflict, the man of color is without the bedrock of guilt out of which the marginal man can carve an identity when all else fails; indeed, the guilt that colors his marginality often becomes the hallmark of his identity. Those who are subjected to racial categorization, by contrast, find their very existence threatened by social exclusion.

The psychological concomitant of racial visibility is personal invisibility. When a categorical status is internalized without another set of cultural values even to cause conflict, there are no social alternatives available to serve as a source of identity. The individual experiences a sense of nonexistence rather than of marginality, and there is no positive response from within that can offer any psychological resolution. The resulting tension is all but intolerable; its consequences for Negroes in American society have not begun to be encompassed within a sociological framework, although they have been considered on occasion by psychologists and discussed at length by litterateurs. There are also (and have been for a long time) the militant ideologists and black revolutionaries who have taken time from their engagement in action to describe the expe-

---

[3] Louis Wirth, "Culture Conflict and Misconduct," in Albert J. Reiss, Jr., ed., *On Cities and Social Life* (Chicago: University of Chicago Press, Phoenix Books, 1964), p. 240.

riences they have endured; and they write as they have lived, with an intensity given to few observers. It is perhaps because the essence of invisibility is so difficult to convey that invisibility is suffered with such excruciating intensity. The lack of an adequately expressive language exacerbates the emotions. Only the very gifted can find the words to transcend what they have endured and with their creativity communicate to us something of their experience.

Even for the most creative men, this is not easy. Ralph Ellison writes of himself:

> For I found the greatest difficulty for a Negro writer was the problem of revealing what he truly felt, rather than serving up what Negroes were supposed to feel, and were encouraged to feel. And linked to this was the difficulty, based upon our long habit of deception and evasion, of depicting what really happened within our areas of American life.[4]

What does happen to the Negro? What is the nature of his experience with nonexistence? Richard Wright harks back to William James for confirmation that there is "no more fiendish punishment" than complete social exclusion. Without specifying a particular minority situation, James simply explained, "[If others] acted as if we were nonexistent things, a kind of rage and impotent despair would ere long well up in us, from which the cruelest bodily tortures would be a relief."[5] The writer, by the very nature of his work, can create an identity out of the depths of this nothingness; the very act of acknowledging such a reality surmounts its unreality.

Others lack the literary means of surviving so desperate a search for identity and suffer the emotional consequences of being nobody. "In the social jungle of human existence there is no feeling of being alive without a sense of identity."[6] In Harlem and elsewhere, they are "nowhere," and they say so, knowing only one thing for sure, that they don't know who they are. Their existence is suffused with its own uncertainty.

> When Negroes are barred from participation in the main institutional life of society they lose far more than economic privileges or the satisfaction of saluting the flag with unmixed emotions. They lose one of the bulwarks which men place between themselves and the constant threat of chaos.[7]

[4] Ralph Ellison, *Shadow and Act* (New York: Random House, 1953), p. xxi.
[5] Quoted by Richard Wright in St. Clair Drake and Horace R. Cayton, *Black Metropolis* (New York: Harper Torchbooks, 1962), p. xxxii.
[6] Erik H. Erikson, *Identity: Youth and Crisis* (New York: Norton, 1968), p. 130.
[7] Ellison, *op. cit.*, p. 299.

Without institutional participation to give him a sense of direction, the individual feels he is nowhere. He has no recognized place in society, and his identity drifts in a capricious reality where even the most common assumptions are questionable.[8] The person can achieve no affirmative sense of self that is in accord with the images of the world. He is so out of joint with the world that he experiences the extreme of disjuncture.

> In our society it is not unusual for a Negro to experience a sensation that he does not exist in the real world at all. He seems rather to exist in the nightmarish fantasy of the white American mind as a phantom that the white mind seeks unceasingly, by means both crude and subtle, to lay.[9]

No Negro has ever written without documenting his desperate pre-occupation with invisibility. Whether they describe it as "inaudibility," as did W. E. B. DuBois, or consider it a form of "namelessness," as did James Baldwin, they struggle to regain a personal identity surrendered to the visibility of color. They wage their battle against categorical status with words as weapons, dredging up the metaphors with the greatest difficulty from the depths of their experience. "In most cases, the black man lacks the advantage of being able to accomplish this descent into a real hell."[10] A man who is nowhere may find nothing with which to make art, or even ideology, out of nightmare. It takes a rare talent to create something out of nothingness, and the black man may not be able to structure the chaos within and to shape a self out of his experience. If he is incapable of sustaining the inner turmoil precipitated by the search for identity, he may never achieve a sense of authenticity about his manhood; he may never succeed in becoming a man. If he is constantly confronted with the dilemma of turning white or disappearing, as Frantz Fanon has depicted it, he may not be able to find a possibility of existence; he may not even be able to conceive of one. How then can he make himself seen and heard as an individual?

[8] *Ibid.*, p. 300.
[9] *Ibid.*, p. 304.
[10] Frantz Fanon, *Black Skin, White Masks* (New York: Grove Press, 1967), p. 10.

Violence as a Source of Identity

Up to a point the Negro acts by reacting, and his reaction is a rejection of those who attempt to define him and therefore to delimit his reality. Beyond that point, he may through violence escape the nonexistence imposed by categorical definition. Like a protagonist in a Richard Wright novel, the victimized self asserts its existence through an act of violence; it is the only action available to him when he chooses to act rather than to react. The victim of categorization then feels he exists; he can feel so because he has begun not only to hurt, but also to hate. He cries "I am" —with a vengeance. Perhaps even more significant, he begins to know he exists because he can see in action the consequences of his existence. This may account for the intensity of his violence more than the desire for vengeance that Fanon attributes to it.[11]

Perhaps there is something inherent in the status of victim that invites violence. Erikson suggests that the status "is transcended by human revolt, the inner realignment by intense contact with historical actuality."[12] Such revolt may be a means of legitimating the past, but violence does not necessarily take a revolutionary direction in vindicating the self. Even in its most disorganized form, however, it is a way of achieving visibility. It may be the victim's only way of expressing himself and exacting response, for he is not otherwise taken seriously. "The Negro is a toy in the white man's hands; so in order to shatter the hellish cycle, he explodes."[13] This could well be the case because the conceptualization of him as victim is even more victimizing than the categorical treatment that imposes the status.

The concept itself is a demeaning one that deprives the individual of dignity and denies his responsibility. Destructive of common humanity, it is a contemptuous form of pity.[14] No one is a "victim" who assumes responsibility for himself and his responses, even when he does not have the power to control the consequences for his situation. This sense of

---

[11] *Ibid.*, p. 225.

[12] Erikson, *op. cit.*, p. 298.

[13] Fanon, *op. cit.*, p. 140.

[14] This is part of Ralph Ellison's quarrel with Irving Howe, literary and social critic; Ellison complains of being reduced to (and by) the ideas of others about him. Most difficult to escape are the sympathetic views that conceive of him as nothing more than a victim. For his side of the exchange with Howe, see Ellison, *op. cit.*, pp. 107–43.

responsibility for the self is a source of dignity in the human condition, perhaps the sole source for some, and it is denied by social definition of the victim. Hence the impelling need for rebellion. It is, if nothing else, a rebellion against victimization; the shout of the rebel drowns out the cry of the victim. It is the function of such rebellion to transcend the victimized self of the past, but it is no simple matter to suppress one's former self. Thus there is the violence that may seem gratuitous, to say the least. It is an act of affirmation for its own sake, for the sake of the self and its sense of strength, however spurious it may prove to be.

The consequences of some forms of oppression may become more immediate than the oppression itself. Whatever the ostensible changes in their social situation, men must still contend with the consequences of the past, even after (and if) oppression has passed. The mark of the oppressed is that he must struggle against the shadows of his past as well as the conditions of the present. As he fights, he may find that he improves his immediate position more readily than he dispels the memory of his oppression. He seeks to lay the ghost of his humiliation, the subjective meaning of which may be more overwhelming than the social experience of it. Thus the rebel cannot be understood solely in the context of the objective reality he is striving to overcome; finally he is oppressed by his own psychological reality—or lack of it.

The consequences of the minority situation are intensified for the Negro by the stark contrast between the visibility of his color and the invisibility of his person. Some consequences are unique to him, as unique as his history with the peculiar institution of slavery in America. Having been subjected to enslavement, the Negro has a sense of shame not readily understood in psychological terms of the guilt of marginality. He is guilty only by an accident of birth that imposes upon him a historical association with forebears who were slaves. Haunted by ancestral slavery, the Negro may find his experience incommunicable, in part because of its uniqueness and in part because of its very nature. Since the experience of slavery was not shared with other groups, the consequences may remain mutually unintelligible. It is questionable whether the experience of slavery is readily explicable since it is beyond the pale of all that is essential to the human condition. The source of suffering peculiar to the slave, after all, lay in being "dehumanized." There are few words to delineate the nature of such suffering precisely because it cannot be defined in human terms. The categories of sociology, for example, are conceived to encompass human problems. How does one describe the sense of nonexistence of someone who is not defined as human—and who is treated as chattel?

One can understand then that Negroes have more reason than exclusion for associating only with each other. It is enough that they have shared the experience; they do not have to explain its consequences to understand each other. As long as they can confine their existence to each other (and can find some existence with each other), they do not have to suffer a sense of unintelligibility in the futile attempt at explanation to compound their sense of shame in their experience. As Fanon points out, and he says this as a psychoanalyst, a black psychoanalyst, rather than as the revolutionary he was to become before his death,

> For the Negro there is a myth to be faced. A solidly established myth. The Negro is unaware of it as long as his existence is limited to his own environment; but the first encounter with a white man oppresses him with the whole weight of his blackness.[15]

As long as Negroes are among their own, they have no occasion to experience the essence of their being through others who are alien to them. Nevertheless, they cannot avoid some awareness of their blackness and its consequences. In his clinical experience, Fanon found that even a normal Negro child, having grown up in a normal family, becomes abnormal upon contact with the white world. The sense of inferiority is heightened among the more educated.[16] The need may be greater therefore among the educated to lash out against a world that has more than impressed them with their own inferiority, that has oppressed them with it.

In-group isolation, however, cannot be sustained indefinitely in the United States, and in the case of the Negro the consequences of categorical status have been so long institutionalized that they are internalized without interaction. The black man now does not have to meet the white man to know his blackness; he experiences it without personal encounter. Acculturation breaks down the protective walls of his isolation, leading him to judge himself in alien terms. The marginal man feels guilty having to violate one or another of the conflicting norms that he has internalized. The invisible man feels ashamed for the "real" self that doesn't show and of everything else that does show, symbolized by his color.

It is thus true that few whites understand the black man; they have not shared the past that is peculiar to his color, and therefore they cannot project themselves into his person in the present. This further exacerbates the Negro's sense of nonexistence. Even those whites who regard him as human do not always know how to treat him because they are not certain that their projections will fit. Social interaction requires mutual intelli-

[15] Fanon, *op. cit.*, p. 150.
[16] *Ibid.*, pp. 25, 109, 143.

gibility. If one rejects the categorical response and stereotyped reaction, one must be able to take the other person into account on the basis of accurate anticipations and valid projections. One must anticipate the other's response in order to respond to him, but if one cannot understand the response, interaction breaks down. For the black man, the experience of being "nonhuman" is part of his humanity; it must be taken into account when he responds, and is responded to, as a person. The preparation for interaction, like interaction itself, is thus a two-way process; there not only must be willingness (and ability) to understand, but there also must be willingness (and ability) to explain. Rarely does communication between black and white achieve a meaningful level, especially on the issue itself, that is, on the nature of being black.

If there is ever to be such dialogue, it does not seem yet to have begun. In so far as blacks and whites talk at all, they talk at each other, sometimes shouting in the frustration of incommunicability. When the sound and fury subside, little has been said that makes sense to the other. It is not so much that the Negro is nameless any more, but that his suffering is. The namelessness that renders such suffering unintelligible intensifies it; there is no ready label that makes it more tolerable by defining it. It needs to be specified at its source, not because that solves the problem, but because it permits an acceptance of the past. Its damage cannot be undone, but the past can be incorporated into the present, thus providing the potential for a different future.

> It is a sentimental error, therefore, to believe that the past is dead; it means nothing to say that it is all forgotten, that the Negro himself has forgotten it. It is not a question of memory. . . . [The past] remain[s] with him, indivisible from himself forever, part of the passion that drives him wherever he thinks to take flight.[17]

James Baldwin writes of his self-imposed, if temporary, exile that he was seeking some way to make the specialness of his experience connect him with other people rather than divide him from them. He felt as isolated from Negroes as from whites, "which is what happens when a Negro begins, at bottom, to believe what white people say about him."[18] It is the irreparable scar of the Negro's condition. His outlets are desperately constricted, and in his isolation, he turns first upon whatever most represents to him his own emasculation.[19] The devaluation of self may be

[17] James Baldwin, *Notes on a Native Son* (Boston: Beacon Press, 1955), p. 29.
[18] James Baldwin, "The Discovery of What It Means to Be an American," *The New York Times Book Review,* January 25, 1959, p. 4.
[19] Baldwin, *Notes, op. cit.,* pp. 71–72.

so severe as to undermine every relationship with others, even those with whom he has shared his special experience. Negroes have struggled to survive, and they have succeeded in doing so. But in American terms simply to survive is not to succeed. Lacking the sufficiency of success, they learn to hate themselves and each other.

Playing the Role of Inferior

There is perhaps nothing more revealing about the nature of his condition than the mask the Negro dons to cover the mark of his oppression.

> It is part of the price the Negro pays for his position in this society that, as Richard Wright points out, he is almost always acting. A Negro learns to gauge precisely what reaction the alien person facing him desires, and he produces it with disarming artlessness.[20]

That the Negro behaves differently with whites than he does with other Negroes all but goes without saying by now. The costs and consequences of such duality, however, are not so clearly established and substantiated by psychologists and sociologists. Fanon points out that all affect is exacerbated in the Negro. He is full of rage because he feels so small. Suffering from an inadequacy in all human communication, he is chained to an unbearable insularity.[21] He is in a state of tension in all dealings with whites. "To protect himself from his own fears he has devised a mask which he assumes in the presence of all white persons."[22]

Horace Cayton looks behind that mask and finds an oppression phobia, a complex of fear and hatred which is itself cause for further fear. There is no component of paranoia in this for punishment is ever present in the Negro's environment. He fears the psychological and physical violence that has brutalized his personality, and he hates whites as the source of such fear. While resenting his subordination, he also feels guilty about his hatred and afraid of being punished for it. He is bitterly hurt, and this tangle of feelings intensifies his emotional conflict.[23] "The final result

[20] *Ibid.*, p. 68.

[21] Fanon, *op. cit.*, p. 50.

[22] Horace R. Cayton, "The Psychology of the Negro under Discrimination," in Arnold M. Rose and Caroline B. Rose, eds., *Minority Problems* (New York: Harper & Row, 1965), p. 212.

[23] *Ibid.*, p. 213.

is a wretched internal life."[24] His situation leads to rage, whose immediate effect is (or at least has been) fear of its consequences. The rage and the fear may become almost interchangeable,[25] and they require controls on the self of which whites are free. Without such controls, the emotions might erupt and endanger the Negro's situation further.

The subjective aspect of social discrimination, as elucidated by Kardiner and Ovesey, is a constant in the Negro's life, an unrelieved irritant. He is always subject to a negative image of himself emanating from the behavior of others toward him. Its influence is painful in its intensity, and the individual must maintain some sort of internal balance in order not to be overwhelmed by it. In order to continue functioning, he must also maintain some sort of social facade. Whatever his adaptation and whatever its effectiveness, it is a perennial source of preoccupation, although it may be at a low level of awareness.[26] "This fact in itself, the necessity to exercise control, is distractive and destructive of spontaneity and ease."[27]

It is the enforced enactment of an inferior role that divides the Negro from himself and from others. There is impairment of both the individual's acceptance of himself and of his interpersonal relationships.[28] The acting may not prevent the internalization of inferiority; it may only prove to be dissociative, resulting in a confusion of identity in which the mask becomes the self, and fear is the only manifestation of rage. If there is insufficient ego strength, the Negro may not be able to maintain a separation between his basic personality structure and his socially defined role. Crippled by weak ego development from earlier family disorganization, those who are psychologically vulnerable may succumb to mental illness under the impact of such severe emotional stress.[29]

J. Saunders Redding has written poignantly of the burden imposed upon the Negro, a burden of shame and outrage that requires all his energies to bear. It is a burden he can never lay down; the consequences set in with the first consciousness of categorical status, and they are never normal.

[24] Abram Kardiner and Lionel Ovesey, *The Mark of Oppression* (Cleveland, Ohio: World Publishing Co., Meridian Books, 1962), p. 81.

[25] *Ibid.*, p. 304.

[26] *Ibid.*, pp. 302–3.

[27] *Ibid.*, p. 81.

[28] For a descriptive summary of the many social and psychological consequences of such role-playing for the Negro, see Thomas E. Pettigrew, *A Profile of the Negro American* (Princeton, N.J.: Van Nostrand, 1964).

[29] Thomas F. Pettigrew, "Negro American Personality: Why Isn't More Known?" *The Journal of Social Issues*, Vol. 20, No. 2 (April 1964), p. 16.

They will aver that they live *normal, natural, wholesome* lives, even in the South. They will point out their "normal" interests in their home lives. They will tick off the list of their white friends. They will say, truthfully enough, "Oh, there are ways to avoid prejudice and segregation." I have no quarrel with them (nor with any others): it is simply that I do not believe them. Having to avoid prejudice and segregation is itself unwholesome, and the constant doing of it is skating very close to a psychopathic edge.[30]

For decades social scientists have been delineating the consequences of categorization for Negroes. Since they failed to trace these consequences to their source in shame, they have missed the essence of the black experience. However pallid the sociological perception of the Negro condition may be, its consequences are analogous to those of a chronic disease, draining the energy and consuming the self.

The series of studies sponsored by the American Council on Education in the late 1930's found that no Negro youth escaped the consequences of his categorical status, although some personalities were more completely enveloped than others. Not even the relatively sheltered youngster from the upper class was free of conflict. "His apparent objectivity covers up inner dread of and resentment about humiliating experiences."[31] In his summary of these studies, Robert Sutherland points out that the disorganizing effect of such conflict is everywhere. Upper-status Negroes, for example, may compensate by being excessively concerned about their status within their own group. Those who are successful may even deny the existence of any conflict, because its effects are so subtle they can't see the consequences for their own personalities.[32]

In her unusually sensitive study of a southern town, *After Freedom*, Hortense Powdermaker depicts the explicit reactions of Negroes to the duality of their existence—and nonexistence. Although her observations were made in the late 1930's, her perceptions of Negro role-playing remain as valid now as they were astute then. At that time there was still a generation born into slavery and socialized into submission. Most members of this generation are now deceased; while they lived, they continued to accept complete dependence on whites.[33] More typical of the response we are now discussing is the behavior of those who were middle-aged at

[30] J. Saunders Redding, *On Being Negro in America* (Indianapolis, Ind.: Bobbs-Merrill, Charter Books, 1962), p. 25.

[31] Robert L. Sutherland, *Color, Class, and Personality* (Washington, D.C.: American Council on Education, 1942), pp. 74, 52.

[32] *Ibid.*, p. 75.

[33] Hortense Powdermaker, *After Freedom* (New York: Atheneum, 1939, 1968), p. 325.

the time of the study, those who are now members of the older generation. They didn't believe in white superiority, but in dealing with whites, they always acted as if they did. It was this accommodation that permitted them to get along.[34]

The dual role played by these Negroes was deliberately enacted and explicitly articulated. Unlike their fathers, they were not ignorant; through the mass media, they had grown increasingly aware of a world outside the local domination of the whites in their community. They saw some Negroes succeed and began to gain confidence in the potential of the race. These middle-aged Negroes were prudent, however, and kept their convictions to themselves. They derived some satisfaction from a secret sense of superiority about fooling the whites with their acting. Playing at inferiority, however, was a costly compromise with the reality of subordination.

> For this type of Negro, daily forced into acts of humiliation, large and small, the fleeting sense of superiority may help toward maintaining self-respect.
> To the majority of middle-aged Negroes, however, such secret satisfaction is meager recompense for the lack of respect from others. . . . The way they put it, with monotonous insistence, is: "I want to be treated like a human being."[35]

Even then younger Negroes resented the practice of social deception. The very need to do so wounded their self-esteem, and so they avoided contact with whites whenever possible.[36] All Negroes chose each other's company in order to forget what they knew only too well, that they were Negroes. Whites reminded them of the fact in every way. With an elaborate system of social usages, whites kept Negroes in their place. Negro resentment cut deep, but survival required its concealment. Powdermaker, as an anthropologist, confirms independently the observations of psychologists and psychiatrists previously cited:

> Such circumstances impose on the Negro a constant need to keep guard over his feelings. Whether he pretends to accept his role or merely refrains from open resentment, the compulsion to constant surveillance is there. To lose one's temper means to run the danger of being "mobbed," and this is a constant anxiety for the rebellious Negro. Since he finds so much to try him, efforts at control may result in the sullen manner of which so many Whites complain.[37]

[34] *Ibid.,* p. 327.
[35] *Ibid.,* pp. 327–30.
[36] *Ibid.,* p. 331.
[37] *Ibid.,* p. 347.

Such continual control with its constant censorship of impulse has the potential for explosiveness, the eruption of dangerous emotions. The control itself may sow the seeds of violence, as it does in so many of the novels written about the southern Negro. There are, of course, accommodations to ease the acuteness of the situation. "But despite the accommodations the element of strain persists, felt more or less consciously and more or less keenly by every member of the colored community."[38] The increasing awareness of the strain has exacerbated it; the awareness becomes part of the strain.

The Negro's "dual personality" was further documented by John Dollard in a different study of the same community. As Negroes knowingly enact the role they are forced to play with whites, they become adept at concealing their feelings. They learn to get along with whites by outwitting them. They study whites closely to learn their susceptibilities and then tell whites what they think whites expect to hear.[39] Negroes can scarcely afford to be as inaccurate in their perceptions as whites are in their stereotypes, since it is their survival that is at stake. If nothing else, the need to survive heightens acuity. According to Dollard, the latent hostility that is always there is only expressed indirectly, and more often than not it is displaced on to other Negroes.[40]

Some time later in still another town, Hylan Lewis's findings dovetail those of Powdermaker and Dollard. The change of locale signifies no change in the situation for the Negro, and this participant observer finds the same underlying problems and perceives similar patterns of response as the earlier investigators. Lewis describes the Negro subculture in Kent as a "tough" one in which there is significant blocking of goals.[41] In this culture

> much of life consists of adjusting to, rationalizing, making consistent, or combatting the force and implications of ethnic role and status. Group consciousness, and a not-always-too-comfortable identification with one's own, derive from the facts of minority status.[42]

Again, the adjustment to categorical status takes the form of presenting one self to whites and another, presumably "real" self, to Negroes.

[38] *Ibid.,* p. 370.

[39] John Dollard, *Caste and Class in a Southern Town* (Garden City, New York: Doubleday Anchor Books, 1957), pp. 257–60.

[40] *Ibid.,* pp. 285, 287, 289.

[41] Hylan Lewis, *Blackways of Kent* (New Haven, Conn.: College and University Press, 1964), p. 153.

[42] *Ibid.,* p. 195.

Since the former is not only a stylized but a subordinate self, it does not coincide with the latter. The disparity between them may account for the high proportion of random and disorganized behavior observed among Negroes.[43] In any case, the lack of restraint within the in-group contrasts markedly with the behavior required in intergroup relations. Among themselves, Negroes are touchy and querulous, manifesting the aggressiveness of a respect-starved group whose members will resort to violence in their quest for acknowledgment even from each other.[44]

The Rage Behind the Mask

Few Negroes transcend their situation. They are either trapped in the role of victim and accept its categorical status as their sole reality, or they rebel, choked with rage and confined to violence as their only alternative to accommodation. Torn between two, equally untenable, polar responses, they rarely understand themselves or their plight. Negro psychiatrists are only beginning to reveal the fear and hatred behind the masks of black men; they cannot always explain what they find, let alone offer any hope of healing the scars of centuries.[45] How do you restore dignity to those who have lost out on human possibilities?

Too risky to express, the Negro's rage is repressed at great cost to his psychic development. The effort alone of repression contributes to the emasculation that is so enraging. The passivity necessary for survival suppresses self-assertion and thus destroys more than the aggressive drive. Alvin Poussaint specifies some of the consequences of the adaptations learned in response to the disproportionate punishment for expression of

[43] *Ibid.,* p. 208.

[44] *Ibid.,* pp. 194, 221.

[45] For a recent psychiatric statement, complete with case studies, on the emotions engendered by the Negro condition, see William H. Grier and Price M. Cobbs, *Black Rage* (New York: Basic Books, 1968). The authors trace contemporary psychological consequences to their historical source in the institution of slavery. The early, and heartrending, onset of such consequences can be seen even in the writing of the youngest of children, as evidenced in *The Me Nobody Knows: Children's Voices from the Ghetto,* Stephen M. Joseph, ed. (New York: Avon, Discus Books, 1969). A dramatic instance of the individual evolution and intellectual justification of these emotions can be found in Eldridge Cleaver, *Soul on Ice* (New York: Dell, Delta Books, 1968).

anger.[46] The results are self-defeating; the techniques that permit one to survive are not those that contribute to success. Echoing earlier findings of David McClelland,[47] Poussaint points out that a trained incapacity to be aggressive leads to low aspirations among Negroes. The feeling of inadequacy is self-fulfilling. Not only is there less academic achievement, there is also less entrepreneurial inclination; Negroes are less likely to go into business than members of other minority groups.

> Central to the entrepreneurial spirit is assertiveness, self-confidence and the willingness to risk failure in an innovative venture. A castrated human being is not likely to be inclined in any of these ways.[48]

The rage that is turned inward is not thereby defused. Anything can set it off, and it is then found in its most disorganized form of riots, an outlet for the accumulated aggression of suppressed hostility. The initial studies of those who participate in riots are at least suggestive on this point. Isolated Negroes, Negroes with intense feelings of powerlessness and dissatisfaction, are more prone to violent action than those who are less alienated.[49] These are Negroes who lack any meaningful contact with whites, and violence has become their only means of communicating with the larger society. It not only expresses anger, it may even exert control, if briefly. Such behavior may well be related to the effects of emasculation, although research in this area to date remains questionable in both its methodological approach and its substantive formulation.

There is a pertinent study of "field-dependency," which attempts to measure the extent to which a person's perceptions are influenced by the surrounding environment. All the boys tested, Negro and white, with and without fathers, manifested similar masculine interests in standard tests, reflecting as much what they would like to be as what they were in fact. Those from homes in which the father was absent had higher field-dependent scores. That is to say they manifested more dependency, revealing characteristics, such as passivity, which are associated with femininity. Confused about their sexual identity, these boys have a compen-

[46] Alvin F. Poussaint, "A Negro Psychiatrist Explains the Negro Psyche," *The New York Times Magazine,* August 20, 1967, pp. 52–53 ff.

[47] See Pettigrew, "Negro American Personality," *op. cit.,* for a summary of these and other studies.

[48] Poussaint, *op. cit.,* p. 57.

[49] H. Edward Ransford, "Isolation, Powerlessness, and Violence: A Study of Attitudes and Participation in the Watts Riot," *American Journal of Sociology,* Vol. 73, No. 5 (March 1968), pp. 581–91.

satory drive toward hypermasculinity. The sample in this study is too small to be more than suggestive, but there is one point that may prove to be of considerable significance, if further confirmed; as it is, it adds weight to the observations already cited. Negro boys, even those with fathers, made significantly higher, more field-dependent scores than white boys.

The authors suggest this reflects that the "demasculinization" of the Negro is inherent in his status. It is a function of his position in society, independent of the presence or absence of a father. It is a generic feature of Negro life that sets in very early in childhood. Most Negro youngsters therefore grow up feeling that any real initiative is a waste of effort since they can't change the social system that structures their individual lives. In their passivity, they have no interest in practical goal-directed action.[50] Their action is "expressive," and the expression may be violent. Violence fulfills a stereotype of virility, thus compensating for the sense of emasculation.

If the violence is not itself instrumental, it has some purpose in establishing a masculinity eaten away by years of invisibility. Malcolm X writes in his autobiography of what it was like to be treated as a pet by whites when he was young. It apparently never occurred to them that he was a human being with intelligence and sensitivity who could understand what they were saying.

> But it has historically been the case with white people, that even though we might be *with* them, we weren't considered *of* them. Even though they appeared to have opened the door, it was still closed. Thus they never did really see *me*.[51]

No white man ever sees a black man as he sees himself, or anyone of his own kind. The consequence of this, claims Malcolm X, is that the Negro can never aspire; he is forced, within the confines of the ghetto, merely to survive. No man engaged only in survival, and without hope of success, respects himself as a man. "Almost everyone in Harlem needed some kind of hustle to survive, and needed to stay high in some way to forget what they had to *do* to survive."[52]

Herein lay Malcolm's meaning even for those Negroes who did not count themselves among his followers—they regarded him as a man. In

---

[50] Allan G. Barclay and D. R. Cusumano, "Testing Masculinity in Boys Without Fathers," *Trans-Action*, Vol. 5, No. 2 (December 1967), pp. 33–35.

[51] Malcolm X, with the assistance of Alex Haley, *The Autobiography of Malcolm X* (New York: Grove Press, 1964), p. 27.

[52] *Ibid.*, p. 91.

fighting his battles and theirs, he restored self-respect. He struggled for something more than survival; he strove for selfhood, for himself and others. Ossie Davis pays tribute to Malcolm X by declaring that he was "that rarest thing" among Negroes, a true man. "White folks do not need anybody to remind them that they are men. We do! This was his one incontrovertible benefit to his people."[53]

The appeal is more than polemical. Part of its sociological significance has been elaborated by Lee Rainwater:

> To those living in the heart of a ghetto, black comes to mean not just "stay back," but also membership in a community of persons who think poorly of each other, who give each other small comfort in a desperate world. Black comes to stand for a sense of identity no better than these destructive others. The individual feels that he must embrace an unattractive self in order to function at all.[54]

Confined to the ghetto, with its pervasive poverty and physical deterioration, the Negro's sense of impotence is reinforced. It is an existence of relative isolation. Worse than being totally cut off from the larger society, residents of the ghetto are subject to the one-way communication of the mass media that serves to remind them of their real deprivation, their institutionally imposed failure to achieve the dominant values on public display.[55] In this context, acts of violence are an assertion of visibility, an affirmation of humanity. Rioting may be the only way to relate to the larger society, to insist upon one's existence and one's right to be treated as a man.

The sheer ugliness of the ghetto has been graphically described by Kenneth Clark as indicative of its psychic state. "People seem to have given up in the little things that are so often the symbol of the larger things."[56] The ghetto is an all-encompassing psychological as well as physical reality that consumes its residents. People are so defeated that their sense of powerlessness is self-fulfilling, perpetuated by their own immobility. Apparent irresponsibility is rooted in hopelessness.[57] Perhaps the most pervasive characteristic of ghetto psychology is its cynicism, a frequently valid reaction to the exigencies of survival. Nobody believes

[53] Ossie Davis, "On Malcolm X" in Malcolm X, *The Autobiography, op. cit.,* pp. 459, 457.

[54] Lee Rainwater, "Crucible of Identity: The Negro Lower-Class Family," *Daedalus,* Winter, 1966, p. 205.

[55] Kenneth B. Clark, *Dark Ghetto* (New York: Harper Torchbooks, 1965), p. 12.

[56] *Ibid.,* p. 27.

[57] *Ibid.,* pp. 57, 67.

that anyone can be motivated by other than self-serving interests. "According to the laws of the ghetto, everyone has an angle."[58] And everyone has to have an angle in order to survive.

Clark confirms that Negro males have to struggle against their categorical status simply to believe themselves men; they have been emasculated by the inferiority of social subordination, and there is ample evidence of it in their sexual relations.[59] Hence the reality of the resentment that Negroes feel about lives they lead without meaningful purpose or effective pursuit; and hence the intensity of their hatred for those who have done this to them. The ultimate loss is the capacity to dream; not just the American dream is killed, but any dream, and along with it all aspiration. Without a dream, there is a sense only of a living death, for there is no life without hope. Richard Wright wrote dramatically in a short story in *Eight Men*:

> Yet I knew—with that part of my mind that the whites had given me—that none of my dreams were possible. . . .
> What could I dream of that had the barest possibility of coming true? I could think of nothing. And slowly, it was upon exactly that nothingness that my mind began to dwell, that constant sense of wanting without having, of being hated without reason. A dim notion of what life meant to a Negro in America was coming to consciousness in me, not in terms of external events, lynchings, Jim Crowism and the endless brutalities, but in terms of crossed-up feeling, of emotional tension.[60]

After enough "wanting without having," there is an end to wanting, and only an endless anxiety remains, the eternal disquiet of daily horror. College students working with young children in Mississippi on summer projects observed that these children seemed to have no daydreams; they wanted nothing, perhaps because they knew of nothing to want. A few had fantasies about going away, but "away" was so far off and fuzzy that it signified no place in particular. It is all the more difficult to get some place when you don't know where you are going. And as Charles Silberman points out, "For the youngster growing up in Harlem or any other Negro slum, the gates of life clang shut at a terrifyingly early age."[61]

Finally it is a sense of powerlessness that accounts for the Negro's feeling of emasculation. Whites not only control his life chances, but control

---

[58] *Ibid.*, p. 159.

[59] *Ibid.*, p. 68.

[60] Quoted in Charles E. Silberman, *Crisis in Black and White* (New York: Random House, Vintage Books, 1965), p. 49.

[61] *Ibid.*, p. 49.

them in a way calculated to "keep him in his place." The defense against such impotence is withdrawal; he cannot fail if he does not try, so he gives up trying. The identity of Negroes suffers from their inability to influence the decisions that affect their lives. Wright explains this social emasculation quite simply. When Negroes are moved to better themselves, they are not in a position to ask, "Can we do it?" Instead they must ask, "Will they let us do it?" The very nature of the question drains the will and destroys manhood. "If you act at all, it is either to flee or to kill; you are either a victim or a rebel. And almost all were victims."[62]

Authenticity and Survival

By now most observers agree that the Negro is not only inescapably black, he is also inextricably American. This implies that a problem in cultural authenticity compounds the problem of social exclusion for the Negro. The severity of his past oppression deprives him of a critical resource in coping with the stigma of his present status. If, as Jean-Paul Sartre conceives of it, "authenticity consists in having a true and lucid consciousness of the situation in assuming the responsibilities and risks that it involves, in accepting it in pride or humiliation, sometimes in horror and hate,"[63] then the Negro's authenticity does indeed lie in horror and hate. His heritage of slavery offers him no source of pride, and the emotional consequences are as consuming as his categorization is demeaning. This is no abstract philosophic dilemma; its social reality is concretely destructive.

If one is not accepted as *a* man, but as *the* Negro, then in Sartre's terms it is inauthentic to attempt to deny or escape the condition.[64] The Negro must choose himself as Negro, and as such assert his being.[65] Presumably when the Negro stops running away from himself, he ceases to be ashamed of himself. This is not necessarily the case, however, because there is no cultural content to his condition that he can call his own; authenticity does not then offer an affirmative alternative for self-assertion. Sartre's analysis, of course, was in terms of the Jew (and the Euro-

[62] Quoted in *Ibid.*, p. 102.
[63] Jean-Paul Sartre, *Anti-Semite and Jew,* trans. by George J. Becker (New York: Grove Press, Black Cat Book, 1948, 1962), p. 90.
[64] *Ibid.*, pp. 91, 101.
[65] *Ibid.*, pp. 136–37.

pean Jew at that) and his distinctive heritage. By contrast, the Negro's unique history in American society left him deliberately decultured by the systematic processes of slavery, depriving him of a viable culture from which to derive social honor and self-esteem independent of his subordination. For him to share the dominant values of American culture means to suffer the stigma of his color; he has no other self-image with which to oppose his categorical status.

The deculturation by slavery was designed to leave the Negro no alternative definition of himself, and thus no basis for rebellion. There is now no other heritage left as his social legacy. He has become exclusively American, and yet he remains excluded from access to all that he has learned to value. Under conditions of oppression, there is nothing to counter the ensuing isolation without an independent set of cultural values. In the extreme, the nature of one's heritage may make a critical difference. More than a source of pride, it may become a condition of survival in degradation. One may be demeaned and depleted, but one cannot be deprived of one's thoughts. The thoughts that permit a man to hold his head high under any circumstance are a function of his history and heritage. This accounts, as we shall see in a later chapter, for the recurrent renaissance of African interest among American Negroes. The culture (whether acquired by breeding or reading) need not instruct one in how to survive; few cultures remain relevant so indefinitely as to anticipate all situations that may eventually have to be survived. It does offer, however, the reasons for survival—the values worth surviving for in order to live by them.

In survival the why precedes the how; when one wants to live, one finds a way to do so. There may be cultural heroes to serve as role models and a source of inspiration. They represent the translation of the past into the present—and a desired projection into the future. As such, cultural heroes personalize the tradition and thereby render it viable. Their precedent becomes possible for others, thus providing for both individual initiative and cultural continuity. The Negro's problem of identity in the present is compounded by a past that lacks sufficient sources of satisfying identification. Because there are so few historical figures with whom he wishes to identify, he has few options for his own identity. The absence of a clear cultural identity creates special consequences for the contemporary Negro community. In Part IV we will contrast the characteristics of the Negro community with those of ethnic communities deriving from a distinctive cultural heritage.

PART II

THE FUNCTION
OF COMMUNITY

Chapter 3

The Nature of Community

THE tensions of the minority situation find some resolution in the context of community. Within their own community members of a minority come to terms with the social deprivation and psychological derogation imposed by their position in the larger society. They cope with the inherent frustrations with varying degrees of effectiveness, which is in part a function of the institutional structure of the minority community. The destructive responses already discussed may be restructured into organized patterns of behavior. Minority members are not often destroyed by their situation, nor do they necessarily become destructive because of it. The fact that they live in communities provides them with the social support that permits constructive action. Their shared circumstances obviate the isolation that might otherwise be incurred in the experience of exclusion and may even alleviate the incumbent sense of alienation.

The underlying conflict between the dominant and the minority group results from the unequal and inequitable distribution of values. Such conflict is resolved by patterns of accommodation that are institutionalized in the minority community. The resolution of conflict becomes part of the social order as reciprocal expectations for behavior. For a society to remain stable, all of its members must accept the established structure. Obviously then there is always a problem in motivation for members of minorities, whose situation lacks the legitimacy that safeguards social stability. It is the minority community that socializes them to their position in the larger society, mitigating its consequences for them while assuring (if not accepting) the continued monopoly of values enjoyed by the dominant group.

The Concept of Community

Any explanation of the relationship between the dominant and the minority group must bridge the theoretical gap between the sociological sources and the psychological consequences of the emergent situation. Psychological theories explain the attitudes and behavior of individuals, while sociological theories explain social processes and the relations among groups. Their respective premises are not interchangeable because a group is not simply a plurality of individuals, but a structured pattern of interaction. The reduction of one level of explanation to the other leads to a confusion of intention and consequence in which psychologists overlook the structured imperatives of the social situation and sociologists overstate the rational pursuit of social interests.

Ultimately it is the relationship between the individual and society that must be explained; it is not enough merely to describe one or the other.

> Until recently, however, the dominant bias in American sociology has been toward formulating theory in terms of variables that describe initial states, on the one hand, and outcomes, on the other, rather than in terms of processes whereby acts and complex structures of action are built, elaborated, and transformed.[1]

The hiatus between the psychological and the sociological, between initial states and consequent outcomes, must be bridged by structural concepts delineating the social conditions under which given patterns of response occur. This focuses sociological attention appropriately on the social form individual expression takes, that is, the structure of alternatives available in any situation. As we shall see, the concept of community specifies intervening structural variables linking the individual to his society through the institutional form given to patterns of social response and to the social relations among groups.

Role analysis focuses on a specific aspect of the individual's participation, whereas community studies consider the full range of institutional participation.[2] The concept of role relates the person to others in his position as role player; he fulfills the expectations inherent in his position and thereby interacts with others in reciprocal positions who share the

[1] Albert K. Cohen, "The Sociology of the Deviant Act," *American Sociological Review,* Vol. 30, No. 1 (February 1965), p. 9.

[2] Maurice R. Stein, *The Eclipse of Community* (Princeton, N.J.: Princeton University Press, 1960), p. 112.

norms defining their respective patterns of behavior. Arensberg and Kimball, long-standing proponents of community study, point out that those who use role theory apply its concepts as attributes associated with an assumed set of fixed positions in a relatively stable institution. The individual is either ignored or submerged as part of the position. Furthermore, the processes of change cannot be explained when the structure of society is seen only as sets of linked roles in interaction.[3]

The concept of role does not encompass the social setting in which the individual lives. It implies therefore a greater fragmentation of social persons and their social lives than they actually experience.

> Community studies seem to escape such distortion arising from artificial abstraction and suspension of data from real processes. They do not remove the social and cultural data they encounter from the web of connections, functions, mutual supports, complementary placements, etc., they seem to have in the life of the people of the community undergoing study.[4]

Although people interact in groups, they live in communities. Community is the more inclusive concept since it encompasses the variously institutionalized groups, more or less organized, and having more or less formally defined roles. The individual does not live in society as a whole, but in a particular community. It is the community that serves as the setting for the institutional patterns of group life, and thus the concept is able to specify the relationship between groups and institutions.

As a microcosm of culture the community provides the structure of roles and relationships embodying the cultural pattern. It is the natural unit of organization, and therefore the study of community reveals the system of institutions and their stratification.[5] The community is a living aggregate of persons following a common way of life as they act out together their various roles from cradle to grave. It makes possible the transmission of culture that assures survival.[6] Community study is thus the study of social and psychological conditions of interaction in its natural setting,

> the study of human behavior *in* communities; that is, in the natural contexts made up of natural and full human cooperative living, of living intergenera-

[3] Conrad M. Arensberg and Solon T. Kimball, "Community Study: Retrospect and Prospect," *American Journal of Sociology,* Vol. 73, No. 6 (May 1968), p. 700.

[4] *Ibid.,* p. 692.

[5] Conrad M. Arensberg and Solon T. Kimball, *Culture and Community* (New York: Harcourt, Brace & World, 1965), pp. x, xi.

[6] *Ibid.,* pp. 21–22, 97.

tional and intersexual relationships, of ongoing cultural and interfamilial communication and transmission.[7]

It is this on-going quality that allows for the consideration of change within the context of community.

The concept of community thus encompasses a total way of life. It is a complex of behavior composed of all the institutions necessary to carry on a complete life. "The community establishes collective bases for solutions to life problems."[8] The institutional patterns of the community incorporate the legitimate social arrangements that distribute rewards and sanction conformity to the shared norms. The way of life is a distinctive one, characteristic in its institutional configuration.

> A community is not only a collection of people, but it is a collection of institutions. Not people, but institutions, are final and decisive in distinguishing the community from other social constellations.[9]

Men living together develop in common some degree of distinctive characteristics setting off their community from others in some meaningful way.[10] It is distinguished not by a single institution, but by an order of institutions. Thus the community is not an unstructured congeries of activities, but a characteristic pattern of life representing a structured system of social forces brought into some kind of equilibrium.[11]

Some integration within and among individuals is implicit in a shared way of life. The concept of community suggests the concept of identity as the other side of the theoretical coin; inherent in a way of life is the idea of a social person. "The degree to which the self is developed depends upon the community," specifically upon its capacity to envision and embody values that deepen and enlarge individual experience.[12] The culture of a community is associated with the realization of values. Hence in studying any community, one must understand the values that are at

[7] *Ibid.*, pp. 30, 42.

[8] Don Martindale, *American Society* (Princeton, N.J.: Van Nostrand, 1960), pp. 105, 108.

[9] Robert E. Park, *Human Communities* (New York: Free Press, 1952), p. 66.

[10] Robert M. MacIver, *Community*, 3rd ed. (New York: Macmillan, 1931), pp. 22–23.

[11] Don Martindale, *Community, Character and Civilization* (New York: Free Press, 1963), p. 159.

[12] George Herbert Mead quoted in Gertrude Jaeger and Philip Selznick, "A Normative Theory of Culture," *American Sociological Review*, Vol. 29, No. 5 (October 1964), p. 657.

stake and the conditions of their realization.[13] Such a conceptualization not only considers the community as a way of life (rather than a series of separate and segmented institutions), it suggests the ways in which individuals experience themselves as social persons (rather than as fragmented role players).

For Max Weber the communal relationship is based upon a sense of solidarity resulting from the emotional or traditional attachments of the participants. It is not enough to share common characteristics or a common situation; even racial distinctions do not in any way imply a communal relationship. People may react to their shared situation in the same way, they may also have a common feeling about it without it leading to the creation of community. "It is only when this feeling leads to mutual orientation of their behavior toward each other that communal relationship arises among them."[14] A community of language, derived from a common tradition, facilitates mutual understanding and thereby promotes all types of social relationships. Language is not in itself, however, sufficient to bring about communalization, but it is a necessary prerequisite.[15]

With the emergence of conscious differences vis-à-vis others comes the experience of community. People begin to feel that they belong together when they acquire a consciousness of kind. Such social bonds are characterized by emotional cohesion and continuity in time. In explicating the concept as it has been developed in much nineteenth- and twentieth-century thought, Robert Nisbet points out that community encompasses all forms of relationship involving a high degree of personal intimacy and depth productive of a sense of commitment.

> Community is founded on man conceived in his wholeness rather than in one or another of the roles, taken separately, that he may hold in a social order. It draws its psychological strength from levels of motivation deeper than those of mere volition or interest, and it achieves its fulfillment in a submergence of individual will that is not possible in unions of mere convenience or rational assent. Community is a fusion of feeling and thought, of tradition and commitment, of membership and volition.[16]

[13] *Ibid.*, pp. 664, 666.
[14] Max Weber, *Basic Concepts in Sociology,* trans. by H. P. Secher (New York: Citadel, 1963), pp. 91–94.
[15] *Ibid.*, p. 94.
[16] Robert A. Nisbet, *The Sociological Tradition* (New York: Basic Books, 1966), pp. 47–48.

Such a concept, of crucial concern in classical sociology, might well be of continuing interest to contemporary sociologists, albeit in somewhat altered form. Indeed, as we shall see, it proves to be pivotal in the study of minorities. The subjective feeling of belonging together leads to a sense of shared social fate. Equality is the essence of community, and as equals people become implicated in each other's existence.[17] Their equality may be the function of little more than exclusion by others, as in the case of some American minorities. This social definition of inequality in dominant terms, however, can be sufficient to serve as a source of community for the members of a minority.

The integration of any community does not presuppose stability; its social processes include conflict as well as cooperation. The theoretical tendency to abstract phenomena out of their social context and thereby to fragment reality falsely has led to a countervailing tendency to impose an equally spurious integration with the use of such concepts as equilibrium in an ad hoc analysis. The concept of community precludes such sociological artifice by encompassing the dynamics of change. It includes the dimension of time, permitting a consideration of changing circumstances and patterns of response, and this is, after all, what constitutes historical change in social structure. The community changes with the changing situation and goals of its members and with the consequent changes in its social resources and institutionalized means. These internal conditions of a community vary with its external position in the larger society. The relationship between the community and the surrounding society is, of course, critical in the minority situation since it is its disadvantaged social position that is the raison d'être for the minority community.

There is a dynamic relationship between conflict and change in which power is a critical variable. No one way of life can fulfill the needs of all the members of a complex community. There are therefore the internal differentiation and social heterogeneity that lead to variations in patterns of behavior. Conflict occurs when the pursuit of shared, but scarce, values by one group precludes their pursuit by another group because of the latter's restricted access to the institutionalized means of achievement. In a differential power situation competition becomes conflict. There is then conflict between those with a vested interest in the status quo and those who are deprived by it. The provision of new social alternatives, when

[17] *Ibid.*, pp. 80, 106.

possible, permits change and prevents the disintegration of the community. When change is internalized within the individual and conflict is externalized within the community, neither need disintegrate. It is thus the function of community to provide the means of resolving conflict and of incorporating change.

The Status Community

Status is conferred by others on the basis of shared values, ranking persons as equals or nonequals. Shared status therefore means social equality, which is to be regarded as a peer by those who share the same values. In distinguishing between class and status, Weber conceptualized the status situation as every typical component of life fate that is determined by a specific positive or negative social estimation of honor. "In contrast to classes, *status groups* are normally communities. They are, however, often of an amorphous kind."[18] Social honor, which may be connected with any shared quality, is expressed in a specific style of life expected from all those who wish to belong to the same circle. Linked to this expectation are restrictions on social intercourse that are ultimately endogamous in character.[19] The status group is the bearer of conventions; it originates and conserves a style of life. Its social honor, therefore, rests upon distance and exclusiveness so that it can maintain its monopoly of ideal and material goods or opportunities.[20]

The status community that emerges out of a shared style of life is based on a social definition of equality, whatever criteria of eligibility are employed; it functions to protect the prestige of its members. Birth is the initial determinant of life chances. One is born into a particular family, which is in turn part of a community. In an open stratification system, there is potential for mobility so that one's social position may not be permanently fixed at birth. The distribution of life chances within a community varies then with the relative consideration given to achieve-

[18] Max Weber, "Class, Status, Party," *From Max Weber: Essays in Sociology,* trans. by Hans H. Gerth and C. Wright Mills (New York: Oxford, Galaxy Books, 1958), pp. 187, 186.
[19] *Ibid.,* pp. 187–88.
[20] *Ibid.,* pp. 190–91.

ment versus ascription (characteristics, that is, for which one has worked versus those to which one was born). The style of life of a community requires a certain class level, but class does not imply status so it does not in itself lead to the formation of a community. Class provides the material basis for community, and as such it may be one of the values stratifying it.

Community once connoted territoriality, but this is no longer necessarily so. Communality rests increasingly on the shared interests of social nearness rather than common residence. The common values that coordinate the behavior of members of such a status community provide the shared expectations that make for mutual intelligibility. Members act on the premise that others will judge them in terms of these common values; this, of course, does not preclude conflict of interests among them.[21] The institutions that make possible a shared way of life are defended by a communal ideology justifying the status of the participants.

> Perhaps the retention of a mythology that allows a minimum of collective self-esteem and justification is the only real alternative to social disintegration. People need to believe in the value of the communities in which they live, the goals that they seek, and the satisfactions they receive.[22]

Philosophic conceptions of community claim that it is just this feeling that members of a group have about themselves that sets them apart from others. Theirs is a relationship not shared with others, and loyalty to it requires commitment to their common way of life. Paradox is thus the essence of community; it is the *shared* uniqueness of social peers whose status is reflected in their communal identity. This status is protected by the exclusion of nonequals. In this way the community not only upholds the social honor of its members, it reinforces the stratification system by perpetuating the social distance among people in different positions. It is the principle of closure, embodied in the exclusion of nonmembers, that maintains the communal monopoly on its style of life.

Weber delineated the closed social relationship as one capable of guaranteeing its monopolized advantages to its members. When the values are appropriated on a permanent basis by a given group, they become more or less inalienable. In the closed community, therefore, membership tends to be determined by family ties.[23] The principle of birth is not

---

[21] Jessie Bernard, *American Community Behavior* (New York: Holt, Rinehart & Winston, 1949), pp. 7–8.

[22] Stein, *op. cit.,* p. 295.

[23] Weber, *Basic Concepts, op. cit.,* pp. 98–99.

the basis of every restrictive relationship, but it is, of course, the crucial premise operative in the minority situation. The motivation for all such social restrictions is "the maintenance of quality and eventually that of prestige and the opportunity deriving from it to enjoy honor and possibly even profit."[24] The status community thus tends to consolidate within it the values of wealth, power, and esteem and to establish exclusive access to these values by social closure.[25] As the community crystallizes, it protects its strategic position and consequent privilege with the enforcement of endogamy.

Closure is central to the significance of the status community. In effect the enclosure enacted by exclusion constitutes community. By drawing social boundaries between members and nonmembers, closure delimits the eligibility for the communal way of life and thus defends its worth. It enhances the status of a style of life by reinforcing its scarcity value. The social honor of the status community is upheld because the prestige of its shared position is protected from usurpation.

The scarcity value of a way of life exists by virtue of exclusion, independently of any intrinsic value it may have. A way of life may have no particular worth over and beyond its exclusiveness; participation in it is restricted, and that may define its worth (at least for the participants), even when communal life loses its cultural distinctiveness. The mass media of modern society have helped to bring about considerable homogenization of its constituent communities. Each community remains nonetheless ethnocentric, convinced of its superiority even while conforming to a way of life that no longer rests on an ideology of difference. The social commitment survives its ideological defense, and people continue to live separately even when their lives have become much the same.

Insofar as there is a characteristic way of life, community enclosure minimizes the potential for social change. There is no more effective protection of ethnocentric commitment than the invisibility of alternatives. When members of a community are permitted to know social alternatives, other possibilities for action become visible to them. In the absence of such knowledge, rational choice is not possible because there is no awareness of the connection between social conditions and their consequences. Effective change is thus prevented. Members of a community are all the more capable of chauvinistic conformity when they

[24] *Ibid.,* p. 101.
[25] Don Martindale, *American Social Structure* (New York: Appleton-Century-Crofts, 1960), p. 460.

do not know of any other way to live, and they are less likely to be aware of alternatives when their community is not contaminated by the influence of strangers. From Plato on, those concerned with the stability of communal life, ideal or otherwise, have wanted to avoid conflict by safeguarding against the adoption of new values. In this way membership is not lost to a mutually exclusive way of life; but so also is the creativity of a community sacrificed for there is no source of innovation and none of the flexibility necessary for adaptation to changing conditions.

The principle of closure operates through the informal social intercourse of the members of a community. The limits of intimacy are established by their commensalism and endogamy. Peers are defined by their willingness to break bread together and to marry; the ultimate measure of social acceptance in any community is marriage, and all its social prerequisites and prerogatives. Those who lack the necessary qualifications either of ascription or achievement are excluded from participation in the community, and thereby from marriage with its members.

The Dominant Group as a Status Community

The ascribed status that determines the style of life of the dominant group by social definition precludes the participation of minority members. The closure of the dominant group takes the form of discrimination, the categorical exclusion of minorities from the major institutions that make up the way of life of the larger society; the ideological defense of such closure is prejudicial in nature. The social processes that determine the relationship between the dominant and the minority group are themselves no different from those that characterize any intragroup and intergroup relations. What differs are the criteria of eligibility, and they are categorical. The dominant community is thus a status community in which membership is based on lineage. Minority members are excluded from its way of life by an accident of birth that deprives them of the necessary ascription. There is no shared status between the dominant and the minority group, and hence there is no shared community.

The minority community is in this sense a counterformation, a reaction to the closure of the dominant community. Its essential raison d'être is exclusion, although it may have a sacred or secular ideology justifying its institutions in terms that are independent of the images of the dominant group. But if the survival of the minority group is at stake in the formation of its own community, so may it also cease to exist with the end of exclusion. So long as categorical criteria remain relevant, the minority community affords its members an existence that does not threaten the exclusiveness of the dominant group. It also helps to defend the minority's honor from the inferiority imposed by such exclusion; self-exclusion makes tolerable, if not acceptable, the social exclusion of the minority situation.

Historical as well as contemporary circumstances account for whether or not a minority group is able to wrest concessions from the dominant group and lay claim to some share of its values. The dominant group may grant such concessions when the minority group has sufficient bargaining power that some economic or political interest of the larger society becomes vulnerable. The minority community is then formed around such values as it can gain. Even when the dominant group grants "separate, but equal" values in law, however, the values are seldom equal in reality, and the status of the dominant community is thereby preserved intact. The alternative is for the minority to create a community on the basis of its own resources. The economic feasibility of doing so frequently rests on specialized ethnic occupations, described by Weber as socially despised.

When the minority group provides its own values, they are, of course, not equal in status to those of the dominant group, if only because they are still separate. The minority community may represent the stratified distribution of acculturated values, but even those dominant values that are embodied in minority institutions are not integrated into the social organization and stratification of the dominant community. The social distance between dominant and minority group is maintained as long as minority members continue to participate exclusively with each other in their own institutions without claiming social recognition in the larger society.

To some extent acculturation is an economic necessity since few minority groups have the self-sufficiency to support a full range of separate institutions. The resulting competition for scarce, but increasingly shared, values produces pressure for further acculturation, advancing it from the economic to the social level. This rarely leads to assimilation, however, as we shall see. Some separate identity is retained even without cultural content. Because of the minority situation such an identity incurs invidious social consequences long after its ethnicity has disappeared.

In a genuinely pluralistic society, assimilation need not be an issue; there would be no social penalty for a special identity. As it is, it is more an ideology of some minority members than an actuality for any of them. It is the hope of a segment of the minority community to solve its social problem by eliminating the situation that is seen as its cause. Thus some minority members desire the eventual disappearance of the ethnic group as a separate entity, and hence the loss of their special identity. They aspire to assimilation, which is not only to be culturally indistinguishable from the dominant group, but to be included in its institutional participation, and finally in its primary relations.[26]

Since the relationship between the dominant and the minority group is a result of the accommodation of their conflicting interests, any change in the status of the minority group leads to a breakdown in the accepted pattern of intergroup relations. Accommodation may take the form of subjugation in which the minority group has no access to dominant values, of segregation in which unequal values are granted by the dominant group, or of pluralism in which equal values are established by the minority group. The nature of the minority community varies with its capacity to create independent parallel institutions. The mobility of minority members thus means that a previously accepted pattern of accommodation is no longer applicable to their situation. Their achievement changes their status, and that in turn changes the structure of their community. Their new status prompts them to make new claims on the dominant group. The renewed emergence of intergroup conflict leads to a redefinition of the minority situation—and some modification of the existing pattern of accommodation.

The structure of the minority community thus reflects the status of its members, and it incorporates any change in that status by institutionalizing patterns of accommodation that embody the responses to changing circumstances. The minority community constitutes, in a word, a continuing adaptation to its socially disadvantaged situation. As such it has a multiplicity of functions that we will explore in the next chapter. We will find some functions that survive minority acculturation, but few that survive dominant exclusiveness. There remains little point in a minority community if and when its members are included as social equals in the status communities of the dominant group. In most instances, however, such integration is hardly imminent, whatever the qualifications of the minority; its exclusion continues on the grounds of categorical ineligibility —and so does its community.

[26] For a discussion of the different types of assimilation, see Milton M. Gordon, *Assimilation in American Life* (New York: Oxford, 1964), particularly pp. 60–83.

Chapter 4

The Function of the Minority Community

THE minority community is a status community like all status communities, but its shared status is a depreciated one. It is formed not so much out of its own exclusiveness as out of the exclusiveness of others. The minority community is characterized therefore by the equality of its social inferiority, an inferiority imposed by exclusion. The common categorical status of its members takes precedence over any achieved status of individuals; it is an ascribed status that is negatively evaluated, and as such it leads to the formation of communities that crosscut class lines in the larger society. The communities are themselves internally differentiated, with some members being more negatively evaluated than others.

The institutions that provide the basis for the communal way of life are stratified by class. By contrast to the status community that is founded upon economic homogeneity, the minority community encompasses a variety of social groupings that have in common only their ethnic birth. The stratification system of any minority community is a function of the way in which its particular ethnic background limits the achievement of members. Each community has a characteristic level of access to social values; each stratification system thus distributes values differentially.

The Formation of the Minority Community

The variations in style of life among and within minority groups will be examined in Parts III and IV. At this point we will look only at the general structure of their communities and the specific functions. In the next chapter we will trace the concrete historical emergence of the minority community, but first we should seek its generic sociological source in the social structure. Why does it come into being? The Weberian question still pertains in this context: "Under what conditions is there communalization?" The same reactions to a shared situation are not a sufficient condition of community under any circumstance. It requires the mutual orientation of social interaction and, in the case of minorities, this is likely to be brought about by their categorization. Categorical treatment cuts them off from social alternatives, and they have no choice but to form their own communities.

Weber points out that the extent to which any communal action emerges depends upon cultural conditions, especially upon conditions of an intellectual nature. There must be sufficient contrast in life chances so that there are visible connections between the causes and the consequences of a social situation. People, in other words, must be aware of their situation in order to act upon it; its consequences must be recognizable so that the contrast in life chances is not accepted as absolutely given.[1] Continual categorization appears to create such an awareness among members of a minority group, and their resulting sense of relative deprivation may then serve as the basis of communalization.

Robin Williams, Jr., describes some of the processes involved in communalization as he seeks to explain how an aggregate, or a collection of individuals with no relationship among themselves, becomes a collectivity, or an interacting group.[2] Due to historical circumstance, there is the initial categorization of those considered to have some important characteristic in common. Identifying symbols with social visibility are used as the basis for categorical definition. This is, of course, the source of the minority situation, and the ability to impose such categories on others is part of the dominant group's power to subordinate. Persons in the same category are typically found (or believed to be found) in occupations or other social roles that are recognizably different from those associated with other categories. Consequently they develop distinctive interests and values as well as specific modes of behavior. These differences in turn reinforce the initial definition of the category.

[1] Max Weber, "Class, Status, Party," *From Max Weber: Essays in Sociology,* trans. by Hans H. Gerth and C. Wright Mills (New York: Oxford, Galaxy Books, 1958), p. 184.
[2] The following discussion is drawn from Robin M. Williams, Jr., *Strangers Next Door* (Englewood Cliffs, N.J.: Prentice-Hall, 1964), pp. 18–19.

As a result, members of a category acquire a sense of common identity, which tends to increase interaction among themselves and to reduce contacts with others. Such social closure makes it even more likely that others will treat them as a unit; this treatment further enhances the new collectivity's cultural distinctiveness and social separateness. It is not a completely closed social system since it is economically and politically dependent on the larger society. As a subordinate group, it must not only maintain relationships with others, it must accept the dominant rules of the game. It is forced into a one-way adaptation to a common set of constitutive norms regulating necessary relations between the dominant and subordinant group.

> A fully developed collectivity . . . is a *people,* and is characterized by 1) a distinctive culture; 2) tests or criteria of membership; 3) a set of constitutive norms regulating social relations both within the collectivity and with outsiders; 4) an awareness of a distinct identity by both members and nonmembers; 5) obligations of solidarity, such as enforced requirements to help members in need and to resist derogation by outsiders; and 6) a high capacity for continued action on behalf of its members or of itself as a unit. In its most comprehensive development such a collectivity may become a potentially self-sufficient society, able to meet all internal needs from its own resources and to perpetuate itself as a functioning system from generation to generation.[3]

Not all minorities have crystallized into such complete communities, but they all do develop into collectivities in varying degrees. They start off as culturally or physically (or both) distinctive and self-conscious aggregates with hereditary membership and a high level of endogamy. Subject to discrimination by the dominant group, members of a minority become a collectivity. If outsiders act toward an aggregate as if it is a collectivity with an identified and definite membership, it becomes one. If its members are treated alike, they become so in many of their interests and values. And their increased awareness of common interests leads to an increased likelihood of concerted action. Hence minority communities emerge whose shared institutions make possible common activities. Because members of these communities are to some extent isolated from the larger society, their feeling of interdependence is intensified. The sense of unity within a specific community is extended to include members of the same minority in other communities, thereby enhancing the potential strength of any collective action to improve their situation.[4]

[3] *Ibid.,* p. 18.
[4] *Ibid.,* pp. 304–5, 236.

It is through such processes that the sense of shared fate of a minority group leads to the emergence of a communal social structure. Members are shored up by forces of defensive solidarity, finding both protection and fulfillment within the boundaries of their own community, at least in so far as it is possible to do so. (The minority community, as we will see, may lack sufficient institutionalized resources to provide for its members adequately.) The community becomes internally differentiated as its members achieve varying levels of mobility and thereby come into contact with the dominant group. Religious differentiation also appears to suit the stratified life styles.[5] The lives of minority members may be so fully enacted within their own community that the ethnic group remains a significant reference group even after acculturation. Ethnic bonds may retain their emotional strength even while losing their cultural distinctiveness.

> It is within the ethnic grouping that all individuals form their first relationships, their deepest dependencies, and the most important bases of emotional ambivalence.[6]

It is critical to understand the careful distinctions Weber makes among kinds of status communities in order to avoid contemporary confusions about the nature of caste. Only when the consequences of status are fully realized is there caste. There are no castes among American minorities, for neither their ethnic differences nor their status distinctions are guaranteed by any sacred ideologies and religious rituals. Weber discusses the fact that "pariah" peoples form communities. Although they are socially segregated, they acquire a specific occupational tradition and are frequently tolerated for their economic indispensability. Such ethnic communalization does not, however, constitute a caste situation. A caste structure transforms the horizontal and unconnected coexistences of ethnically segregated groups into a vertical system of superordination and subordination. In such a position, the ethnic community cannot cultivate a belief in its social honor.[7]

The minority situation, whatever else it is, is not a caste structure and the contrast is crucial. Even pariah people, who must acknowledge the greater honor of higher status groups, are allowed some belief in their own honor, and genuine ethnic coexistence permits each community to

[5] J. Milton Yinger, "Social Forces Involved in Group Identification or Withdrawal," *Daedalus:* Spring, 1961, pp. 254–55.

[6] Williams, *op. cit.,* p. 19.

[7] Weber, *op. cit.,* p. 189.

consider its honor the highest.[8] Rarely is a society so pluralistic that this is really possible, but at least there can be mutual disdain. The sense of dignity of the negatively privileged may rest only on their hopes for an afterlife, another existence different, of course, from their worldly life, but it is dignity nonetheless, whatever its source. The social honor of a pariah people frequently has religious reference; it needs no more to prevent the acceptance of dominant images. Such a group may be despised, but it does not despise itself. Its religion offers a powerful potion to self-esteem, even to the extent of the glorification of suffering.

> The situation of the pariah people and its patient endurance were thus elevated to the highest station of religious worth and social honor before God, by receiving the meaning of a world historical mission.[9]

When men are subjected to a continual barrage of negative experiences, both major and minor, it is not surprising that they should be drawn to one another. But there is also significance in this fact for the dominant community. Since a community is a way of life monopolized by its members, to share it indiscriminately is to risk the peculiar properties of the community itself. Members are therefore always reluctant to receive strangers. "The very existence of an alien with ways of life different from those of the community is a kind of threat—for the alien is living proof that social life is capable of other kinds of organization."[10] The emergence of the minority community diminishes this threat to the dominant group at the same time that it resolves the tensions of its members' social subordination.

The Sociological Functions of the Minority Community

The categorization of any group gathers its own momentum; it is not a matter of individual volitions acting in concert. The way in which one is identified in the larger society affects the way in which one identifies one-

---

[8] *Ibid.*

[9] Max Weber, *Ancient Judaism*, trans. and ed. by Hans H. Gerth and Don Martindale (New York: Free Press, 1952), p. 376.

[10] Don Martindale, *American Social Structure* (New York: Appleton-Century-Crofts, 1960), pp. 385–86.

self—as well as where one is located in the social structure. The interdependence of their shared fate shapes the lives of the members of the minority community.[11]

> Within the ethnic group there develops a network of organizations and informal social relationships which permits and encourages the members of the ethnic group to remain within the confines of the group for all of their primary relationships and some of their secondary relationships throughout all the stages of the life-cycle.[12]

As institutions become ethnically enclosed, they acquire a vested interest in maintaining themselves. They may do so beyond the point of their initial functions when the purposes of the minority community are no longer served.

The basic social unit of this community is the family, since its institutional structure is founded upon the involuntary and inescapable fact of ethnic birth. Because the boundaries of the community are defined by ancestry, it has considerable impact on personality development. E. K. Francis argues that the ethnic group is an extension of the "we-feeling" of the primary group. It permits the self-sufficiency and the segregation that the family alone is unable to provide.[13] The minority community formed by the ethnic group practices self-exclusion as a protection against the social exclusion of the dominant group. Its institutions and ideologies provide a way of life that is independent of the categorical status of its members. Their social honor is thereby secured against dominant derogation.

In its incipience, the minority community developed out of the distinctive institutions of the ethnic group. The terms "ethnic" and "minority" therefore are frequently used interchangeably, and properly so historically. Among the groups that were transformed into minorities in American society, after all, were those characterized by cultural differences. Their solution to the problems experienced in their socially disadvantaged situation was, of course, the formation of separate communities. With acculturation, however, minority communities do not continue to be ethnic. (Nor do all ethnic groups remain minorities.) As we trace patterns of change through several generations, we will no longer be able

[11] Milton M. Gordon, *Assimilation in American Life* (New York: Oxford, 1964), pp. 29–30.

[12] *Ibid.*, p. 34.

[13] E. K. Francis, "The Nature of the Ethnic Group," *American Journal of Sociology*, Vol. 52, No. 5 (March 1947), p. 399.

to treat the minority community and the ethnic community as synonymous. The growing distinction between them will begin to make a critical difference in the contemporary situation of the various groups; their respective social structures vary accordingly, as we will see in later chapters.

"Every ethnic group presupposes an ideology, however vague and unreflective it may be." Once the minority community has become real, that is, institutionalized as a social fact, it finds new rationalizations for its coherence if its ideological basis is challenged.[14] The ideology, among other things, defends the special identity of community members in an attempt to safeguard their group survival. Such survival is usually justified in terms of the way of life offered by the community and the realization of values it makes possible.

The life chances of minorities are more likely to be enhanced when the minorities themselves can provide their own values than when values are granted as grudging concessions by the dominant group. Paternalism always rankles, perpetuating its power in the very dispensation of special privilege. Values thus gained bear the stamp of inferiority implicit in the process. Separate values, by contrast, whether the same as or different from those of the dominant group, offer the chance of equality. With access to such values, members of the minority community are afforded the possibility of independent achievement. Insofar as they exercise their capacities, they can fulfill aspirations denied to them in the larger society. Participation in the minority community thus enables them to live more fully, to live as if dominant exclusion did not exist.

By freeing its members of some of the deleterious consequences of their minority situation, the community offers them a sense of autonomy that makes possible aspiration and achievement. Being able to control some of their life chances effectively expands those chances and their capacities. Ultimately the very achievement that the minority community helps to bring about may lead, if not to group assimilation, at least to individual integration into the dominant community. It is the boomerang built into the ideology of group survival; insofar as the function of group survival is fulfilled, the grounds for community are undermined by diminishing its necessity—unless, of course, discrimination continues to any great extent. However, as Martindale points out, the pressures from the surrounding society are variable and frequently inconsistent. The same

[14] *Ibid.*

processes that led to the formation of the community in the first place may help to bring on its decline in the future.[15]

Although the minority community may not retain its cultural integrity, it is initially characterized by indigenous social patterns. The dominant patterns are eventually blended with, or refracted through, the particular heritage of the ethnic group. With time the community is subdivided into groupings based on social class, and class may come to be more significant in influencing behavior than ethnicity. There may be the whole spectrum of social classes within the community, or only a partial distribution, but by no means are all members of a minority group alike. With regard to participation in primary groups, therefore, they tend to confine themselves to their own class segment within their own ethnic group, or what Gordon calls their "ethclass." It is here that they find a social affinity based on behavioral similarity.[16]

Oscar Handlin has shown much historical sensitivity in discerning the functions of the ethnic enclave.[17] The diversity of the American population has always been such that no single integrated community could have been created. The prevailing looseness of institutional forms has allowed numerous smaller communities to develop that perform functions important to individual lives. Among these were the ethnic groups that satisfied the emotional desires for personal association and enabled common action with organized means. The continuity of experience was disrupted by migration, and the ensuing isolation exacerbated human crises. Organizations deriving from a common pool of ethnic membership appeared in order to meet such needs. Although they served discrete ends, these organizations helped to restore a sense of stability and solidarity based on traditional patterns.[18]

Not all ethnic groups were aware of their identity upon their arrival in the United States; some acquired a sense of identity only after they were here. Even when the boundaries of membership were not quite clear, however, the ethnic group permitted men to organize their lives on their own terms. It minimized compulsion and maximized choice, providing the means for cooperative action without requiring undue social restraint. This rather fluid pattern of association, as Handlin depicts it,

[15] Martindale, *op. cit.,* p. 429.

[16] Gordon, *op. cit.,* pp. 38, 48, 52–53.

[17] There is perhaps no more poignant portrayal of the immigrant experience than Oscar Handlin's *The Uprooted* (Boston: Little, Brown, 1951).

[18] Oscar Handlin, "Historical Perspectives on the American Ethnic Group," *Daedalus,* Spring, 1961, pp. 223–25.

maintained a fine balance between those forces that connected members of the ethnic community to the larger society and those that isolated them. Over time the ethnic differences that set them apart diminished, and the minority community then protected its social identity by de-emphasizing its particularity.[19] The community thus continued to fulfill its special functions for minorities even in the absence of ethnicity.

It is perhaps its link with the past that gives the minority community its emotional significance. Since members of a minority group are forced to associate with each other and even to live in segregated areas, they not only begin to regard themselves as a community, but they come to feel a sense of responsibility for one another. "All of them tend to possess a transmitted remembrance of how the community developed."[20] There is always the memory of how they were received in this country and the discrimination they encountered in settling here. It is this shared history, as we shall see, that constitutes a major focus of the socialization into minority status. The separate institutions of the minority community, however, do not preclude relationships with the larger society. Most minority communities lack economic self-sufficiency, for example, and their members are frequently dependent upon the dominant group for a source of livelihood.

Although there have been innumerable studies of immigrants and their adjustment, few have taken into account the way in which the social organization of their respective communities affects their patterns of response. There has been one sociological investigation along these lines, carried out in Montreal, Canada, that is of particular interest in its concern with the impact of institutions upon individuals; it thus highlights the functions of community. In studying relatively recent arrivals, Raymond Breton finds that the nature of the ethnic community influences their social relations.

An ethnic community may consist of a network of interpersonal relationships with no supporting institutions, in which case the immigrant must establish his institutional affiliations in the dominant community. There is institutional completeness, by contrast, when the ethnic community can perform all the services required by its members.[21] Such

[19] *Ibid.*, pp. 226–27.

[20] Peter I. Rose, *They and We* (New York: Random House, 1964), pp. 125–26.

[21] Raymond Breton, "Institutional Completeness of Ethnic Communities and the Personal Relations of Immigrants," *American Journal of Sociology*, Vol. 70, No. 2 (September 1964), pp. 193–94.

communities are characterized by their relative number of churches, welfare organizations, newspapers, and periodicals. Those Canadian ethnic communities with a high level of institutional completeness include the Greek, German, French, Hungarian, Italian, Lithuanian, Polish, and Russian. Among those with a low level of institutional completeness are the Albanian, American, Austrian, Belgian, Bulgarian, Czechoslovakian, Danish, Dutch, English, Irish, Portuguese, Spanish, Swedish, and so forth.[22]

Breton interviewed 230 male immigrants, 163 of whom he reinterviewed fourteen months later to determine what proportion of their interpersonal relations were with others of the same ethnic group and what proportion with native Canadians. He asked them, in effect, what they did with whom. This is a critical question for the immigrant since uprooting forces him to reconstruct his network of personal affiliations in a new community. He usually accomplishes this through activities satisfying his immediate needs. Initially the immigrant is drawn into the ethnic community. Its formal organizations minimize contacts with outsiders and thus help to keep his social relations within ethnic boundaries. Those communities with the highest degree of institutional completeness have the greater proportion of members whose personal relations are found mostly within the ethnic group (i.e., 89 percent of members of highly institutionalized communities in contrast to 21 percent of those from groups with few or no formal organizations).[23]

The institutions of an ethnic community are the origin of much social life in which its members become mutually involved and thereby tied together in a cohesive interpersonal network. In fact, Breton finds that the existence of communal institutions increases ethnic cohesiveness, irrespective of their level of acculturation. The sheer presence of churches, for instance, leads to more in-group relations, even among those who do not attend. The ethnic group succeeds in holding its members' allegiance when it can prevent their contact with the dominant community. This occurs through a process of substitution in which ethnic rather than dominant institutions prevail in the immigrants' social life. They may establish a wide range of institutional attachments through their work, but it is the religious institution that has the greatest effect in keeping the immigrant's personal associations within the ethnic community. The church has a predominant role in the community; it serves as the center

22 *Ibid.*, pp. 195–96.
23 *Ibid.*, p. 196.

of many activities and a source of reinforcement for national sentiments.[24]

A community's capacity to control the social integration of its members is thus a function of its institutional structure. It is not so much a matter of having many formal organizations, but of having some organizations rather than none at all. There is expansion in the interpersonal network when the ethnic group ceases to be an informal system and acquires the first elements of formal structure; therein lies the significance of community. This expansion continues as the formal structure develops, but the increments are smaller than the initial one. If the immigrant, therefore, is a member of an ethnic group with organizations of its own, he is three times more likely to have acquired associates within his group than if he belongs to a group that lacks a formal structure (i.e., 62 percent in contrast to 20 percent).[25]

The formal structure not only reinforces the cohesiveness of existing informal networks, it enlarges them by attracting new immigrants to the community. A high degree of institutional completeness gives the community a greater capacity for the absorption of newcomers, but it doesn't prevent some members from establishing relationships beyond its boundaries. After a while, many immigrants begin to break their ethnic ties and form new attachments outside the community. (The Breton study finds an increase in relationships with the dominant community after six years in Canada.) The greater the difference between the ethnic group and the dominant group, the more likely the former is to develop institutions to satisfy the needs of its members. The differentiating characteristics of the group constitute the basis for the formation of a clientele for ethnic organizations. Since these characteristics are negatively evaluated in the larger society, they reduce the potential mobility of members of the ethnic group and restrict them to their own community; hence a difference in language, which both symbolizes and embodies other cultural differences, is associated with institutional completeness.[26]

Not all such communities lose their members with time; there is a way of holding them that allows for the alternative of social continuity.

In the continuing relations between the ethnic community and its environment, one of two things may happen when the mutual relation is not such as to evolve into a caste system. The ethnic community may simply eliminate those individuals by a continual whittling-down process, or new

[24] *Ibid.*, pp. 197, 199, 200–1.
[25] *Ibid.*, pp. 201–2.
[26] *Ibid.*, pp. 202, 204.

communities may form between the ethnic and majority community with as characteristic a reshaping of the institutions as was true in the first place.[27]

The greater the social and economic distance between the ethnic and the dominant community, the more likely that through the years there will be a succession of community forms moving closer to those of the dominant community.[28] The pattern of acculturation is asymmetrical for institutions as for individuals, and it is in the direction of the norms and values of the dominant group.

To maintain ethnic identity the community tries to provide a complete set of institutions to occupy the whole of the individual's life. To continue doing so over time the community must change to meet the new needs of its members. Such change, however, is often resisted; for example, the elders of the community want parochial schools to teach youth the traditions in order to prevent them from drifting away to the dominant culture. Nevertheless, it is usually impossible for the ethnic community to provide out of its own resources all that is offered by the surrounding society. The majority of members remain within the ethnic group only if they continue to encounter prejudice on the outside. Otherwise they are tempted by the greater economic and political opportunities in the dominant community.[29]

Even so, it is difficult for the ethnic community to remain unchanged, whatever the resistance of its vested interests. Conditions of external discrimination and a coherent set of internal institutions may combine to maintain the ethnic community for generations. It, nevertheless, undergoes a series of changes, each approximating more closely the social patterns of the dominant community. Each stage of acculturation is also accompanied by the loss of some members. The success of the ethnic community in forming a protective shell around its members is no guarantee that they will want to continue in its way of life. Opportunities in the larger society may be offered to members whose talents are valued by the dominant group. Such successful members of the ethnic community may be assimilated through intermarriage, or they may introduce to their ethnic group the dominant patterns they have acquired.[30]

Individuals have a complex investment in the institutions of the

[27] Martindale, *op. cit.*, p. 429.
[28] *Ibid.*, p. 430.
[29] Don Martindale, *Community, Character and Civilization* (New York: Free Press, 1963), p. 310.
[30] *Ibid.*, pp. 311–12.

ethnic community, and thus a stake in its continuation, regardless of loss in membership. The community may respond to the threat of dissolution by organizing new social forms. In their discussion of the principal ethnic groups of New York City, Glazer and Moynihan point out that each of them maintains a distinct, if changing, identity from one generation to the next. These ethnic differences, which may become a matter of choice as well as heritage, are a function of new creation as much as old forms.[31] The community persists by means of its social innovations.

Although their language and culture may be lost in the first and second generations, ethnic groups frequently remain concentrated in occupational specialties. Even when they are stripped of their original attributes, they are re-created in new social forms and still identifiable as groups, sometimes as interest groups whose rational economic pursuits overlap with the social and emotional ties of the ethnic community. Various values thus continue to be encompassed by ethnicity.

> Concretely, persons think of themselves as members of that group, with that name; they are thought of by others as members of that group, with that name; and most significantly, they are linked to other members of the group by new attributes that the original immigrants would never have recognized as identifying their group, but which nevertheless serve to mark them off, by more than simply name and association, in the third generation and even beyond.[32]

Whatever the changes in the cultural content of its institutions, associational ties have remained, by and large, bounded by the ethnic community. Nationality differences rarely survive the third generation, but religious differences continue to define the limits of community. And religious distinctions are reinforced by economic conditions as well as social affiliations.[33]

There are also external forces that influence the nature of the ethnic community and serve as renewed bases of cohesion. There was the shaping of New York's Jewish community under the impact first of the Nazi holocaust and then of the creation of the state of Israel. Similarly, the integration of the Catholic community was furthered by the reemergence of the parochial school controversy. The Negro community has grown with the migration of southern Negroes since World War I, and the Puerto Rican community with the influx of immigrants since World War

[31] Nathan Glazer and Daniel P. Moynihan, *Beyond the Melting Pot* (Cambridge, Mass.: The M.I.T. and Harvard University Press, 1963), p. vi.
[32] *Ibid.,* p. 13.
[33] *Ibid.,* pp. 300, 313.

II. The differences among these groups in experiences and values are now supported by the existence of separate ethnic communities.[34] The communities, already long established, have also acquired vested interests in perpetuating themselves.

For this reason, most ethnic groups have not pushed their claim for equality to the point where the exclusive institutions of the dominant group would be threatened. Most Jews and Catholics, for example, have not demanded the complete abolition of social distance because they too want to maintain their own communities. They accept many of the lines drawn by the dominant community in order to preserve a special identity shored up by social segregation. Since they prefer not to mingle, they do not try to break down the more informal barriers of the dominant community. They strive, as they have always striven, for an equality of opportunity that does not challenge the established patterns of exclusion.[35] Immersed in their own exclusiveness, the ethnic groups deriving from earlier migrations accept exclusion by others. Such self-exclusion is their accommodation to the categorical closure they have experienced in the larger society, but it is also perforce an acceptance of dominant power and privilege—and of the inequities of discrimination.

The Psychological Functions—and Dysfunctions

Individual responses to the minority situation become institutionalized within the ethnic community and so the psychological consequences of the minority situation become incorporated into social patterns. These patterns in turn acquire an existence of their own, independent of the situation to which they were once a response. They serve as a source of socialization for members of the community, whatever the changes in their circumstances. In so doing, they are perpetuated, often beyond the point of functional adaptation to the minority situation. The appropriateness of the accommodation over time may well become irrelevant as minority members are shaped more by significant influences within their own community than by discriminatory experiences in the dominant community.

[34] *Ibid.*, pp. 292, 298.
[35] Nathan Glazer, "Negroes and Jews: The New Challenge to Pluralism," *Commentary*, Vol. 38, No. 6 (December 1964), p. 33.

In some sense the minority situation is a chronic crisis for which the structure of the community offers coping mechanisms. First and foremost, the existence of the minority community enables its members to pursue at least some goals, however limited by lack of opportunity in the larger society. Its institutionalized means make possible the achievement of ends, albeit selective ends, thus allowing individuals to be rational as well as realistic. Because members of the community have in common the minority condition, with all its categorical circumstances, they also share meanings and values. This meaningful basis for behavior makes possible a style of life that resolves many of the tensions of the minority situation. There is also a communal ideology that offers a raison d'être for the particular position and consequent social patterns of that minority group. The ideological function of the community is psychologically critical since the minority group finds a source of survival in such a system of values.

Members of the minority group are not only socialized into their shared situation, but into the common (and communal) patterns of response. They are therefore mutually intelligible to each other, whatever outsiders think of them. This kind of understanding is what permits their individualized acceptance—or rejection—within the community, by contrast to the categorical response they encounter elsewhere. Part of their protection against discrimination is the discriminating response they offer each other, a selective response taking into account individual differences denied by the dominant group. They do not all look alike to each other—on the contrary. And because of this they find sufficient social support among themselves to alleviate the neurotic sense of aloneness and its attendant anxiety; the individualized interpersonal relations become a source of human dignity. Such communality also makes possible cooperative action in an organized attempt to improve the minority situation.

In the absence of community (or at least of adequate institutionalized resources), there are no values to constrain behavior. The resulting social disorganization leads to the destructive behavior that contains within it the potential for violence. The isolation of the individual without community is such that he may feel unique in his situation and unable to find a way out of his plight.[36] The minority community mitigates against the

[36] This may be why, some years ago, Negroes said of Jean Genêt that he revealed unusual understanding of "Negritude" in his play *The Blacks,* unusual, that is, for a white man. It was not true. What Genêt understood was neurosis, not Negritude, but the consequences of hatred and violence were the same in this instance, whatever the source of the rage.

paralyzing consequences of fear and hostility by providing social peers and appropriate modes of interaction. There is a way of life that permits the continuation of cultural differences and social recognition of achievement in those terms. Social solidarity emerges out of the sense of shared destiny that can channel self-hatred into militant conflict with the dominant group. In all these ways the minority community helps to define, and thereby to delimit, its problematic situation, making it more manageable by institutionalizing patterns of resolution for its tensions.

If group experience is a necessary condition for the stabilization of individuality,[37] then it is the minority community that offers its members criteria for self-validation that are independent of the categorical criteria of the dominant group. In the larger society there is only social confirmation for second-class status; not so in the minority community, which thereby constitutes an alternative to subordination. Pettigrew makes an interesting point in this context. He suggests that highly organized minorities with their own cultures, who are neither fully accepted by the larger society nor are seeking acceptance, typically do not disparage the dominant group; they simply ignore it as much as possible. Such social insulation, of course, is afforded only in middle-class communities. Lower-status groups are too dependent on the dominant group for a livelihood to be able to avoid contact with it.[38]

Even economically disadvantaged minorities, however, do not necessarily become disorganized under the impact of discrimination. They maintain low crime rates, for example, as long as they remain socially and culturally integrated within their own groups. The crime rates begin to rise in some groups as they aspire for dominant values.[39] The stability of the home is crucial in counteracting the effects of prejudice for any minority. The nature of the family may serve as compensation for social restrictions, as it does in several instances where family life is central to the communal structure. Segregation, thus, has its most fundamental influence on Negro personality, for example, in the way in which it affects the functioning of the Negro family, a problem we shall examine in a later chapter.[40]

When there is a strong family at the core of the community, endowed with a cultural heritage, it may be the basis for social improvement. It

[37] Kenneth D. Beane, "The Uses of Fraternity," *Daedalus*, Spring, 1961, p. 233.
[38] Thomas F. Pettigrew, *A Profile of the Negro American* (Princeton, N.J.: Van Nostrand, 1964), pp. 37, 51.
[39] *Ibid.*, p. 155.
[40] *Ibid.*, p. 23.

encourages the efforts of its members, keeping up their pride and organizing familial resources in new situations.[41] Such a family may indeed prove a source of success; the minority community provides role models for social mobility, and it provides the motivation—and perhaps some of the means.

The minority community may be the only place in which its members feel at ease. They opt for ethnic enclosure in an alien world, finding it a haven of refuge in unfriendly surroundings. Although minority members may have to participate in the economic system of the larger society and accept its political structure, they follow more familiar traditions within their own communities. There they establish institutions suited to their special needs. Like all people, members of a minority group feel comfortable only among those with whom they can identify and this usually means each other. They can't relax with outsiders because they can't anticipate what outsiders are likely to do. Because of these barriers to communication, they are on their guard with those who do not share the same ethnic identity, partly in self-defense and partly not to give offense.[42]

This results in differential association in which members of minorities associate primarily with each other. Their contacts with outsiders tend to be impersonal. They frequently lack interest, perhaps due to a lack of confidence, in further contact. This is particularly true in their relations with the dominant group. Members of minorities are raised from childhood on tales of the crimes perpetrated by the dominant group, and they never lose a sense of danger in its vicinity. Their differential association encourages a distinctive perspective that is reinforced by selective perception. Such a characteristic perspective is further facilitated when the minority has its own communication channels. Even when the dominant language is used, special words are employed to convey nuances of meaning unknown to outsiders.

> Within each ethnic community, then, there tends to develop a special universe of discourse. This is a matter of great importance, for human experiences are classified in terms of words.[43]

The world that these words help to create is one with a sense of wholeness. It is a small world, but a human one, and without this haven

---

[41] Glazer and Moynihan, *op. cit.,* p. 88.

[42] Tamotsu Shibutani and Kian M. Kwan, with contributions by Robert H. Billigmeier, *Ethnic Stratification* (New York: Macmillan, 1965), pp. 283, 285, 288.

[43] *Ibid.,* pp. 285, 288.

of community, the humanity of the minority might be lost in oppression. The minority community is more than a buffer between its members and the larger society. It constitutes a social reality in itself, one that is free of dominant images. Its existence renders what the dominant group thinks is true less important than what the minority group knows its reality to be. External expectations are thus less likely to impinge upon minority members wrapped up in their own world. They view life from their own perspective and assess events in terms of the effects on them.

> One of the characteristics of minority peoples is their extreme preoccupation with the affairs within their own world; they have a detailed knowledge of the transactions within their own group but only a vague notion of what goes on outside.[44]

In effect the minority community mitigates against social inferiority by permitting its members to see themselves as persons. Eschewing the categories of the dominant group, they are able to engage in the interpersonal relationships and meaningful behavior that support personality development. The shared minority status of members of the community provides peers who appreciate individual worth and recognize social achievement. With each other they do not have to overstate the legitimacy of their claims to status nor prove their qualifications without social validation.

When the values underlying legitimacy can be taken for granted because they are mutually understood, appropriate social behavior is possible. Each man is able to maintain a positive self-image because of the social acceptance of his minority peers; they are his significant others, not members of the dominant group, and it is their response that he values.

> Within the segregated community a man lives a life in which he is his own master in a world in which men are equal. . . . A person's prestige within the minority group is more or less independent of his rank in the outside world.[45]

Perhaps his status is not entirely independent of the dominant group, but it is enough so to spare his self-esteem—and to save his social honor.

The minority community then offers the sense of security that comes with a consciousness of kind and its concomitant mutual aid. As a reference group, "the minority group becomes the primary audience for whom one performs."[46] It is also more—it is compensation for being socially

[44] *Ibid.*, p. 288.
[45] *Ibid.*, p. 290.
[46] *Ibid.*, p. 291.

despised. Within the confines of the community, there is a sense of superiority, a shared secret frequently explicated in in-group sociability. Such communal chauvinism seems to counteract the consequences of categorical treatment.

> Overt obeisance is not necessarily matched by inward assent. This is especially true where the culture of the minority remains undisturbed. They form conceptions of themselves from the standpoint of their own culture, and because of their enthnocentrism they find themselves adequate and others wanting.[47]

Members of the minority group take particular pleasure in outwitting the dominant group; it vitiates the humiliation of subordination.

They also return the compliment of prejudice with reciprocal stereotypes of the dominant group. This minority reaction is likely to be more than a social defense, or sour grapes. Their exploitation by the dominant group gives minority members grounds for contempt, and therefore their images may be more realistic than categorical. They are all too often tolerated for the illicit, or at least disreputable, goods and services they provide. In catering to such tastes, members of minorities are in a position to perceive, and not to appreciate, the more debased aspects of dominant life.

By and large, however, social distance in intergroup relations reinforces mutual categorization and misunderstanding. The dominant and minority groups are frequently unintelligible to each other in terms of both subjective intention and objective action; hence the distance between them is self-perpetuating. The minority community contributes as much to the social distance as the discrimination of the dominant group. Like any community conscious of its status, it enforces the principle of closure to protect its special identity and thereby precludes the shared experiences that bring about common values and make possible meaningful behavior.

Thus the minority community itself becomes a barrier in intergroup relations. The social rituals of intergroup relations stylize interaction and thus eliminate its affect. It is this consequence that protects the self-esteem of the minority, but so also does it perpetuate the social distance. The community, of course, provides the appropriate modes of expression and patterns of behavior for such ritualization. They are calculated to divest interaction with the dominant group of any ego involvement, thus intensifying communal commitment.

[47] *Ibid.,* p. 294.

These patterns, however, may prove to be dysfunctional for members of the community themselves as well as for their intergroup relations. As institutionalized patterns of behavior, they make up a way of life, one that is more a function of the internal dynamics of the minority community than of its external situation. There comes a point when the community is more enclosed than necessary; its institutionalized patterns contribute to its members' unwillingness to test the changing limits of social reality. Such behavior is more than self-limiting; it may become self-defeating.

> Once the minority community has emerged as a viable social entity, it can be as much a trap as it is a way station. In it the individual member of the minority group can find security and acceptance which he risks if he pioneers in the larger community. He can compete more confidently, for in the larger society he would be judged by the standards of a group which has played the game longer than he has. By the same token, he can achieve prestige which comes more easily because the competition is restricted.[48]

Life within the community, however confining, is simply easier, so few finally even venture out to try themselves in the surrounding society. The outside world is still there, but it is all too readily ignored after a while. The institutions of the minority become unexpectedly effective; they emerge in response to restricted opportunity and then serve to delimit it further. There is a time lag in which patterns of discrimination change more rapidly than the patterns of response. People who are socialized into a particular minority situation rarely attempt to ascertain for themselves whether or not it is still the same as they have been told since childhood; often it is quite different than they were taught. Although the dysfunction of this disparity in awareness is not always so dramatic as social immobility, it is nonetheless limiting to accept the minority situation only as others have experienced it rather than to know it personally. The consequences are pervasive throughout communal life. The deprivation of power, to be sure, sets limits on the possible action of minority members such that their feeling of powerlessness is realistic rather than neurotic. Nevertheless, they are likely to impose upon themselves an impotence that exceeds situational exigency.

The minority community is a small and sometimes stifling world. For all its emotional enrichment (and even experienced expansiveness), it may be socially impoverished to the point of being suffocating. It is

[48] Lewis M. Killian and Charles Grigg, *Racial Crisis in America* (Englewood Cliffs, N.J.: Prentice-Hall, Spectrum Books, 1964), p. 124.

limited and thus limiting; above all it is dull, for such is the essence of its security—the familiarity that produces predictability, and may well breed contempt. Its very sameness is the source of its boredom. Even those communities that do not suffer from "cultural deprivation" may offer too few social alternatives to afford variety for the individual. Erving Goffman, who understands so well the consequences of stigma, includes minority status within the social rubric. Like others, he observes the functions of community, among which are the advantages of acquiring peers with a shared status.

> Knowing from their own experience what it is like to have this particular stigma, some of them can provide the individual with instruction in the tricks of the trade and with a circle of lament to which he can withdraw for moral support and for the comfort of feeling at home, at ease, accepted as a person who really is like any other normal person.[49]

Goffman understands more than the advantages; he is one of the few observers to see the drawbacks; one pays a price for such peers. The minority community functions as a source of individual visibility for its members, who share the categorical invisibility of their subordination. Ah, but the dreariness of such sharing! It is so much the same that fellow-sufferers cannot help but be a bore. "Among his own, the stigmatized individual can use his disadvantage as a basis for organizing life, but he must resign himself to a half-world to do so."[50] One need not experience self-hatred to endure ennui. The variations of the stigmatized theme are so slight that one hears the same thing over and over again; and worse still, one hears only that, especially when stigma is the only thing that people have in common. "The matter of focusing on atrocity tales, on group superiority, on trickster stories, in short, on the 'problem' is one of the large penalties for having one [a stigma, that is]."[51] This exclusive preoccupation may well compound stigma, for such attention neither discharges the onus nor distracts from it.

The sameness of the story told by those who share the same stigma is not the only problematic aspect of such preoccupation. The expectation implicit in their telling of the tale is one of mutual loyalty. They feel that somehow they owe each other something, although this sense of obligation may not always be reciprocated. They expect each other in some

---

[49] Erving Goffman, *Stigma: Notes on the Management of Spoiled Identity* (Englewood Cliffs, N.J.: Prentice-Hall, Spectrum Books, 1963), p. 20.

[50] *Ibid.*, p. 21.

[51] *Ibid.*

way to make up for what the world has done to them—or more accurately, what the world does not do for them.[52] Personal allegiance without question is required in return for sometimes questionable support of the person. The minority community is certainly no house of cards, but it appears to be even more threatened by detachment than other communities. It does not really fall apart under the impact of intellect, but it builds its fences so high that one suspects its fears accordingly. It suggests its own vulnerability by the very excesses of its defenses.

That this is so is doubtless due to the precariousness of any communal honor which must rest on negative status. It is dull when such status is all that members of a minority community share; it is destructive when that status is threatened by detachment. Members of the younger generation are then doubly deprived, first by the dominant group and then by their own community, when they are not permitted to explore their situation. They can learn neither its intellectual implications nor its social limitations. And if they cannot assess their priorities rationally and realistically, they have all the fewer possibilities in the outside world. The probability of mobility is low enough without further constriction of life chances, confined by default to the social context of the ethnic group. In that sense the minority community does devour its young; it kills them with institutionalized kindness that may no longer be individualized.

Constrained by its own community, each generation is inclined to rebel against its elders rather than against the dominant group. Insofar as members of the younger generation are effectively sheltered, they do not experience the restrictions of the larger society; they therefore do not recognize the source in the dominant group. They are protected from the consequences of their categorical status and blame the conservatism of the older generation for the restraints that they do know. Those who have raised them then bear the brunt of their rebellion, rather than those who made the restraints necessary. In Part III, we will examine the dynamics

[52] One of the most graphic illustrations of this expectation can be found in Philip Roth's short story, "Defender of the Faith," first published in the *New Yorker* in 1959, and then reprinted in his collection *Goodbye, Columbus* (Boston: Houghton Mifflin, 1959), pp. 159–200. That this story may be better ethnography than fiction was confirmed by the reaction of the official representatives of the Jewish community. They demurred over its publication, defensive about the washing of such ethnic linen in public. Their reaction to the story was as graphic an illustration as the story itself; it was indicative of their touchiness about in-group attitudes and behavior. As an act of ethnic fealty, Roth was expected to cooperate in the communal conspiracy of silence, the collusion in a "united front" as a defense against the dominant group and its defamation.

of such intergenerational conflict in the minority community. For now we need only observe that the functions of the minority community may not only change over time, they may lose their significance.

As ethnicity diminishes with each generation, the functions continue, albeit in changed form. They can no longer be characterized, however, by any distinctive cultural content, and they may thereby become dysfunctional. Although the minority community still defends against dominant defamation, it no longer protects a particular tradition after acculturation takes its toll. The way of life is no different from that of the surrounding society, and there is growing insecurity about the specialness of the communal identity. Is it really unique? No one dares to ask lest the social premises that members of the community take for granted be undermined by the very question itself. One suspects the vulnerability of their ideology as their defensiveness begins to be self-destructive. When the raison d'être of the community so much as seems to be at stake, there is rejection not only of outsiders, but of some insiders as well.

The strongest opprobrium is reserved, of course, for the intellectuals of the minority community. Their detachment threatens its increasingly unfounded ethnocentrism. They may say what they will about the dominant group; it is, after all, the source of all social problems from the minority's perspective. But intellectuals may say nothing about their own group—unless it is to sing its polemical praises. Should they happen to regard their fellows as merely human, nothing more and nothing less, and try to portray them as they are, then these truth-sayers are regarded as renegades, betrayers of the faith, albeit a fallible, if not indeed failing, faith.[53] At that point the minority community becomes so xenophobic that it treats such members as if they were strangers. And in a sense they are strange to the community, alien to its acculturated anti-intellectualism. They are considered threatening because they embody

[53] There are to date no sociological studies of anti-intellectualism among minorities as such, but various authors provide peripheral documentation for particular groups. Daniel P. Moynihan, in his chapter on the Irish for example, discusses their attitudes toward intellectuals in Glazer and Moynihan, *op. cit.*, pp. 217–87. The strongest indication thus far of the intellectual ambivalence of minorities may be found in their response to the publication of sociological data about their communities. They do not disagree with the findings so much as they oppose their being published; scientific detachment, however sympathetic, is too threatening when it exposes the minority to public purview. For several illustrations of this, see Judith R. Kramer, "Resistance to Sociological Data: A Case Study" in Paul F. Lazarsfeld, William H. Sewell, and Harold L. Wilensky, eds., *The Uses of Sociology* (New York: Basic Books, 1967), pp. 783–88.

cultural alternatives that encourage social change. Interestingly enough, as we shall see, this response was probably less characteristic of the ghetto, secure in its sacred tradition, than of the gilded ghetto, so insecure in its secularism that it is intolerant of intellect.

It may be then that the importance of the ethnic community as such is essentially historical. (It is in fact customarily treated as an historical phenomenon even in the sociological literature, or discussed in the context of more recent immigrants, that is, functional for newcomers, and perhaps only for newcomers.) The earlier ethnic community is at best the source of the contemporary minority community, but it is no longer one and the same thing. Historically there was a time when the ethnic community and the minority community were synonymous, but that remains true only in a few cases, which we will investigate in Part IV.

In most instances the minority community becomes much like other status communities, and sometimes even more enclosed. Defensive about the insecurity of its status, it may flatter with a form of imitation of the dominant group that overdoes the most unflattering features. Because the minority community has so little occasion to close out others (few members of the dominant group come knocking on minority doors since opportunity obviously knocks for them elsewhere), it closes off its own, excluding insiders with an outside perspective, however acquired. Members of the minority community may thus treat each other as categorically as they have been treated in the larger society. It is as if they have been on the outside looking in too long to have learned any other principle from the dominant group than the principle of closure. As a result they shut out those of similarly categorical status whom they cannot somehow swallow up communally.

Such parochialism is perhaps as endemic as it is pervasive; it may inhere in an inevitable conflict between intellect and ideology. Yet the minority community persists. What's in a name? Something still—something more than Shakespeare perceived and possibly even more than sociology conceives, at least in the name of a minority. In its name there is the exclusion that remains after acculturation and achievement qualify the minority for inclusion. Members of a minority group may be prepared to participate in the larger society, but they may still not be permitted to do so. At that point, exclusion rests on the difference between a descriptive label and a derogatory label. The minority member is not just named as such; he is in effect called a name. The minority community thus endures. It eases the social exclusion that survives ethnic segregation and has not yet been dissolved by economic restructuring. And it acquires a character of its own, whatever its cultural attributes, or lack of them.

> Ethnic groups . . . are continually recreated by new experiences in America. The mere existence of a name itself is perhaps sufficient to form group character in new situations, for the name associates an individual, who actually can be anything, with a certain past, country, race. . . . A man is connected to his group by ties of family and friendship. But he is also connected by ties of *interest*.[54]

There are variations in the structure of minority communities due in part to differences in the historical conditions of their emergence. The nature of the communal structure helps to shape its contemporary circumstances by its influence on the relationship between the dominant and the minority group. Since minority institutions embody the communal response to its shared situation, they have consequence for intergroup as well as intragroup relations. We will now turn to an overview of the social structure of the minority community. Part III will include a consideration of its institutional dynamics, its social conflicts and consequent changes. Later we will look at another variety of community in which there is insufficient institutional basis for its social structure. These will constitute the racial variations on the prototypical minority theme of community.

---

[54] Glazer and Moynihan, *op. cit.*, p. 17.

PART III

THE MINORITY COMMUNITY

Chapter 5

The Ethnic Enclave

THE minority community as we know it today had its origins in the ghettos of the first generation. The uprooting of the immigrants led to the formation of ethnic enclaves to meet the needs of their alien status. Their way of life was adapted to their shared experiences in a new world. Indeed, their alien status became the basis of integration for their community, since traditional values eventually lost their meaning in a secular society.[1] Nevertheless, these values were significant in the emergence of the ghetto. It was the existence of the ghetto that tempered the transition from one culture to another, buffering strangeness with communal familiarity. Uprootedness was the characteristic quality of the immigrants' community, no longer situated in its accustomed land; the changed life transformed its institutions over time, but the initial intent of the first generation was to keep intact those institutions it could, thereby sustaining its cultural identity.

All ethnic communities are to some extent physically segregated and socially isolated, but the ghettos established by the immigrants were also culturally insulated. The practice of closure functioned to perpetuate distinctive values. The enclosed and encompassing way of life of the ghetto was not yet an acculturated one, unlike that of the gilded ghetto of the second generation, whose mobility into middle-class status leaves little ethnicity to preserve. The relatively complete enclosure of the ghetto was the source of its communal strength and social cohesion. Religion and the family, supported by a variety of voluntary associations, constituted the institutional core of the immigrant community. These institutions

[1] Don Martindale, *American Social Structure* (New York: Appleton-Century-Crofts, 1960), p. 386.

79

were defended by an ideology that justified their intrinsic worth in sacred terms. Values given such institutional embodiment and ideological justification proved to be virtually impregnable in the first generation. The immigrants could not conceive of cultural alternatives to their own values, which were thus protected from the influence of the larger society. Critical social change within the minority community did not begin until the acculturation of the second generation.

Its Historical Emergence

Although there was some transferability of institutional structure across the Atlantic, migration usually required some social reorganization around minority status. Only Jews, a perennial minority, brought with them communal institutions already adapted to centuries of exile. Other immigrants had a way of life that had originally been part of the dominant patterns of their native countries. As peasants and laborers they had been without economic privilege, but they had had a homeland. Part of the shock of uprooting was its loss; psychological security had been sacrificed in the search for opportunity. Minority status was a new experience necessitating a major adjustment on the part of most immigrants. It was all the more difficult to adjust when much of their way of life was found to be irrelevant in an industrial setting; frequently personal and social disorganization ensued.

A large proportion of the immigrants were unskilled, but they provided certain essential, if disvalued, services. They were thus concentrated in specialized occupations, tolerated for the profitable exploitation of their labor, but never granted personal acceptance. This economic location in low-status jobs reinforced their social segregation, which was further compounded by their physical aggregation in particular places, such as the poorest slums of the big cities.

Gathered together in these ethnic enclaves, the immigrants found a new source of social integration in institutions that were formerly peripheral to their native existence.[2] Usually it was the religious institution, once comfortably taken for granted (and often conveniently ignored), that

[2] *Ibid.*, pp. 391–92, 395.

became the core of the community around which their way of life was reorganized. As with the Jews, religion became increasingly critical to the group survival of other more newly formed minorities. Herein is to be found the historical emergence of the characteristic minority community. It is not a re-creation of the original community found in the old country, but an adaptation to minority status. A way of life evolves out of traditional patterns to meet the problems presented by the surrounding, and alien, society. Once established, this way of life tends to perpetuate itself.[3]

The earlier ghettos of American society owed their existence to the social functions they fulfilled for the minority group rather than to the legal enactment of the dominant group. The defensive insulation of the ghettos protected the immigrants from unnecessary contact with the dominant group, which inevitably proved to be an unpleasant experience. Not just the Jews, but all new arrivals, sought the isolation of the ethnic enclave to temper the impact of their alien status. Among themselves, they moved freely and acted naturally, avoiding trouble with others, while following their own traditions. Robert Park, one of the on-the-scene sociological observers in Chicago, saw the city in the following way.

> A mosaic of segregated peoples—differing in race, in culture, or merely in cult—each seeking to preserve its peculiar cultural forms and to maintain its individual and unique conceptions of life. Every one of these segregated groups inevitably seeks, in order to maintain the integrity of its own group life, to impose upon its members some kind of moral isolation.[4]

There were, of course, the social and cultural consequences of such isolation that the younger generation later sought to escape. The urban research of the 1920's and 1930's, however, found that, at the time, "the ethnic community was a gigantic sociological defense mechanism which facilitated the survival and adjustment of immigrants."[5] The way of life of each ethnic community socialized the individual to a common core of values; insofar as its culture remained integrated, the ethnic community was reflected in the integration of the personality it made possible. Eventually social change in the direction of the dominant society was encompassed by its institutions and incorporated by individuals.[6]

[3] *Ibid.,* p. 428.
[4] Robert E. Park, *Human Communities* (New York: Free Press, 1952), pp. 99–100.
[5] Everett V. Stonequist, "The Marginal Man: A Study in Personality and Culture Conflict," in Ernest W. Burgess and Donald J. Bogue, eds., *Contributions to Urban Sociology* (Chicago: University of Chicago Press, 1964), p. 325.
[6] *Ibid.,* pp. 328, 331.

The adjustment of the immigrants was nonetheless severe, often pain-fully so. Stonequist suggests the areas in which they suffered the most wrenching changes. The immigrants were, as he sensitively describes them, *dépaysé,* homesick in their distance from the familiar environment of their homeland, removed from relatives and friends still there. They were also *déclassé;* they had lost status in their migration and, handicapped by dif-ferences of language and culture, had to compete with older settlers in a new society. Perhaps most difficult of all was the fact that they were *déraciné.* They endured a profound uprooting of sentiments and values, accompanied by some disorganization of the subconscious life. With this the immigrants often lost more than status; they lost self-confidence.[7] The problems were too overwhelming for the average immigrant to be as-similated, but he did manage to make a workable adjustment, at least within the confines of his own social world, where he felt like a person in the traditional terms that he understood.

> This status in the immigrant community gives him self-respect and stability; here his marginality is eased because it is shared by others in a like situation. The immigrant community's culture gradually changes and provides him with a cultural framework.[8]

The communities of the first generation developed characteristic fea-tures which remained much the same as long as there were new immi-grants to replenish the population—and discrimination to force them to associate with each other.[9] These communities were of low economic status and sometimes without leadership; they often lost their most suc-cessful members when the price of success was the severing of group ties. There were, nevertheless, mutual benefit societies to assist the residents of the ghetto in sickness and death and to serve as social gathering places. There were also food shops and restaurants that offered local news and gossip along with traditional dishes. Characteristic patterns of thought were reinforced in this informal interaction within the in-group.[10] When the group was large enough, there was a press in the native language that brought news of the old country and interpreted the affairs of the new. There were also traditional forms of entertainment and indigenous pro-fessional men serving the ethnic group. The community became so com-plete, in a word, that its members almost never had to leave it; they never

[7] *Ibid.,* pp. 334–35.
[8] *Ibid.,* p. 335.
[9] Carolyn F. Ware, "Ethnic Communities," *Encyclopedia of the Social Sciences,* Vol. 5, pp. 607, 611.
[10] *Ibid.,* p. 611.

thought in terms other than those of their own community, in part because they never met any other people.[11]

Because of the increased importance of religion, the first thing to be built in the ghetto was usually the church. "To many an immigrant his religion is the only experience which he can carry unchanged from his old home to his new." Often a parochial school followed in order to perpetuate the religious affiliation in the next generation.[12] The church became crucial as the one institution that was completely transferable; even the traditional structure of the family was threatened by its transplanting. And its religion was a source of comfort to the first generation in the stress of uprooting, explaining, as always, the inexplicable in the sacred terms of the supernatural. Its authority had not yet been effectively challenged by secularization.

With few indigenous institutions surviving migration, religion became central to ethnic identity. As the family was the focus of interpersonal life, so the church was the core of communal life in the new world. There were, of course, a variety of voluntary associations surrounding and supporting these two institutions, but the immigrants were still aliens in a strange land with little left that was familiar to them. They were no longer at home in a rural society; as minorities in an industrial economy, they had to take on new occupational pursuits and eventually become part of dominant political patterns.

Although their children might venture out, most immigrants remained ensconced within the ghetto. They learned enough English to get along economically, but otherwise shut themselves off socially in the shelter of their own self-contained world. The immigrant was often so enclosed that he had little awareness of anything outside his ethnic enclave.

> In the colony he meets with sympathy, understanding and encouragement. There he finds his fellow-countrymen who understand his habits and standards and share his life-experience and viewpoint. In the colony he has a status, plays a role in a group. In the life of the colony's streets and cafés, in its church and benevolent societies, he finds response and security. In the colony he finds that he can live, be somebody, satisfy his wishes—all of which is impossible in the strange world outside.[13]

Exclusion from the institutions of the larger society instilled a sense of special identity even in those groups that did not have one upon arrival

---

[11] *Ibid.*, p. 612.

[12] *Ibid.*

[13] Harvey W. Zorbaugh, *The Gold Coast and the Slum* (Chicago: University of Chicago Press, 1929), p. 141.

in this country. As members of the same group banded together in immigrant colonies supported by a continued influx from the old country, they began to constitute a separate community. There they preserved some of their own cultural patterns, while the dominant group remained largely indifferent and sometimes hostile to them, concerned only with their exploitable economic skills. Because the immigrants were treated categorically as a separate entity, they learned to think of themselves as such —and acquired an appropriate ethnic identity. Many a self-respecting peasant felt the loss of status when he no longer lived on the land, but worked at a low-paying job in industry. He found some compensation in the social interaction of the ethnic enclave within which the immigrants re-created the communal life of the native village as much as possible. Their ecological separation permitted the development of an integrated community that had little contact with the dominant group.[14]

Whether urban or rural, the immigrant colonies developed a form of communal life oriented toward their own ethnic existence and the use of their native language. There was the formal organization of the church and related associations, combining mutual aid and sociability for the *landsmann*, to replace the informal patterns of village life; enmeshed in these associational activities was a network of ethnic friendships. And underlying the structural continuity of the immigrant community was, of course, the family. The ghetto thus provided a kind of decompression chamber in which newcomers, at their own pace, could make a workable adjustment to American society.[15] In the cities acculturation was retarded by the size of the ethnic group and the strength of the dominant group's prejudice. Acculturation was further delayed in rural areas that were physically isolated from any surrounding Americans; there parochial schools using the native language often preserved the ethnic culture for several generations.[16]

Most immigrants were neither willing nor able to be assimilated, and certainly not rapidly. Only the early immigrants of Protestant background were soon absorbed into the dominant group; they created no new structures themselves, but fitted into the prevailing institutional forms, whose prior existence they accepted.[17] The "old immigration" arrived early in the nineteenth century and located on the land, where there was still op-

[14] Charles F. Marden and Gladys Meyer, *Minorities in American Society,* 2nd ed. (New York: American Book Co., 1962), pp. 83–84.
[15] Milton M. Gordon, *Assimilation in American Life* (New York: Oxford, 1964), pp. 105–6.
[16] *Ibid.,* pp. 108–9.
[17] *Ibid.,* pp. 126–27.

portunity for them. The "new immigration" from southern and eastern Europe didn't come to this country until the 1880's. They were largely Catholic and of peasant origins, entering a society by then advanced in urbanization and industrialization. It was they who settled in the large cities of the northeast and midwest, where they worked at the unskilled levels of industry.[18]

Most sociologists agree that the rapidity of the immigrants' assimilation depended upon their own cultural traits as well as their reception in the United States. They were assimilated more quickly when they resembled Americans, were not too numerous, arrived over a long period of time, and dispersed throughout the country. When large numbers were concentrated in cities, they retained their own culture within the ghettos of the first generation and only began to acculturate in succeeding generations.[19] One study, however, suggests that the difference between "old" and "new" immigrants may have been a function of demographic conditions and time of settlement more than a function of cultural distinctions. It may have been the resources and opportunities available in the larger society at the time of the group's arrival that were critical in determining the terms of a group's survival.[20]

The culturally distinctive institutions of the immigrants were the necessary, if not sufficient, conditions of community in the minority situation. In embodying values alternative to those of the dominant culture, these institutions acquired special significance as an independent source of social honor. Such institutions emerged out of the voluntary migration of the first generation, whose uprooting led to the establishment of ghettos in American society organized around ethnic specialization as well as segregation. Within these enclaves indigenous institutions were adapted to the exigencies of life in the new world; one critical adjustment was to minority status itself, which was a new experience for all immigrants except Jews.

Without such institutional resources, there is an absence of community, or at least of an adequate community, with all the ensuing consequences of personal and social disorganization. The absence of community leads to greater variations than its presence since the very presence of com-

[18] John Sirjamaki, *The Sociology of Cities* (New York: Random House, 1964), pp. 222–23.

[19] *Ibid.*, p. 227.

[20] Stanley J. Lieberson, "The Old-New Distinction and Immigrants in Australia," *American Sociological Review*, Vol. 28, No. 4 (August 1963), pp. 564–65.

munity is structuring. When there is community, therefore, there are institutional similarities that transcend cultural differences. Hence one can speak of a prototypical minority community, whatever its ethnic origin, and describe its changes, whatever their pace. The social patterns of community are similar, although the rate of change varies with the point at which acculturation sets in and the extent to which mobility follows. We will delineate these patterns in this section, tracing the emergence of the ghetto in the first generation of various nationality groups through to their merging in the gilded ghettos of the minority religions. Then we shall try to ascertain the developments within this prototypical minority community in the third generation and beyond, at which point it may begin to dissolve into another sort of status community.

By contrast, each case of inadequate community must be described as the particular alternative to community that it is. This we shall do in Part IV, where we will treat both the deculturated groups and, if you will, the commuting groups. The Negroes and Indians, the Puerto Ricans and Mexicans each represent a different form of inadequate community, as we will see, although their lack of sufficient institutionalized resources often has the same social consequences. Their members, for example, have less basis for individual identity when they lack the communal capacity to cope with the involuntary imposition of categorical status. Members of the prototypical minority community, however, can achieve personal identity, although its social grounds may shift with the changing status of their community.

The ghetto community of the first generation continued to embody the traditional values of its country of origin, even though some institutional reorganization was required to do so. The principle of closure in the ghetto operated to protect its cultural insulation and social isolation. Avoidance of all but the most impersonal economic contact with the dominant group (and even that was not always necessary) minimized the potential for cultural conflict and thus helped to preserve the distinctive values of the ethnic group. The immigrants maintained their social honor in part by refusing to recognize the legitimacy of dominant values. They paid the price of special identity with the economic services they provided in exchange for tolerance of their separate existence; their group survival rested upon the profitable exploitation of their labor by the larger society.

The immigrants performed a necessary, if socially despised, function as unskilled laborers. Such economic necessity, however, inevitably brought about some modifications in their communal institutions, although their social survival continued to be premised upon their cultural distinctiveness. Those nationality groups who lacked economic self-sufficiency, most particularly those who settled in urban areas, thus were not capable of sustaining their self-imposed isolation entirely. The exchange of the marketplace itself forced some concessions to dominant values.

Traditional values, nevertheless, prevailed in the ghetto; they constituted the source of prestige in its ranking system. Few class distinctions emerged in the first generation's struggle for survival. Commitment to its own institutions persisted, and traditional values remained the basis for whatever stratification there was within the community. There were, of course, differences among the immigrants based on their time of arrival and consequent degree of Americanization, but these differences were not sufficient to affect the distribution of their life chances. The respected man was still the traditional man, and his status was based upon his adherence to ethnic values—and his concomitant allegiance to the ethnic community.

Eventually the isolating values of the ghetto collapsed under the impact of American life and the possibility of mobility in the general class structure, but the ghettos themselves did not disappear until immigration declined, leaving them with no replenishment of residents. Even before then, however, the economy and education of the larger society served as secularizing influences, a source of acculturation to alternative values, which were already desirable by definition of their dominant status. Ultimately, the economic mobility of future generations provided the basis for an acculturated minority community, a community of the marginal men descended from immigrants; but this was not to happen until well into the twentieth century.

The Jewish Ghetto

The perennial minority status of the Jews has all but made them the quintessential minority. The patterns that emerged in their situation in effect set the precedent that was eventually followed by other groups. What remained characteristic about the Jews was the acceleration of their pace of adjustment to American society; their historical conditioning afforded them a more rapid accommodation than was possible for others. Lacking such resources, other groups, that ultimately were to make up the modern Catholic community, had to proceed more slowly. It was not just the cultural shock of uprooting that impeded their ready adjustment; it was the imposition of minority status for which nothing in their past had prepared them. Without a homeland for centuries, the Jews, by contrast, had a set of institutions already adapted to exile. Other groups first had to modify their institutional forms not only to live in a different society, but to do so without dominant status. However deprived they had been in their native lands, they had not been minorities. Hence they also lacked a common identity, remaining for a long while separate nationality groups, albeit Catholic ones. Jews, although also of mixed backgrounds, shared an identity welded out of their minority status in whatever country they had originated.

Jews thus are distinguished from other ethnic groups by their habituation to segregated living. The history of European ghettos reveals their function in providing institutional shelter in a hostile environment. The social patterns and the personality types, and most especially the sacred ideologies of the ghetto offered the basis for ethnic solidarity under almost any circumstances. Although there were tendencies toward emancipation even in Europe, it was in America that there was a diminished emphasis on the observance of religious ritual that finally led to the decline of the institutional structure of the ghetto.[21] In the time of the Babylonian captivity, Judaism was transformed to meet the needs of exile. As a pariah people, Jews were permitted to make a living, to enter into business, or to engage in crafts, but they were cut off from their formal political and economic foundations of community life.[22]

Ancient religious customs were revived, according to Weber's interpretation, and fixed as unbreakable ritual, thus intensifying the sacred basis of community. The synagogue was its core institution, fulfilling both religious and educational functions. Dietary restrictions were imposed with special strictness; it was ritually defiling to eat with gentiles and thereby to come under their influence. A quorum was necessary for correct religious observance, which helped to prevent dispersion into rural occupations.[23] The ghetto was originally granted as a right rather than imposed by force. The concentration of Jews in areas of medieval cities, for in-

[21] Maurice R. Stein, *The Eclipse of Community* (Princeton, N.J.: Princeton University Press, 1960), p. 39.
[22] Martindale, *op. cit.*, p. 420.
[23] *Ibid.*, p. 421.

stance, was a reflection of their needs and practices. The spatially separated and socially isolated community offered the best opportunity to follow religious precepts and to engage in the numerous functions that tied the individual to his communal institutions.[24]

Its segregation also facilitated the social control of the community over its members. They engaged in forms of trade and money exchange required by the economy, but prohibited by medieval Christianity.[25] Their relations with gentiles were thus those of externality and utility, and life beyond the ghetto did not touch the life within; trade relations were possible when no other form of contact could take place. Wherever situated, and whenever, the ghetto remained a closed community, in-bred and self-perpetuating. Its inner solidarity lay in the cohesion of family life, and families in turn gained status within the community through the organization of the synagogue. The community was both specialized and highly integrated; its life was well organized, with ritual playing a critical institutionalizing role.[26]

> The real inner solidarity of the ghetto community always lay in the strong family ties. In this inner circle deep bonds of sympathy had been woven between the members through a colorful ritual. Here each individual, who was just a mere Jew to the world outside, had a place of dignity, and was bound to the rest by profound sentiments.[27]

What the ghetto lacked in breadth of horizon, it made up for in the depth of attachment to tradition and sentiment as well as in the consequent strength of familial and communal bonds. Although it was not always surrounded by a wall, the ghetto was almost completely cut off from the world outside, thus preventing the infusion of external, and alien, influences.[28] "The life of the immigrants in the ghetto is so circumscribed and they are so integrally a part of it that they are unaware of its existence."[29] Not unless they left the ghetto did the immigrants become fully conscious of themselves and their minority status. Their community, however, remained intact as long as the larger society treated it as an entity, thus

[24] Louis Wirth, "The Ghetto," in Albert J. Reiss, Jr., ed., *On Cities and Social Life* (Chicago: University of Chicago Press, Phoenix Books, 1964), p. 86.

[25] Martindale, *op. cit.,* p. 421.

[26] Wirth, *op. cit.,* pp. 87, 89–90.

[27] Louis Wirth, *The Ghetto* (Chicago: University of Chicago Press, Phoenix Books, 1928, 1956), p. 37.

[28] *Ibid.,* pp. 222, 226.

[29] Wirth, "The Ghetto," *op. cit.,* p. 96.

reinforcing its communal capacity to act corporately. The ghetto was always "not merely a physical fact, but also a state of mind."[30]

The sociological studies of the Jewish ghetto in American society, the foremost of which was Louis Wirth's, are well known by now, but there was also a sympathetic outsider who observed the Lower East Side of New York as a journalist. Hutchins Hapgood's account in 1902 conveys some of the qualities of life in the ghetto, capturing the color that characterized its vitality.[31] Orthodox traditions were maintained almost in their purity, although men were forced to earn their bread by working in sweatshops or peddling from pushcarts. As peasants lost status when they no longer worked the land, so Talmudic scholars lost their self-esteem when they had to support themselves and their families.[32] The social structure of the eastern European *shtetl*[33] had freed them from a need for an occupation, and many could not make the adjustment to the economic demands of a secular society.

There was a high proportion of skilled workers in the needle trades, but they aspired for self-employment and in lieu of that, worked for other Jews. In so far as they wished to continue their orthodox observances, they were not employable in the larger society. The immigrant also belonged to one of hundreds of lodges on the Lower East Side, which "curiously express[ed] at once the old Jewish customs and the conditions of the new world."[34] There were Yiddish newspapers exerting an intellectual and educational influence in keeping immigrants abreast of world events of special interest. There were also Yiddish theaters that portrayed American customs and often satirized orthodox ones. Yet the ghetto remained immersed in its own traditions, maintaining institutional forms that had changed little since medieval times. Modern ideas may have been conveyed by some of the communal media, but they did not affect the way of life.

Nevertheless, these influences leave the man pretty much as he was when he landed here. He remains the patriarchal Jew devoted to the Law and to

[30] *Ibid.,* pp. 97, 98.
[31] Hutchins Hapgood, *The Spirit of the Ghetto,* Preface and Notes by Harry Golden (New York: Schocken Books, 1966).
[32] *Ibid.,* pp. 3, 7.
[33] *Shtetl* refers to the small towns and villages in which Jews characteristically lived in eastern Europe. For a description of the traditional culture of these Jewish communities, see Mark Zborowski and Elizabeth Herzog, *Life Is With People* (New York: International Universities Press, 1952).
[34] Hapgood, *op. cit.,* pp. 10, 13.

prayer. He never does anything that is not prescribed, and worships most of the time that he is not at work. He has only one point of view, that of the Talmud; and his esthetic as well as his religious criteria are determined by it.[35]

There is still a ghetto to be found among the Hasidim of Williamsburg. They are able to maintain their social isolation in the midst of a modern metropolis, as Solomon Poll points out, because the non-Hasidic Jewish community serves as a buffer between the Hasidim and the dominant society, deflecting the values of the outside world before they can penetrate the ghetto. Its cohesion, therefore, remains more dependent upon internal identity than upon external pressures.[36] The Hasidim have not only transplanted their entire culture to a new setting, they adhere to their traditional values to an even greater extent than in Europe, anticipating perhaps a more serious threat of secularization in American society.

"So strong are religious sentiments that not only religious affairs but secular activities as well are controlled and directed mainly by religious prescription and authority."[37] Even economic practices are determined by the injunctions of orthodox religion. Occupational roles complement and supplement religious observances, providing an acceptable livelihood for individuals as well as economic support for the communal religion. The members of the community are not identified by occupation, however, but by religious performance; it is still the intensity and frequency of observance that constitutes the source of status among the Hasidim.[38]

Oriental Counterparts

Chinatown has long been one of the most exclusive ethnic communities in American society, a tightly knit, in-grown ghetto that is only now beginning to lose members of the younger generation in greater number. The Chinese population has tended to concentrate in segregated areas in large cities such as New York, Los Angeles, and most particularly San

[35] *Ibid.,* p. 16.
[36] Solomon Poll, *The Hasidic Community of Williamsburg* (New York: Free Press, 1962), pp. 10–11.
[37] *Ibid.,* p. 248.
[38] *Ibid.,* pp. 258, 252.

Francisco. Although a smaller proportion now live in Chinatown than formerly, its social structure has remained largely the same, with only some modification in institutional function. Until recently the Chinese have been highly insulated, maintaining their own distinctive organizations, which, among other things, mediated indirectly the instrumental relationships with the dominant community that were unavoidable.[39] There were relatively few Chinese, and they were determined to preserve the way of life and the language of their ancient culture. Although much like the Jews in this respect, their reasons were different: they did not conceive of themselves as permanently exiled, they still hoped to return to their homeland.

The life of the Chinese centered entirely on their own communities, whose economic basis rested upon such specialized businesses as restaurants, laundries, and gift shops that did not compete with dominant enterprises. They had originally been recruited for railroad building and then agricultural work, but they encountered the increasing hostility of organized labor after 1870. Since there were so few women on the west coast at the time of the frontier conditions, the Chinese began to fulfill the demand for domestic and personal services;[40] others became small tradesmen.

Although more Chinese have found white collar and skilled jobs since World War II, their voluntary segregation remains institutionalized. The system of organized solidarity is a strong one, and it supports the individual in many ways.[41] There is still an elaborate network of associations dominating the lives of those who live in Chinatown or whose business or social life brings them into contact with the associations. These associations not only perform familial and welfare functions, but also exercise communal control by settling local disputes, thus by-passing legally constituted dominant authority. The Tongs, once the stronghold of illegal enterprise, have become respectable merchants' associations, promoting the interests of Chinese business.[42]

Chinatown is almost an ideal typical case of the enclosed ghetto whose

[39] Marden and Meyer, *op. cit.*, p. 181.

[40] Paul C. P. Siu, "The Isolation of the Chinese Laundryman," in Ernest W. Burgess and Donald J. Bogue, eds., *Contributions to Urban Sociology* (Chicago: University of Chicago Press, 1964), p. 430.

[41] D. Y. Yuan, "Voluntary Segregation: A Study of New York Chinatown," in Milton L. Barron, ed., *Minorities in a Changing World* (New York: Alfred A. Knopf, 1967), p. 269.

[42] Marden and Meyer, *op. cit.*, pp. 173–74.

ethnic segregation is reinforced by occupational specialization; it is so striking in this instance that it gives communal life its distinctive quality. Siu's study of the Chinese laundryman conceptualizes the occupation as an accommodation to the immigrant situation. It was undesirable, but easily learned, manual labor that he drifted into because he had no choice. He hadn't been a laundryman in his native country, but laundry was one of the few alternatives left when he was forced out of competition with other groups. It was isolating work, but this very isolation permitted him to retain his cultural identity.[43]

The isolation was a function of more than the institutional patterns of the laundry. It was also a function of the attitudes of the sojourner, who always expected to return to China, however long his residence in the United States. Such an orientation toward the homeland strengthened ethnic solidarity, encouraging the Chinese to associate exclusively with each other, most particularly with members of their own kinship group with whom they enjoyed warm and spontaneous relations based on shared sentiments and traditions.[44] This has begun to change recently. One study of 164 families in Chicago in 1950 found only half of them still living in Chinatown. Those who worked in establishments catering to the general public were already more acculturated than those who owned or worked in Chinese stores. About a third of the families were entirely English-speaking, and children were increasingly disinclined to follow Chinese ways.[45] Another study suggests the extent of acculturation among American-born Chinese college students in whom the depth of attitudinal change is such that their characteristic emotional control is replaced by American expressive spontaneity.[46]

The history of the Japanese in the United States shows striking sociological similarities to that of the Chinese. The early immigrants were single young men, many of whom went into domestic service or other menial work on the west coast, mostly in California. Some owned small shops, while still others went to work as laborers on large farms. Capable of considerable adaptability, they began to transform themselves and their way of life, organizing for cooperative action such as a demand for higher wages. This succeeded in arousing the opposition of organized

[43] Siu, *op. cit.,* pp. 429, 431.

[44] *Ibid.,* pp. 441–42, 437.

[45] Marden and Meyer, *op. cit.,* p. 177.

[46] Stanley F. M. Fong, "Assimilation of Chinese in America: Changes in Orientation and Social Perception," *American Journal of Sociology,* Vol. 71, No. 3 (November 1965), p. 272.

labor so more of them became tenant farmers, concentrating on truck farming since they were accustomed to intensive cultivation. When they began to buy land, they were excluded from farm ownership as aliens in 1913. They then leased small scattered units of land adjacent to urban communities to use as gardens; they carved out for themselves a special noncompetitive niche in the production of fruits and vegetables for the cities of the west coast, using family labor. Not only were the Japanese thus economically specialized, as were other immigrants, but there was also ethnic continuity in their channels of production and marketing.[47]

There were also Little Tokyos, ghettos established in the large cities to provide goods and services to those engaged in the produce industry, who were refused service elsewhere. The shops were small family businesses with little capital. Since there was so small a range of income there were few class differences among the Japanese. This reinforced the strong sense of community based on their highly integrated culture. Preserving their traditions enhanced in-group solidarity and enabled the Japanese to develop their competitive strength much as the Jews had done—and almost as rapidly.

Acculturation proceeded apace with the increasing urbanization of the Japanese. The traditional family, patriarchal and cohesive, had been the chief agency of social control. It embodied norms of mutual helpfulness expressed in themes of filial piety and respected seniority. Children were encouraged to pursue their education, but their marriages were still arranged in terms of familial continuity.[48] They chafed at parental authority as well as their own contained status. Although the rejection of traditional patterns would have led to the slow disintegration of the ghetto over time, as it did in every other instance, the Japanese ghetto was brought to a more abrupt end by the internment of its members during World War II. Until then, the Nisei, the children of the immigrants, had been unable to break away from their established communities, where at least they were able to find relatively secure employment in ethnic occupations, especially during the depression.[49]

The vulnerable economic position of the Japanese made it easier to evacuate them, and thereby to undermine their communal resources. The disruption in the continuity of group life, in effect, spelled the end of the

[47] Carey McWilliams, *Brothers Under the Skin,* rev. ed. (Boston: Little, Brown & Co., 1951), pp. 150–53, 155–57.

[48] Leonard Broom and John I. Kitsuse, *The Managed Casualty* (Berkeley, Calif.: University of California Press, 1956), pp. 2–3.

[49] *Ibid.,* p. 7.

ghetto. The Nisei, once educated in the culturally conservative Japanese language schools and already straining at the family's traditional authority, gained their autonomy in relocation. They had long since internalized American values, playing acculturated roles in organizations that remained ethnically circumscribed only because of dominant exclusion.[50] Now, after the war, they began to relocate, taking white collar and skilled jobs in the larger society and participating in it for the first time as citizens.

Many Nisei now live in Chicago, forcibly freed of the sanctions of the once self-contained and tightly controlled Japanese community. The compatibility of Japanese and American value systems led to a ready economic adjustment. Although there is greater informal contact with the dominant group, intimate sociability is still confined to the in-group.[51] The marginality of the Nisei is not entirely resolved, however. The parents who helped their children to achieve long-range goals expect them to fulfill filial obligations in return. This expectation is felt deeply by the Nisei, who experience a conflict of values as they strive for greater participation in the American middle class.[52] They want to act as individuals, but experience strain as members of the family.

Catholic Nationality Groups

Other nationality groups also lived in their own ethnic enclaves; although all Catholic, they lived separately for several generations. The communities of these immigrants were not actual re-creations of their respective villages in the old country. In the transplantation of the culture, peripheral institutions became primary, the most crucial one being religion. Ironically, in a sacred society the church could be taken for granted; in America it became the source of social organization for the first generation. (The family, of course, remained the focus of tradition and interaction.) Ultimately, the church, as the core of communal cohesion for each group, was able to serve as the source of unity for the different nationalities making up the same minority religion. In part, its institutional importance

[50] *Ibid.*, p. 6.
[51] William Caudill and George De Vos, "Achievement, Culture, and Personality: The Case of the Japanese Americans," in Bernard E. Segal, ed., *Racial and Ethnic Relations* (New York: Thomas Y. Crowell, 1966), pp. 79–80.
[52] *Ibid.*, p. 82.

increases in the minority community, which requires strong social solidarity. Religion has the power to become the "united front" for the minority group.[53]

The Irish, who eventually became the leaders of other Catholic groups, were among the first of their religion to arrive here. They had a generation of adjustment to American life before the others began to settle, and they had the added advantage of being English-speaking.[54] There was a sizable Irish Catholic community in New York, for instance, in the early nineteenth century. Those who made up the mass migration of the mid-century, therefore, found patterns established for them that created their identity. Among other things, the Irish dominated New York political life beginning in the 1870's and controlled the local Democratic organization.[55]

Instead of accumulating family property, the Irish built the church at great cost in men and money. They transformed Catholicism from a despised sect of the eighteenth century into the largest religious organization in contemporary America. All the economic surplus that might have built a solid middle class in the nineteenth century went to build the church. The community itself lacked leadership; the Protestant Irish were assimilated into the dominant community, and the celibacy of the clergy deprived the Catholic Irish of that class of ministers' sons who contributed so much to Protestant achievement.[56] The Irish Catholic church, organized around parishes established in the last century, was different in culture, if not in theology, from Roman Catholicism. In Ireland, the church had acquired historical significance in the attempt to establish itself in a country dominated by English Protestant culture. It therefore developed many of the characteristics of sectarianism. It retained this defensive character, along with its unusual importance, among Irish immigrants in the United States. There could be no easygoing attitude toward a church that was both parochial and puritanical.[57]

The church sustained (and continues to do so) an attempt unique in organized American religion to maintain a complete and comprehensive

---

[53] Spanish-speaking groups are the most casual about Catholicism, and therefore the least susceptible, up till now, to religious unity with other Catholic minorities. We will discuss the characteristics of their situation in Part IV.

[54] Marden and Meyer, op. cit., p. 385.

[55] Nathan Glazer and Daniel P. Moynihan, Beyond the Melting Pot (Cambridge, Mass.: The M.I.T. and Harvard University Press, 1963), pp. 221–23.

[56] Daniel P. Moynihan, "The Irish of New York," Commentary, Vol. 36, No. 2 (August 1963), p. 95.

[57] Glazer and Moynihan, op. cit., p. 232.

educational system. This effort absorbed much of the community's resources, seriously straining them; but both the church and the community were separatist in attitude toward the dominant, and non-Catholic, community. The schools were considered essential in preserving this isolation, and thus worth the investment. A conservative clergy stood apart from the social issues of the day, and the church's prestige diminished as it became an Irish church, enveloped in its own insularity.[58] Irish nationalism, a "hodgepodge of fine feeling and bad history," filled the cultural void within the community. Nationalist organizations, serving as a source of social cohesion, pursued the American interests of the immigrants. Irish identity declined with the decline in immigration.[59]

Nationalism among the Irish did not include a respect for the intellect. This was a working-class community whose derision of the "highfalutin" encompassed a contempt for learning. The excessive respectability of the lace-curtain fringe of the community led to a condemnation even of the flowering of Irish literature in the late nineteenth century. The best of the young began to leave the community, their sensibilities offended by a culture that had little to recommend it to those without a religious vocation;[60] their perceptions sought the broader horizons of the wider society.

The Poles made up another Catholic migration to the United States, rather different from the Irish and all but immortalized in the sociological literature by Thomas and Znaniecki.[61] They arrived relatively late in the nineteenth century as peasants from rural areas, and settled in industrialized urban centers, mainly around the Great Lakes. Lacking knowledge and skills, they could obtain only the lowest-paying positions and the lowest-rental housing in undesirable neighborhoods. There was a wide social gap between the Polish immigrants and the dominant group. Their culture was primarily a feudal one, both Catholic and patriarchal, characterized by strong kinship ties and in-group control based upon a relatively unified pattern of behavior that was resistant to change.[62]

---

[58] Moynihan, *op. cit.*, pp. 96–97, 104.

[59] Glazer and Moynihan, *op. cit.*, pp. 241, 251.

[60] Moynihan, *op. cit.*, p. 98.

[61] For a full depiction of the quality of Polish life see the monumental work by William I. Thomas and Florian Znaniecki, *The Polish Peasant in Europe and America* (Chicago: University of Chicago Press, 1918).

[62] Helena Znaniecki Lopata, "The Function of Voluntary Associations in an Ethnic Community: 'Polonia,' " in Ernest W. Burgess and Donald J. Bogue, eds., *Contributions to Urban Sociology* (Chicago: University of Chicago Press, 1964), p. 204.

The traditional social system disintegrated in transplantation. "In the process of migration a large part of their traditions and folkways is lost or profoundly altered."[63] Folk life, deeply embedded in the church, was imbued with a sense of sacredness lost in a secular society; established customs were meaningless in the new context. Family life was weakened as its institutionalized obligations became attenuated by more individualized relations.

> In the American setting many of the old ways survive through language, religion and customary practices. But the processes of disorganization that had already begun in the homeland become even more devastating.[64]

The growth of individualism meant that interests were no longer completely identified with the fortunes of the family.

The church was the one institution the immigrants brought from Poland, and it remained a symbol of unity. In the United States the parish became the center of communal life, finally exercising greater social control than in the peasant community. The church thus became the reorganized basis for primary relations among the immigrants.[65]

> The early Poles in America centered most of their organizational and social life around the Church, its institutions, and building, to which they devoted great efforts and sums of money. Thus, the parish was the first organized institution of the Polish-American.[66]

Faced with the existing Irish Catholic hierarchy, the Poles formed their own national parishes and obtained Polish priests, building parochial schools, old age homes, and orphanages along with the churches.[67]

Again we see the church gaining in importance with uprooting. Religion becomes a strong social bond in the new experience of the minority situation, all the more so perhaps as it is faced with the forces of secularization. The Polish immigrants did not form a self-conscious cohesive group upon arrival. They came from different parts of Poland and shared only a consciousness of the Catholicism they held in common.[68] They lived in close physical proximity in this country, however, and their special needs as an ethnic group led to the growth of a variety of voluntary asso-

---

[63] Arthur Evans Wood, *Hamtramck* (New Haven, Conn.: College and University Press, 1955), p. 35.

[64] *Ibid.,* pp. 42–45.

[65] Martindale, *op. cit.,* p. 427.

[66] Lopata, *op. cit.,* p. 210.

[67] *Ibid.*

[68] *Ibid.,* p. 206.

ciations. So complete was the system of institutions that developed in Polonia that it was possible to spend one's whole life within the community without coming into contact with the dominant group. The very existence of Polonia was itself a deterrent to acculturation.

Its ethnic organizations functioned to preserve the community as a distinct entity, providing for the transmission of its culture. Although Polish nationalism did not survive past the early part of this century, neither did assimilation gain in appeal. There persisted a group feeling of separation from the larger society, strengthened by the vested social, psychological, and economic interests in the community which sought justification for its continued existence.[69] Parochial schools in particular were supported to pass on the culture in the hope of preventing the younger generation from leaving Polonia.

The Italians were still another kind of Catholic nationality group, more distinguished by their "Italianness" than their Catholicism. The immigrants were Catholics nonetheless, although less intensely and less actively so than their Irish and Polish counterparts.[70] The mass migration from Italy began in the 1870's; it was the largest such movement. Most of them were peasants and landless laborers from southern Italy, although a few were craftsmen and building workers. They were largely illiterate and village oriented, suspicious of anyone who was not a member of the family.[71] The Italian neighborhoods were made up of kin and town folk, and even the laborers and building workers often worked together in groups under *padroni,* who usually took advantage of their shared ethnic sentiments to exploit them. They worked hard, but without hope of getting ahead, without even aspiration for achievement by their children.

> In the village community there was neither a tradition of self-help nor an expectation of improvement. The Italian immigrants did not assume that their children were as good as anybody else's.[72]

The Italians thus did not create communal institutions of mutual aid. The focus of their life was on the family, upon which they relied exclusively; even their morality was limited to the members of the family, for they did not trust strangers. Their social mobility remained negligible since they valued family interests rather than individual advancement.

[69] *Ibid.,* pp. 205–6.
[70] Marden and Meyer, *op. cit.,* p. 387.
[71] Glazer and Moynihan, *op. cit.,* pp. 182–84.
[72] *Ibid.,* pp. 190–91.

Although they desired material improvement, they saw no role for education, which did not gratify the family directly.[73] The Italians therefore expected their children to leave school and contribute early to the family income. Education was associated with a style of life to which a peasant could not aspire, and the immigrants continued to live in an isolation that was as much intellectual as social. Many of them hoped, however futilely, to return to their native land.[74]

Gans's study of second generation Italians finds that acculturation was nevertheless rapid among their fathers in areas critical to material survival. As farm laborers, the immigrants brought with them a way of life associated with rural poverty. Their characteristic economic patterns, irrelevant in an industrialized America, were quickly jettisoned, and "the ensuing vacuum was filled by things American."[75] In this country they became unskilled factory or construction laborers. They had no choice about their work and certainly no identification with it; it was backbreaking labor that provided only subsistence wages. For all the changes induced by migration, some things remained the same. The family, for example, was still central to their communal existence in American society. It was a significant source of social survival, reinforcing their newly acquired sense of ethnic identity and supporting their continued separateness.

> The studies of the immigrant generation would suggest that the move to America resulted in little change in the pattern of adult life. The social structure which the immigrants brought with them from Italy served them in the new country as well. Those who moved to the cities, for example, settled in Italian neighborhoods, where relatives often lived side by side, and in the midst of people from the same Italian town. Under these conditions, the family circle was maintained much as it had existed in southern Italy.
>
> The outside world continued to be a source of deprivation and exploitation. The immigrants worked in factories and on construction gangs, but while work was more plentiful than in Italy, people had to strive as hard as ever to support their families. . . . Moreover, the churches in the immigrant neighborhoods were staffed largely by Irish priests, who practiced a strange and harsh form of Catholicism. . . . As a result of the surrounding strangeness, the immigrants tried to retain the self-sufficiency of the family

[73] For a characterization of some of the continuing conflicts about mobility, both individual and interpersonal, see William Foote Whyte, *Street Corner Society* (Chicago: University of Chicago Press, 1955).

[74] Glazer and Moynihan, *op. cit.*, pp. 191–92, 195–99.

[75] Herbert J. Gans, *The Urban Villagers* (New York: Free Press, 1962), p. 35.

circle as much as they could. They founded a number of community organizations that supported this circle, and kept away from the outside world whenever possible.[76]

Although the church was the most important formal institution, the Italians were not closely identified with it. The immigrants accepted the sacred symbols, and most of the moral norms, of the Catholic religion, but they were anticlerical. They remained religious at the same time that they rejected the church as a moral agency, seeing it as a human institution so full of frailties that it frequently failed to practice what it preached. Unlike the Irish, the Italians had no respect for the priesthood, which compounded their intergroup ethnic conflict. Italians regarded the celibacy of priests, for example, as problematic, whereas the Irish were themselves accustomed to marrying late or not at all, even in the United States. The Italians expected the clergy to be superhuman morally while still suspecting them of being insufficiently human because of their celibate state. Men attended mass less frequently than women, and when they did, it was out of a sense of religious duty rather than out of any involvement with the local parish.[77] Yet Catholicism had importance even for Italians as for other nationality groups; it was an importance that increased, as we shall see, with the social mobility of future generations.

Ethnic Differences and Cultural Marginality

The values of these early nationality groups were as real in their impact as they were distinctive in their content. Although such values may have disappeared with time, and acculturation, they once had a critical influence on individual behavior and social outcome. "In all complex cultures there are certain traits that are considered appropriate for all irrespective of social position and other traits that are class bound."[78] It was just these shared traits, deeply embedded in the institutional structure of the ghetto, that were significant in the survival of the ethnic group. In determining the daily behavior of its members, such values shaped a special identity

[76] *Ibid.,* pp. 204–5.
[77] *Ibid.,* pp. 110–12.
[78] Celia Stopnicka Heller, "Class as an Explanation of Ethnic Differences in Mobility Aspirations," *International Migration Review,* Vol. 2 (Fall, 1967), p. 36.

that justified a separate existence. The immigrants were different, and were thus defended in their difference from the dominant group. In so far as they continued to prefer and to perpetuate their own values, they remained independent of the larger society, at least socially, if not economically.

Distinctive values were a defining characteristic of the ethnic group, constituting the basis for the community it established. The life fate of its members was formed in the image of what they deemed desirable. Although such values were most often embodied in the religious institution, they were sometimes entirely secular in nature—and in effect. What proved to be at stake in the pursuit of these values was the mobility of the members; their achievement was affected decisively by their commitments. Some groups, like the Italians (and, as we shall see later, the Mexicans), cherished values that were not conducive to mobility. Family obligation, for example, created ambivalence about individual advancement. The price of mobility, if achieved, might mean severing traditional ties with former peers, who were no longer socially suitable; the clan could not accompany the climb up the social ladder of success.

Unlike the Jews and the Japanese, some groups considered those qualities that were more likely to lead to mobility to be the domain of the upper classes. It was not always that they did not appreciate learning, for example, but that they deemed it worse than useless, futile, and therefore frustrating, for those of lower status; it was a luxury only the rich could afford. Jewish and Japanese immigrants, by contrast, valued education as a channel of mobility and stressed it in the socialization of their children; this obtained, whatever their class. They consequently achieved even more than members of the dominant group. Their mobility began in the first generation, although both groups started from an equally impoverished position, and succeeded by the second generation.[79] Thus, the impact of cultural values generic to an ethnic group was such as to affect its social situation independently of internal class differences. As a result, these values also influenced the nature of the relationship with the dominant group. Groups most sensitive about their social honor, for instance, did everything possible to avoid intergroup contact for fear of humiliation.

Cultural values varied among different nationalities of Jews as well as among other groups. Although they all valued mobility, they chose different routes into the middle class. It was the Ashkenazim of European

[79] *Ibid.*, pp. 34–36.

origin (the majority of American Jews) who utilized success in school; the Sephardim of Syrian origin opted for success in the marketplace. One stressed (and still stresses) academic performance, the other business profits.[80] Cultural values, in so far as they persist, continue to influence many other aspects of mundane behavior besides mobility.

> With an orientation to problems usually goes a preferred solution or way of handling them. . . . One behavioral manifestation of this is defense mechanisms—a part of the everyday way individuals have of dealing with their everyday stresses and strains.[81]

The expressiveness and expansiveness of Italians, for example, are reflected in the culturally defined way in which they cope with anxiety by dramatic overstatement. It helps to dissipate the anxiety as it makes bearable the daily deprivations of poverty. The Irish, by contrast, defend against anxiety by denial. Life is bitter and hard, and its inevitable suffering is best ignored; the less said the better.[82] These responses are socially ritualized in the shared terms of the respective groups.

Emile Durkheim suggests that the best evidence for the existence of a norm may be found in its violation—and the incumbent sanctions. So similarly perhaps the best indication of the distinctive values of the ethnic group may be found in the cultural conflicts they created in the second generation. The seeds of marginality were sown early among the children of the immigrants, and with extensive consequence. The first generation, of course, tried to preserve and perpetuate the traditions of the ethnic group, but the younger generation often preferred to adopt the ways of the dominant group. Children sometimes grew to despise their parents for their old world origins and ignorance of American norms. With rejection of the advice and authority of the elders, there resulted conflict that frequently reversed the usual relationship that prevailed between the generations.[83]

The mutual antagonism that developed was fraught with emotional ambivalence. Members of the second generation identified with American

[80] From a study by Morris Gross of New York City school children discussed in *The Washington Post,* Sunday, February 18, 1968, in a feature article by J. W. Anderson, "Ancient Jewish Split Holds New Lesson," B4.

[81] Irving Kenneth Zola, "Culture and Symptoms—An Analysis of Patients' Presenting Complaints," *American Sociological Review,* Vol. 31, No. 5 (October 1966), p. 626.

[82] *Ibid.,* pp. 627–28.

[83] Brewton Berry, *Race and Ethnic Relations* (Boston: Houghton Mifflin Co., 1965), pp. 360–61.

culture (at least among those groups in which youngsters came into contact with representatives of the dominant group, through the public school system, for instance), but they had absorbed some of the traditional culture. Because of the interpersonal relations within the family, "the culture conflict becomes a parent-child conflict."[84] The problem was the more severe, the greater the difference between the ethnic and the dominant culture.

The concentration of immigrants in communities intensified the problems of the second generation. The social isolation that gave security to the parents created conflict for the children. When the children learned that their parents' ways were considered inferior in the larger society, they often derogated the ethnic group as did the dominant group, with the added vehemence of self-hatred. Intergenerational conflict was further compounded by the immigrants' insecurity in their parental roles. They had grown confused about their established rights and duties in the new world and had to face their children as individuals, without the protective cover of traditional roles, under the most trying conditions.[85]

It was more than cultural values that were being tried in the crossfire of conflict. The family itself was often at stake as members of the second generation aspired for dominant values. Their acculturation by the public schools and mass media had risked their alienation from the family. Sometimes there was personal disorganization in the second generation when it rejected the restrictions of the traditional culture, but failed to take on the social restraints of dominant patterns.[86] And sometimes there was simply hope and excitement about the future—along with all the doubt and confusion.

Hapgood describes the strange and fascinating life of the streets as seen by young Jewish boys at the turn of the century. Even before they went to public school, they came into contact with a new world which represented a sharp contrast to their orthodox homes. These influences were at total variance with traditional values and effectively weakened religious orthodoxy, even among those youngsters who attended parochial school in addition to public school.[87] Also among the Jews there was a "tendency to reverse the ordinary and normal educational and economical relations existing between father and son." The father was less able to

[84] Stonequist, *op. cit.*, p. 335.
[85] Marden and Meyer, *op. cit.*, p. 88.
[86] Gordon, *op. cit.*, pp. 107–8.
[87] Hapgood, *op. cit.*, pp. 20, 27–28, 30–31, 33.

make an economic place for himself than his son, who early contributed to his family's support. Since the son spoke English, he served as interpreter for the family, generally taking things into his own hands.[88]

> He is aware, and rather ashamed, of the limitations of his parents. He feels that the trend and weight of things are against them, that they are in a minority; but yet in a real way the old people remain his conscience, the visible representatives of a moral and religious tradition by which the boy may regulate his inner life.[89]

If the elders of the ethnic group sometimes continued to serve as a significant source of conscience (at least as mental images in moral matters), they no longer constituted a relevant community for the second generation. The children of the immigrants chose as their reference group the dominant group. But they were not accepted as social equals in the larger society. Those who were rebuffed, however, did not necessarily return to their ethnic enclaves. They turned to each other as peers and created acculturated communities of their own. Some remained still too sheltered in the second generation to experience marginality, but those who did resolved their conflicts communally; they did not remain chronically caught between two cultures.

The ghetto is a social world now all but gone. One looks at it for the legacy it left, a legacy of values that are now for the most part lost. Although these values are scarcely recognizable to the later descendants of the immigrants, they were once sufficiently real to their direct heirs to cause serious conflict. For the immigrants themselves, however, it was just these values of family and community, church and religion, that helped them to endure. And they had much to endure: uprooting, minority status, and continued poverty. They were sustained by each other, and their shared values, in a hard life of unremitting and unrewarding work. The essential problems of categorical treatment were endless. Most of their tensions remained unresolved, and yet they were not without hope.

The immigrants had survived, and perhaps that was enough. Their values had given survival its raison d'être. It was not so much what they endured that had significance, but why they endured. Nevertheless, what the first generation had to survive was often significant to its children. A slum, after all, was still a slum, and its problems of poverty sometimes drove the second generation to seek success as a means of escape. Survival was no longer enough; it would take money to satisfy those who thought

[88] *Ibid.,* p. 34.
[89] *Ibid.,* p. 37.

poverty was too high a price to pay for piety. Traditional values were accordingly sacrificed for economic pursuits. The children of the immigrants had many reasons to leave the ghetto, but so also did they leave much behind. They left behind all that made the ghetto bearable, for they no longer needed it in a better life. Many ethnic values were thus shed along the way.

Once the second (or perhaps the third) generation was securely established, it attempted to revive some of these values for the sake of maintaining its separate identity, but it succeeded in retaining only the social forms. The essence of the values had disappeared with the spirit of the ghetto, a world that had proven too constricting. The children of the immigrants carried with them only a spurious sentimentality that they resurrected when safely removed from the more sordid realities of the slum that was the ghetto. The values that had once been the basis of group life were eventually distorted by success; they could not be maintained out of their social context. Since the second generation no longer participated in immigrant institutions, it could relinquish their ideological justifications. It required, however, some rationale for continued separate existence as an ethnic group. Increasing secularization undermined the separatist ideology, which was most secure when sacred, and the second generation never found an adequate substitute in its religious institutions. It took the first, and critical, step when it left the ghetto. After that, the pace of acculturation accelerated, which in turn made possible the ultimate potential for assimilation. As there were fewer ethnic values to preserve, there were fewer grounds for social separatism. Eventually, as we shall see, all that remained to justify the existence of the minority community was the exclusion of the dominant group.

Critical as categorical status is in delimiting a minority group, it does not serve as a source of identity in the way that traditional values do. Such status is a dominant definition rather than a minority affirmation, and hence it offers an identity only by default. Should there be an end to social exclusion, there would be little justification for a special identity —or a separate existence. Perhaps this is why there is so much sentimentality about the ghetto in a world in which no one is certain of his identity any longer. It had values, and its members had identity. These values did not change the harsh facts of slum life, they simply rendered these facts secondary; the ghetto was thereby more likely to be transcended than transformed.

Mobility paved the way of the second generation into the middle class, all the more quickly for those groups whose values supported mobility. Indeed, the stronger these values, the greater the seeds for their disintegration by the very success they made possible. Out of this mobility, however, emerges the prototypical minority community in which ethnicity begins to lose its traditional meaning. We will now look at the institutional patterns of this community and the way in which they resolve the marginality of its members.

Chapter 6

The Prototypical Minority Community

THE ghetto of the first generation eventually gave way to the gilded ghetto of the second or succeeding generation, and its social structure is what we know as the contemporary minority community. The tensions of marginality are resolved by the emergence of an acculturated, but segregated, community made possible by economic achievement. It is still an enclosed community, but its values are increasingly those of the dominant group. Insofar as there is mobility into the middle class, there is the development of parallel institutions and internal stratification. The second generation (or the generation that first comes into meaningful contact with dominant norms) experiences both the cultural conflict of mutually exclusive alternatives and the social conflict of differential status audiences; the often contradictory values of the dominant and the minority groups mean that they rarely recognize each other's respective attainments.

Marginality and Mobility

The marginal men of this generation make up the membership of a community now adapted to the middle-class style of life of American society, with institutions modified to meet its requirements. This minority community, situated in better urban neighborhoods, is able to emulate the social structure of the dominant group because of its members' increasing concentration in middle-class occupations; this affords the income necessary for an acculturated life. The community provides both access to values whose priority has been reordered and appreciative peers to serve as audience for achievement. Thus shared patterns of behavior resolve cultural conflicts, and mutual communal acceptance resolves social conflicts. The minority community thereby offers its members an institutional context in which to enjoy the social consequences of economic achievement and all its accoutrements of status.

The incorporation of dominant values into the communal structure is a result of the earlier acculturating contacts of the second generation. The principle of closure continues to protect the minority's social isolation at the same time that the community begins to provide access to dominant values. For all their acculturation, members of the second generation do not reject their special identity. They therefore establish new forms for their religious institutions so that the identity will be perpetuated; the younger generation is inculcated with it in order to guarantee the continuity of the community, as religion, rather than ethnicity, becomes the basis for its minority status.

They adapt their religion to their new status by reducing its scope and significance to that of another institution, a specialized one that must compete with a variety of secular institutions. It is no longer the basis for a sacred way of life, although it may remain central to communal sociability. Traditional welfare activities are transformed into formal social organizations, which reinforce the in-group sentiments that in turn support the institutional structure.

The acculturated community with its separate, but equal, values is a mutually acceptable accommodation of the conflict between the dominant group and the minority group. By living together, marginal men no longer feel caught between two worlds; their tensions are eased by sharing the values of success in a segregated existence in which their special identity and social honor are still protected by self-exclusion. Such a community is also advantageous from the perspective of the dominant group because it increases the cultural consensus of the larger society without increasing the social participation in it. The exclusiveness of dominant values is not threatened, although their uniqueness is undermined; their status is maintained by a social rather than a cultural monopoly.

The community of the second generation is thus a response to its members' minority status in the dominant stratification system; it provides the social recognition along with the realization of values which they are denied in the larger society. Material values of class may be acquired in the impersonality of the marketplace, but the honorific values of status must be granted in the context of interpersonal relations. Peers are the pre-requisite of prestige; the appropriate acknowledgment of economic achievement requires social equality. The fulfillment of minority aspirations is not likely to be appreciated by a dominant group that refuses to recognize their worth.

The structure of the minority community changes as the structure of opportunities changes in the larger society. Class distinctions emerge in the second generation that begin to affect the distribution of life chances. Higher-status members gain greater access to dominant values than do lower-status members. The differences between them are based more on financial accumulation than on occupational variety; because there is still ethnic specialization in the second generation, they are in similar occupations, but some are more successful in their economic pursuits than others. Since they are all sons of immigrants, there is no difference in the family lineage between high- and low-status minority members in this generation. It is money, and more often than not, money alone, that differentiates one from the other.

There may be conflicting principles of organization operating in the social interstices where dominant and minority structures overlap. There are then conflicting economic and ethnic considerations underlying their respective stratification systems. Minority members may thus be subject to contradictory demands in dominant and minority terms. Such conflict is heightened for high-status minority members because of their increased interaction with the dominant group. Although they value the good opinion of the dominant group, they are deprived of its social recognition and the consequent prestige. Minority members have to decide in which status community their social chances lie, if indeed they have any choice at all.

Even when the values of the dominant and the minority group no longer conflict, there is conflict for the minority member between closure within the minority community and lowered status opportunities in the dominant community. The conflict between organizational principles of overlapping stratification systems is resolved in the minority community by the creation of contrasting life styles. Its way of life is no longer homogeneous as its members strive for increased access to dominant values within minority institutions. Status groups in the community therefore may be distinguished by their level of acculturation and the accompanying life style which are a function of their mobility—or lack of it. Such status distinctions are manifest in the plethora of socially differentiated organizations.

Ethnic groups have often been compared sociologically in terms of their economic advancement and the resulting adaptation of the internal organization of their communities; such advancement is correlated with length of residence in this country.[1] In summarizing the Warner and Srole study of Yankee City, Stein suggests some factors retarding mobility: an original intention of temporary settlement, a family structure with patterns of maintaining customary status and of parental determination of that status, later arrival in the city (concomitant with changed local conditions), large size of group (which increases dominant resistance), and proximity to the homeland (commuting slows acculturation).[2]

By contrast, the factors accelerating mobility derive from similarities in cultural aspects and social organization to the dominant group. Even when these similarities exist, however, the minority is usually characterized by two somewhat divergent social systems that reflect generational change, the younger generation being always more acculturated than the older generation. The pressure toward acculturation rests in large part upon the adoption of American consumption patterns. The desire for more mass-produced commodities begins to motivate change in areas other than economic. The church, of course, still stands as a bulwark in defending the integrity of ethnic patterns, but even it changes, losing its distinctive national features in the process. Exclusively ethnic associations are increasingly confined to the first generation as its children are acculturated by dominant institutions. Industry permits the second generation to begin to move into the economic mainstream of American society, and the public schools provide the technical skills necessary for such advancement.[3]

The marginality brought about by mobility is not always resolved by the re-creation of the minority community. Some members of the second generation find alternatives to the accepted community in other (and sometimes deviant) social forms.[4] There are those who acquire access to dominant norms through illegal means and who may thereafter derive their social support from associates in organized crime. They may finally accumulate enough money to gain the social acceptance of the minority

[1] One well-known study is reported in Volume 3 of the Yankee City series, W. Lloyd Warner and Leo Srole, *The Social Systems of American Ethnic Groups* (New Haven, Conn.: Yale University Press, 1945).

[2] Maurice R. Stein, *The Eclipse of Community* (Princeton, N.J.: Princeton University Press, 1960), p. 76.

[3] *Ibid.*, pp. 77–78.

[4] For a conceptual elaboration of alternative modes of individual adaptation, see Robert K. Merton, "Social Structure and Anomie," in *Social Theory and Social Structure*, rev. ed. (New York: Free Press, 1957), pp. 131–60.

community itself. Since the minority community has so few other criteria of class (education, and the occupational difference it makes, is sometimes also significant), it may be even more materialistic in its values than the larger society—enough to permit its social judgments to be bought, if the price is high enough.

There are also those who reject dominant values in favor of the non-material values of art and intellect. Indeed marginality may be a source of creativity, when it encourages the detachment necessary for perceiving the patterns underlying the fragments of experience. It is the perception of such patterns, after all, that makes possible some interpretation of the human condition. There has always been an affinity between the position of the marginal man, who lives in two mutually exclusive worlds, and the perspective of the intellectual, who stands apart from any social world. The shared values of intellectuals provide the basis for communication, if not community; they associate with each other, finding emotional release while sustaining the tensions of detachment necessary for their perspective on the world. They are part of neither the minority community nor the dominant society. The social support of informal circles founded upon shared tastes affords them sufficient stability to live without the conformity of community.[5]

The intellect is itself marginal to all communities. As such, it is not a monopoly of any particular occupation. There is therefore not necessarily any shared style of life among intellectuals, but rather, individualized interpersonal relations. Intellectual marginality is a voluntary matter premised on the conscious choice of different values rather than the involuntary imposition of social categories. It may thus serve as a channel of mobility. The acquisition of status may actually be the unintended and even unanticipated consequence of the pursuit of nonmaterial values. It may be granted in the dominant society to the achievement of intellectual aspiration. Taste, often acquired along with advanced education, is then more important than money.

The basis of community has begun to shift in American society, and eventually this shift affects the minority community, if not in the second generation, then in the third generation. The traditional community was always the community of locus. Birth in a given place, whether a midwestern town or an eastern city, was a significant determinant of style of life. Since closure was likely to operate within a particular territorial area,

[5] For a somewhat different view of "the intellectual community," see Milton M. Gordon, *Assimilation in American Life* (New York: Oxford, 1964), pp. 224–32.

social mobility often required geographic mobility. Increasingly the modern community is one of status based upon occupation rather than location, ultimately making possible the greater inclusion of minority members. The very structure of the community thus changes with class mobility.

Unlike the status community that emerges out of class factors, the minority community is, of course, founded upon ethnic birth as its status determinant. It may therefore encompass a relatively full range of class differences, and is thus a more heterogeneous community than the one based on class alone. The minority community constitutes a resolution of the disparity between class and status created by the continued negative evaluation of ethnic birth even for those who achieve economic mobility. It is for this reason that the stratification system of the minority community overlaps the stratification of the larger society. Class mobility is accessible even to minority members (albeit less so than to the dominant group), but those who are successful are still socially excluded and hence deprived of status. They have no choice but to create their own community, which proves to be the prototypical minority community whose members acknowledge each other's achievement.

This community, because it is internally differentiated, is characterized by contrasting life styles, which give rise to a proliferation of organizations, reflecting the dual stratification systems of the minority and dominant groups. Exclusion from alternative status communities perpetuates itself because minorities are unable to learn the patterns of behavior that would qualify them for participation in the dominant group; they thereby have less opportunity to acquire a shared style of life. This situation may well increase the desire for material values among minority members; wealth, for example, serves as a quantitative substitute for the qualitative criteria of status of which they are deprived. The status aspirations of the second generation, as we will see, begin to be fulfilled by its children. It is the third generation, schooled in social subtleties, that incorporates some of the nonmaterial values of the dominant group. The process of acculturation, however, starts with the material ones.

The Jewish Community

Their relatively rapid mobility into the middle class afforded the Jews an acculturated community by the second generation. Unwilling to sustain the isolation of a sacred tradition, they had incurred the tensions of marginality sooner than most. They thus required a new communal resolution earlier than others. Fortunately they were also better prepared to establish one. The Catholic nationality groups were only securely working class by the second generation. Although some emergence of pan-Catholicism may be found among them sooner, an acculturated community transcending national origins does not really crystallize until the third generation. At this point there is sufficient educational and economic mobility to provide the middle-class status (albeit lower-middle-class) that is prerequisite to the prototypical minority community.

By the third generation Jews, of course, have advanced still further, reshaping their community around more sophisticated concerns of status. There also begin to be those who merge into the status communities of their occupational groups, creating for the first time a genuine potential for assimilation. Salaried professionals and specialized experts employed by bureaucratic structures may participate socially with non-Jewish colleagues; nevertheless, few Jews, even among young organization men, are yet assimilated. What is critical in the second generation, however, is its advancement into such middle-class occupations as managers and proprietors in retail and wholesale trade and light manufacturing, and increasingly in the professions.[6]

A recent summary of census data indicates that Russian-Americans (most of whom are Jewish) outrank not only other minorities but also members of the dominant group in educational and occupational achievement. Although the greatest advance was made by the Jews, the sharp differentials in formal schooling that obtained among nationality groups in the parental generation do not persist among native-born sons.[7] Glazer and Moynihan amplify these findings with a description of New York Jews (who constitute, along with those in the surrounding suburbs, one-half of the total population of Jews in the United States). The vast majority are descendants of Yiddish-speaking immigrants from eastern Europe, whose common experiences were reflected in shared characteristics. They had brought with them little more than a religious tradition intensified

[6] For a general summary of the social characteristics of Jews, see *Ibid.*, pp. 173–95. See Judith R. Kramer and Seymour Leventman, *Children of the Gilded Ghetto* (New Haven, Conn.: Yale University Press, 1961) for a particular study of second and third generation Jews in North City as well as a synoptic history of their changing community.

[7] Beverly Duncan and Otis Dudley Duncan, "Minorities and the Process of Stratification," *American Sociological Review,* Vol. 33, No. 3 (June 1968), pp. 357–58.

by isolation. Their communal life remained strongly self-conscious, however, even when fewer of them were still committed to its core institutions.[8]

Jewish immigrants, like most immigrants, came with few skills and no money. They started in American society as workers and peddlers, and they achieved remarkable success. The Jews of New York have a larger lower-middle class than is found elsewhere, where Jews make up a smaller proportion of the population. Even so, 24 percent are proprietors, managers, and officials; 15 percent are professionals and semiprofessionals; and 25 percent are in white collar and sales occupations.[9] They are prominent in clothing manufacture, department stores, and entertainment; they are now also found in light manufacturing, real estate, and building. In other cities, second generation Jews are characteristically small businessmen in their own or family businesses, or they are independent professionals, in part because the large private bureaucracies do not employ Jews. (Since social clubs are closed to Jews, so are many corporate businesses.)[10]

Although members of the second generation are relatively educated, they are not yet residentially integrated. In New York City, the neighborhoods in which they live are four-fifths and nine-tenths Jewish. Even the suburbs show a marked ecological concentration along religious lines, and Jews continue to express a preference for residing in neighborhoods that are at least 50 percent Jewish. Living in close physical proximity, they exert pressure on each other to participate in communal institutions, particularly the synagogue and a variety of philanthropic and social organizations. "But the religious institutions are so strong because they serve the social desire to remain separate to begin with."[11]

Jews thus stay together and support common institutions in order to maintain their separateness. Although they don't want their children to be any more religious than necessary, they want them to be sufficiently Jewish to avoid intermarriage. The function of the synagogue, therefore, is to transmit a sense of special identity to the next generation. In its orientation toward children, the synagogue offers Jewish education to implant the self-consciousness that (presumably) prevents assimilation.[12] In this way it is the communal institutions that now create the social needs rather

[8] Nathan Glazer and Daniel P. Moynihan, *Beyond the Melting Pot* (Cambridge, Mass.: The M.I.T. & Harvard University Press, 1963), pp. 138, 141–42.

[9] *Ibid.*, pp. 144, 146.

[10] *Ibid.*, pp. 151, 154, 149.

[11] *Ibid.*, pp. 156, 160–61, 163.

[12] *Ibid.*, pp. 164, 175–76.

than the needs that create the institutions. These institutionally created needs in turn perpetuate the community.

> While at one time the problem of Jewish identity was no problem for the individual who lived a distinctively Jewish life in his home, his synagogue, and the community, today there is little that marks the Jew as a Jew except Jewish self-consciousness and association with fellow Jews. . . . The parents favor residence in a neighborhood that has such a high density of Jewish families that the probability of their children marrying a Jewish person approaches certainty.[13]

Although there are still some distinctive patterns of behavior associated with being Jewish (such as a strong family life, a low rate of alcoholism, and a high degree of political liberalism), second generation Jews are, in effect, less "Jewish" than their fathers.[14] Perhaps they think of piety as synonymous with poverty, for in their prosperity, they observe less of religious orthodoxy; they have in fact shed most of the customs characteristic of the ghetto. Ironically, along with this acculturation, as Glazer and Moynihan point out, "there are tendencies to caution and withdrawal."[15] It may be that as the threat of assimilation increases, so does the defensiveness that is unnecessary in isolation.

The social and economic situation of the second generation is similar in metropolitan areas throughout the country. Fifty percent of the Jews in Detroit, for example, are self-employed in family-type enterprises. This is so in spite of the fact that Detroit is a one-industry city in which one out of five employed persons works for one of the three leading automobile companies; much salaried employment is still closed to Jews, particularly in large-scale corporations. Linked to such discriminatory economic practices is an inbred social life based on restricted neighborhoods and clubs.[16] Chicago as well has decidedly Jewish neighborhoods that are correlated with degree of acculturation. The area of first settlement disappeared with upward mobility, but it was replaced by a high-status residential area, suggesting, at least in part, the voluntary nature of Jewish settlement. Jews continue to choose neighborhoods with high in-group density in order to encourage endogamy.[17]

[13] *Ibid.,* p. 164.

[14] *Ibid.,* pp. 164–65.

[15] *Ibid.,* p. 180.

[16] Arnold Foster, "Detroit's Old Habit," *The ADL Bulletin,* Vol. 20, No. 9 (November 1963), p. 2.

[17] Erich Rosenthal, "Acculturation Without Assimilation? The Jewish Community of Chicago, Illinois," *American Journal of Sociology,* Vol. 66, No. 3 (November 1960), pp. 276, 283, 285, 287.

The contrasting communal acceptance that Jews enjoy in the Bay area of San Francisco has been accompanied by somewhat higher rates of intermarriage than is found in the rest of the country. (The national average is 13 percent; in San Francisco, 17.2 percent of Jewish marriages are mixed, and on the Peninsula 20 percent.) Yet the relative freedom of social movement has not led to assimilation. The integration in which local Jews take pride is something of an illusion. As elsewhere, discrimination still exists in social clubs and in private corporations. Jews maintain their own exclusive clubs, and even those who intermarry remain active in them, thereby retaining their identity. Jewishness is a function of just such organizational activity for the second generation. Only in the younger generation are there some who are once more challenged by the religious issues themselves rather than their social institutionalization.[18]

The synagogue is now the center of social life; about 60 percent of American Jews are affiliated, and more attend on High Holidays or take part in some of its secularized activities. They join synagogues (and related community centers) in order to participate in Jewish affairs as Jews and to gain status as members of the community. They thus remain aware of themselves as Jews.[19] According to Gordon, the nearest thing now to an over-arching institution in the Jewish community is its philanthropy, a well-organized system of fund-raising. Its social network strengthens the endogamous nature of the informal relations among Jews; primary groups remain within the bounds of the minority community.[20]

> The acculturation, thus, has drastically modified American Jewish life in the direction of adaptation to American middle-class values, while it has not by any means "dissolved" the group in a structural sense. Communal life and ethnic self-identification flourish . . . while at the same time its members and, to a considerable degree, its institutions become increasingly indistinguishable, culturally, from the personnel and institutions of the American core society.[21]

In a 1958 survey of the Detroit area, Gerhard Lenski found this communal bond among Jews to be very strong, perhaps more so than for any other group. As in other cities, Jews are preponderantly middle class and geographically concentrated. Ninety-six percent of them have relatives who are all or nearly all Jewish, and 77 percent of them have friends

[18] Walter Blum, "The Fear of Intermarriage," *San Francisco Examiner, People,* August 8, 1965, p. 5.
[19] John Sirjamaki, *The Sociology of Cities* (New York: Random House, 1964), pp. 243–44.
[20] Gordon, *op. cit.,* pp. 176, 178, 181.
[21] *Ibid.,* pp. 194–95.

who are all or nearly all Jewish.[22] In every other way they are like members of the dominant group. Jews bear a greater resemblance to Protestants than do Catholics; they differ only in the strength of their kinship bonds and the degree of their attachment to their own community.[23]

The cohesiveness of the family is thus still a distinctive characteristic of the Jewish community. Although the family follows the nuclear pattern of the dominant group, relatives keep in closer touch with each other and visit more often.[24] This does not begin to change until the third generation. A recent study of an upper-middle-class suburb reports that Jewish housewives, as compared with non-Jewish housewives, manifest more extended familism measured by the interaction with kin households (i.e., the degree to which services had been given and received).[25]

The differences are striking, reflecting the considerable degree of cohesion among Jewish families. One hundred and fifty Jewish and 150 non-Jewish households were studied; 78 percent of the Jewish households, 35 percent of the Catholic households, and 14 percent of the Protestant households had at least twelve households of kin in the metropolitan area. Seventy-one percent of the Jewish households, 33 percent of the Catholic households, and 16 percent of the Protestant households reported regular interaction with at least five kin households.[26]

The Jews upon arrival in this country did have some slight advantage in terms of their urban skills and occupational status. The gap between them and other groups widened appreciably between 1910 and 1940 so that Jews achieved higher occupational status than the population at large, while Italians, for example, continued to have a lower status. Part of the reason for the mobility of the Jews is the structure of their family and the nature of their community. It is true, of course, that they valued education and its consequent attainment. What is significant about this value, however, is that in its traditional form, religious learning and familial satisfactions were not separated; the sacred scholarship of one was supported by the others in the family because it was a source of shared

[22] Gerhard Lenski, *The Religious Factor* (Garden City, N.Y.: Doubleday, 1961), pp. 33–34, 72.

[23] *Ibid.,* p. 319.

[24] Charles F. Marden and Gladys Meyer, *Minorities in American Society,* 2nd ed. (New York: American Book Co., 1962), p. 400.

[25] Robert F. Winch, Scott Greer, and Rae Lesser Blumberg, "Ethnicity and Extended Familism in an Upper-Middle-Class Suburb," *American Sociological Review,* Vol. 32, No. 2 (April 1967), p. 265.

[26] *Ibid.,* p. 267.

status. For Italians, by contrast, school and learning were an alien pursuit removed from everyday experience.[27]

The Jewish family was traditionally close knit, "but it was the entire Jewish *shtetl* community rather than the family which was considered the inclusive social unit and world."[28] Since all Jews were bound to each other, the physical proximity of the family did not have to be stressed, although it was certainly to be preferred to separation. This was doubtless a consequence of their perennial minority status that had long accustomed them to dispersal in the Diaspora. The traditional definition of their mutual obligation to each other as Jews reinforced their membership in the community as well as in the family. What they had received, they were to pass on to others.

> The dynamics of benefice for the Jews was not in the nature of reciprocal exchange. Parents' gifts to their children were to be paralleled in the next generation. In the home, as in the community, giving must move in a descending spiral. . . . [It served] to maintain the constituency of fundamentally equal persons, and in this way, to enrich the community.[29]

The traditional culture was thus so embedded in the structure of the community that its continuity was not threatened by economic mobility any more than it was by geographic dispersal. The sense of personal responsibility existed along with a communal responsibility for the individual that helped to ease the precariousness of exile. There has always been great social pressure on the successful to assume such communal responsibility; they in turn have responded with pride to the rewards of recognition thus earned. This reciprocity has contributed to communal identification at the same time that it has sustained the individual members.[30]

Catholic Groups

The Irish, at least of New York, are relatively evenly distributed by now economically and socially; this normal occupational distribution is unlike

[27] Fred L. Strodtbeck, "Family Interaction, Values, and Achievement," in David C. McClelland, Alfred L. Baldwin, Urie Bronfenbrenner, Fred L. Strodtbeck, eds., *Talent and Society* (Princeton, N.J.: Van Nostrand, 1958), pp. 138, 149–50.
[28] *Ibid.*, p. 151.
[29] *Ibid.*
[30] *Ibid.*, pp. 155, 157.

that of other groups. Moynihan points out that the historical distaste of
the Irish for commerce persists in the United States, although they are well
represented in Wall Street law firms. It is perhaps the traditional influence
of the church that has led the Irish to shy away from business. Catholicism's early injunction against usury reflects an ambivalence about the
making of money that stands in sharp contrast to the Protestant ethic.
As merchants, the Irish have been overwhelmed by Jewish competition.
What businesses they own tend to be family affairs, founded by working
men, involving the organization of manual labor, in forms that may have
begun small and grown larger. The Irish have prospered nonetheless in
contracting, real estate, and banking. They have carried over their talent
for political bureaucracy into business organization. They work in the
large corporations, where there is stress on personal qualities and the
accommodation of conflicting interests, and some involvement in politics.[31]

Although the majority of Irish have climbed out of the working class,
it has only been to the next higher social rung; there are still, for instance,
a plethora of Irish policemen and politicians in New York, occupations
that are not sufficiently lucrative to permit mobility out of the lower
middle class. Even within the large corporations in which Irish are employed, their advancement has been slow. Their lower-middle-class orientation stresses security more than success, and communal leadership is still
considered the prerogative of the clergy as the church continues to maintain its institutional importance. With a less positive attitude toward work
than Jews, the Irish, like other Catholics, accept positions with less status.
And when they are successful in political careers or civil service, little
improvement is possible from one generation to the next. As functionaries,
the Irish lack the potential for material gain of entrepreneurs.[32]

Moynihan suggests that there is something painful for a group like the
Irish to become lower middle class. Their working-class vitality is sup-
planted by social resentment, the cumulative effect of which is a sense of
displacement. (This is most acute in politics, where their power in New
York has declined with their proportion of the population.) The resentment that accompanies their lower-middle-class respectability may account
for the continued tendency to alcohol addiction.[33] The self-discipline required to move into the lower middle class is not always rewarded by
success sufficient to compensate for the loss of a colorful life. Frustration

[31] Daniel P. Moynihan, "The Irish of New York," *Commentary,* Vol. 36, No.
2 (August 1963), p. 99.
[32] Glazer and Moynihan, *op. cit.,* pp. 256, 258–60.
[33] Moynihan, *op. cit.,* pp. 100–1.

may then be expressed in displaced aggression toward lower-class groups whose apparent lack of constraint is envied and thus condemned as licentiousness.

As Catholics, the Irish continue to be partially segregated from the general community. They are defensive about their isolation, yet lethargic in their self-satisfaction.[34] They may find themselves associated with Protestants in formal organizations, but it is only the upper-status Irish who are likely to mingle with the dominant group in primary relations. Although they now lack in-group solidarity as Irish, they continue to experience a minority situation as Catholics.[35] As a nationality group, and an early arrival at that, they are already assimilated; as a religious group, they are acculturated, but not socially integrated into the dominant group.

The Irish still play a dominant role in the church among both clergy and laity, but there is also the emergence of intellectually trained laymen increasingly critical of the hierarchy. Along with a growing proportion of educated Catholics, there is considerable self-criticism. American Catholic intellectuals are concerned with the quality of Catholic institutions and the lesser achievement of Catholics in the physical and social sciences. There is the stirring of intellectual aspiration within the community as its members assess the performance of parochial schools and deem it inadequate in many areas. A crisis is thus developing in Catholic education. A large population is committed to the parochial schools, but their costs, already high, will grow even higher to meet the rising academic and social requirements of a constituency who cannot afford the expense.[36]

Polish Americans remain even more segregated than the Irish, continuing to live in "little Polands" in the second generation. They work in the factories of the Midwest, rarely rising above the level of foreman. There is a high proportion of operators and laborers, although some of the native-born young do succeed in moving to better economic areas. Their community, however, continues to be reinforced by overlapping memberships in church, work group, and lodge, and an elaborate network of ethnic associations.[37] The Polish organizations are primarily concerned with the promotion of sociability, but they also carry on charitable activities and

[34] Glazer and Moynihan, *op. cit.*, pp. 278, 287.

[35] Marden and Meyer, *op. cit.*, pp. 385–86.

[36] Moynihan, *op. cit.*, pp. 104–6.

[37] Harold L. Wilensky and Jack Ladinsky, "From Religious Community to Occupational Group: Structural Assimilation Among Professors, Lawyers, and Engineers," *American Sociological Review*, Vol. 32, No. 4 (August 1967), p. 557; Arthur Evans Wood, *Hamtramck* (New Haven, Conn.: College and University Press, 1955), pp. 19, 23.

provide insurance. Insofar as the traditions of the old country persist in some form, "the Polish character of the community is maintained through its organized social life."[38]

Numerous mutual aid groups have frequently been united into federated insurance organizations, and many of the fraternal groups have become multipurpose community centers; there are even occupational-interest groups based on shared ethnicity. Polish-American organizations, however, now resemble American associations more than the original Polonia groups. Nevertheless they still satisfy certain needs of the members in a way that American associations do not, in part by promoting the use of the Polish language in informal relations.[39]

Like most minorities, the Polish community does not admit to its internal problems for fear of further loss of prestige, but there is some social conflict as in every community. So also is there considerable family disorganization and the chronic drinking by which some seek to drown the frustrations of a hard life and continued, if relative, economic deprivation.[40] Counteracting the problematic aspects of communal life, however, is the reinforcement of a number of parochial schools passing on Polish culture. At one point nearly all Polish children attended parochial grade school, at least for a while, learning Polish history and language. Now the number is declining as more attend public school only. And the function of the parochial school has changed. It has become more like the American Catholic school than a Polish-oriented center of ethnic culture.[41]

Acculturation has been relatively slow among the Poles, but contact with the dominant culture through schools, mass media, and economic activities has led to some changes in the second generation. It has been somewhat different with the Italians. They are acculturated, but even after three generations, remain traditionally bounded by family and neighborhood. Most members of the second generation are workers like their fathers. They still live in the same areas, although the neighborhoods have been improved to suit the higher standard of living. The difference between the two generations in occupation, however, is smaller than in some

---

[38] Wood, *op. cit.,* pp. 173–74.

[39] Helena Znaniecki Lopata, "The Function of Voluntary Associations in an Ethnic Community: 'Polonia,' " in Ernest W. Burgess and Donald J. Bogue, eds., *Contributions to Urban Sociology* (Chicago: University of Chicago Press, 1964), pp. 211–12, 216.

[40] *Ibid.,* p. 214; Wood, *op. cit.,* p. 227.

[41] Wood, *op. cit.,* p. 39; Lopata, *op. cit.,* pp. 207–8.

other groups, and there continues to be a tight network of kinship and friendship binding the community and excluding outsiders.[42]

Second-generation working-class Italians confine their meaningful social and institutional participation to others of the same status and neighborhood. Although their way of life is enclosed, it is acculturated to American working-class standards and styles.[43] There are few cultural patterns that survive, among which are food habits. Italian is still spoken, but it is not being taught to the children. There is no longer any identification with Italian culture, as Herbert Gans confirms in his study, *The Urban Villagers.*[44]

> Assimilation, however—the disappearance of the Italian social system— has proceeded much more slowly. Indeed, the social structure of the West End . . . is still quite similar to that of the first generation. Social relationships are almost entirely limited to other Italians, because much sociability is based on kinship, and because most friendships are made in childhood, and are thus influenced by residential propinquity. Intermarriage with non-Italians is unusual among the second generation, and is not favored for the third. As long as both parties are Catholic, however, disapproval is mild.[45]

The Italian community is a peer group society whose members associate with others of the same sex, age, and status. The primary relations that are found in friendships, cliques, and informal clubs also include those of the family. These are supplemented by a small array of Italian institutions and voluntary organizations which constitute the community and support the peer group. The outside world may determine the second generation's opportunities for work and income, thereby shaping its style of life, but that influence is refracted through the primary group, in which the second generation, after all, lives the most important part of its life.[46]

> Sociability is a routinized gathering of a relatively unchanging peer group of family members and friends that takes place several times a week. One could almost say that the meetings of the group are at the vital center of West End life, that they are the end for which other everyday activities are a means.[47]

[42] Glazer and Moynihan, *op. cit.*, pp. 287–88, 205–6.
[43] Gordon, *op. cit.*, pp. 204–5.
[44] Herbert J. Gans, *The Urban Villagers* (New York: Free Press, 1962), pp. 33–34.
[45] *Ibid.*, p. 35.
[46] *Ibid.*, pp. 36–37.
[47] *Ibid.*, p. 47.

In-group loyalty is, of course, the major criterion for social ranking within the community; it is widened in conformity to the prevalent social practices of the second generation. Members are expected to keep up with group activities and consumer styles, which are characteristically working-class patterns of behavior. In so doing, they cannot depend on others for help for there is little available in a community with limited resources; realistically no one can afford to extend himself to the point of getting caught up in a spiral of reciprocal obligations.[48] These are blue-collar workers whose employment is still insecure, or at least regarded as such. They work for the money they need to enhance the pleasures of peer group life. There is no identification with work—and no ambition for the future. Nor are the social patterns of the Italian in-group oriented toward mobility. Members of the second generation still see much middle-class behavior as status-seeking snobbery that would separate them from their own social world.[49]

Feeling exploited by the outside world, especially on the job, Italians are hostile to the dominant group and prepared to exploit it in return. The ambivalence spills over into the realm of education. There is strong resistance to change and a fear that education will estrange the younger generation from its parents and the peer group society. Children thus acquire little interest in learning.[50] Members of the second generation reject the cultural patterns of the first generation, rural traditions irrelevant in American society; but they do not reject the family-centered social structure, nor do they want their children to do so. They want their children to continue their communal resolutions of marginality; American culture, therefore, is not permitted to penetrate the family circle.

> The rejection of external mobility is largely a rejection of middle-class elements in the outside world. The West Ender has little sympathy for what he believes to be the goals and behavioral requirements of this way of life. Moreover, he rejects the conscious pursuit of status and the acquisition of artifacts that would require him to detach himself from his peers, and to seek ways of living in which they cannot share.[51]

There is little, if any, interest in interacting with the dominant group. It is feared, as much because the second generation still lacks the skills to participate as because it is excluded. The lack of education (few have gone

[48] *Ibid.,* pp. 27, 84, 86.
[49] *Ibid.,* pp. 122–26, 219.
[50] *Ibid.,* pp. 129, 132.
[51] *Ibid.,* p. 219.

much beyond grade school, if that) is itself an obstacle to communication. The second generation went to school as long as they had to attend and then went to work under pressure from a hard-pressed family. Primary education was sufficient to serve as a source of acculturation, but it provided no social ease in the larger society. Italians consequently feel self-conscious about real and imagined deficiencies, rejecting the middle class basically because they refuse to make the required changes in their own lives.[52]

The Changing Ethnic Community

The minority community thus emerges out of the second generation's mobility, at least into the working class, if not the middle class. It is typically a lower-middle-class community, sufficiently acculturated to reduce its members' sense of social difference. Many of the institutions created by the immigrants become a hindrance rather than a necessity in the second generation; some are abandoned, and some are changed. "More and more of these institutions become identified with the religious denomination, rather than the ethnic group as such."[53] In Part IV we will explore to what extent these communal patterns pertain to newer ethnic groups. As we have already seen, even the typical history of the earlier groups varies somewhat with national origins. Yet an overall pattern does begin to emerge for the religious minority community by the second and third generation, whatever the cultural differences in background. We will observe the crystallization of this communal pattern in the next chapter; this does not always occur for racial minorities.

Since the minority community is organized around shared ethnic birth instead of shared economic position, its structure is determined by its position in the stratification system of the larger society. Its own stratification, therefore, is a function of its level of access to dominant values. The structure of the minority community embodies the resolutions of the past and the tensions of the present in patterned responses to the minority situation. The minority community represents the institutionalized resolution of the

[52] *Ibid.,* pp. 220–21.
[53] Nathan Glazer, "Peoples of America," in Milton L. Barron, ed., *Minorities in a Changing World* (New York: Alfred A. Knopf, 1967), p. 146.

tensions engendered by its members' social position. Its structure, therefore, changes with the members' changing situation in the larger society. The structure of the community affects the group's position, thus changing its situation; this in turn requires changes in the communal structure.

Whatever its structure, the community provides a way of living with the minority situation of deprivation (which grows increasingly relative with each generation) and derogation (which is modified, and often muted, by mobility). The growing access to dominant values within the minority community constitutes one of the more successful resolutions of the situation. Even so the community changes to some extent with each generation because both the tensions of its situation and the available means of resolution are different. The situation is changed by the very resolutions of the prior generation, which create new tensions for the next generation as well as new resources for resolving them.

Greater access to dominant values leads to greater diversification within the minority community. There is a proliferation of subcommunities as the status groups within each generation react to their respective situations. Communal sentiment is often stretched thin to cover these internal differences; it is shored up by religious rituals as well as social organizations. When all else fails, the cohesion of an otherwise divided minority community may be restored by renewed conflict with the dominant group, conflict that helps to externalize the inner strains.

The continued existence of the minority community requires the preservation of some special identity, all the more so when its style of life is no longer culturally distinctive. As in the dominant group, members of a minority accept the social priority of the accident of their ethnic birth. Internal differences within the community are thus kept subordinate to its separate identity, and categorical status, reinforced as much from within as from without, perpetuates itself. The self-exclusion of minority members may be supported by their own stereotypes of each other. These stereotypes are used in exacting the fulfillment of communal obligations as payment for protection from the dominant group. Sometimes members of the minority community begin to treat each other categorically as such treatment by the dominant group declines; it may become their only guarantee of communal continuity.

Categorical reactions, whatever their source, are a reminder of the hostility of the outside world that helps to keep members within the minority fold—lest they forget. It is for this reason that the aggressive response of the younger generation may be directed at its own community rather than at the dominant group. After all, when the protective functions of the minority community are fulfilled, the next generation knows more enclosure than exclusion. And self-exclusion, no less than the social exclusion imposed by the dominant group, can induce self-hatred. The enclosed minority may fear its own inadequacies because of self-imposed limitations. Generational conflict is compounded by this ambivalence, and the young are inclined to blame their elders rather than themselves (or the dominant group) for the diminished life chances of their minority situation.

One problem each generation faces is deciding whom to define as social peers in a changing situation. It rejects the older members of the established community because their resolutions are no longer relevant in a new reality. The young may increasingly reject the imposition of social obligations based exclusively on shared birth. They perceive the negative aspects of their known reality and begin to aspire for the less familiar (and thus by definition more positive) reality of the dominant group. There is thus some breakdown of past patterns of accommodation when the new generation refuses to accept the established forms of self-exclusion because they impede the realization of its aspirations; if nothing else, it changes the social forms of self-exclusion.

Once there is a minority community, each generation is socialized within it with minimal contact with the dominant group. The power of the dominant group is thereby protected by invisibility. The older generation, as the embodiment of the minority way of life, thus becomes, in the eyes of the young, the agent of deprivation. Their rebellion, however, may be channeled into the achievement that provides the basis for mobility out of the community. As long as they are still refused social recognition in the larger society, such mobility leads only to the formation of a new minority community offering greater access to dominant values. This community may encompass organized militancy against the dominant group, when it is perceived as the source of deprivation, the group that denies them the status appropriate to their achievement. The alternative response, of course, is the acceptance of the established minority community and its already achieved access to values, whatever the level of attainment; it is an acceptance protected perforce by continued avoidance of the dominant group.

The structural determinant of acceptance or rejection of established patterns of accommodation may well be the stratification system of the minority community itself; the level of access to values within the community affects the aspirations of members of the next generation. Lower status, for example, may impel motivation for mobility since there are no social rewards for remaining in the minority community. The newly acquired qualifications of the mobile do not necessarily mean participation in the dominant community. Insofar as exclusion continues, these characteristics become the basis for a new form of self-excluding minority community. There are still those who accept the old one, however; high-status members, who enjoy greater access to dominant values within the minority community, are more likely to remain in it. They may be too economically secure to be motivated enough for social mobility. Recognizing the legitimacy of the communal claims of their own group, they do not seek the social acceptance of the dominant group. Rather, they continue to confer status among themselves, ignoring the absence of acknowledgment in the larger society.

In later generations, education becomes an increasingly important channel of mobility. Over time there is a subtle change even in its function; it shifts from that of gaining status to that of maintaining status. Education first makes possible the achievement of class values through an advance in occupation, and then it facilitates the acquisition of status values through the attainment of social refinement. College, initially a source of trade training for minority groups, finally becomes a source of taste training, a substitute for family breeding in poise and polish for those who lack lineage. In this context, the nature of the college becomes more important for mobility than its curriculum; not only does its academic prestige have some halo effect for social status, but its informal relations offer socialization into a new style of life not to be found within the minority community itself.

The significance of mobility as the motivation for education (or at least as one of several impelling motives) among minority members is frequently complicated, as we have already glimpsed, by cultural factors of their ethnic birth. Material motives operate for everybody, of course, although not necessarily exclusively. (And there is a difference between intention and consequence; some people gain status as the result of being college graduates, having gone to school simply to learn something.) For the minority member, however, there may be considerable conflict between individual achievement and familial, and even communal, solidarity.

Minority communities that do not reward education compel their college-trained offspring to seek areas offering open channels of mobility. The individual conflicts thus created may diminish motivation by compounding the problems involved in mobility. The risks of mobility include uncertainty of outcome as well as deferred gratification. Combined with the resistance and resentment of peers, the risks may well defeat the aspiration; there is, after all, no guarantee that the goal will be achieved, nor even any assurance that it will prove to be worth the effort, if it is achieved. Finally, it may prove too difficult to enjoy the rewards of success, if one must leave behind family and friends.

The attitude of minority members toward mobility varies with their cultural values, of course, but so also does it vary with the structure of their community. There is greater acceptance of mobility when there is already a middle class within the minority community since this reduces the potential risk of assimilation. The existence of a middle class encourages mobility because it offers role models for others to follow. More importantly, if less obviously, it permits the community to incorporate its more successful members. The negative reaction to mobility is in large part a function of the communal fear of loss of membership. When there are opportunities within the minority community, however, members do not have to seek success outside. And their mobility does not threaten the communal structure; on the contrary, mobility supports it by supplementing the ranks of the middle class.

Doubtless some additional propelling force is needed to induce a person to attempt to change his status. Such an impulse may derive from some combination of social discontent and personal anxiety. In any case, the achievement of one generation creates the resources that allow the next generation the fulfillment of its values. In the process, the older generation feels rejected by any disavowal of established solutions and consequent pursuit of different values. Such interpersonal ambivalence further compounds the reaction—and resistance—to mobility. Nevertheless mobility occurs, at least up to a point; then it may appear as if complacency sets in among the successful. And perhaps it does—along with the vested interests that accompany the acquisition of material values. Yet there seems to be at stake another kind of self-protection of a more personal and less institutional variety. Those who are successful do not strive for more while they still feel insecure about what status they have attained. Fearful of losing what they have gained, they may leave it to their children to qualify for more, if indeed there is still such aspiration. Sometimes the change in reference group incurred by mobility brings on a sense of relative deprivation that motivates further mobility.

The leadership of the minority community is by and large drawn from the ranks of the educated. It is they who most often serve as liaison to the dominant group because their education makes them acceptable as ethnic representatives to the larger society. The interests of the minority may be initially represented by liberal dissidents from the dominant group on the grounds of ideals or ideologies. Leadership is eventually taken over by newly educated members of the community, often operating from the pulpit or through politics. These leaders make claims based on the bargaining power of the minority itself.

Because of its functions, there are ambiguities and ambivalences inherent in the position of leadership. These result from the prerequisite of being acceptable to both the dominant and the minority communities. Such acceptance is frequently premised on mutually exclusive grounds; if a leader is accepted by the dominant group, he may thereby become automatically suspect in the eyes of his constituent minority. If he is not acceptable to the dominant group, he has less chance of effecting change as well as little opportunity for selling out. Leaders are therefore subject to social control by the minority group lest they go too far in accommodating dominant interests (and capitalizing on any personal advantage while they are at it).

There is an additional anomaly in the position of leadership, and that is its vested interest in maintaining the minority situation in order to maintain its status.[54] In effect, the very social structure that makes possible organized communal action ultimately impedes it. Leadership is, after all, premised upon the perpetuation of a separate community. It requires structural continuity, however acculturated the underlying values. By social definition, the status of leader does not exist independently of the stratification system of the minority group.

There may be less of a problem in group survival than leaders anticipate. Minority communities do not necessarily disappear with a decline in discrimination. The sources of community may become self-perpetuating when they are institutionalized into a way of life, and self-exclusion meets needs other than social exclusion by the dominant group. The principle of closure then operates to protect the special identity of the community, with social enclosure assuring its continued separateness, if not its cultural distinctiveness. Without the affirmation of independent values, however,

[54] For a discussion of such vested interests in the Negro situation, see E. Franklin Frazier, "The Negro Vested Interest in Segregation," in Arnold M. Rose, ed., *Race Prejudice and Discrimination* (New York: Alfred A. Knopf, 1953), pp. 332–39.

the minority community is subject to increasing forces of disintegration; there is then less ideological justification for its separate existence. At the point that exclusion becomes more significant than ethnicity, the minority's way of life is determined more by categorical treatment than by cultural uniqueness.

Since there is greater internal differentiation within the minority community than there is in a shared-class situation, there are additional divisive strains. There may also be the stress of economic deprivation compounding the social stresses. Perhaps most significant of all is the fact that the sacred ideologies of an earlier generation are increasingly secularized by an awareness of alternatives. When that happens, it becomes questionable whether members of the minority will confirm their social necessity by cultural choice. Both the paradox and the problem of the minority community is that it is premised on exclusion rather than exclusiveness; its principle of closure derives from being closed out by the dominant group rather than from closing off others from outside. Solidarity frequently becomes spurious when it is based upon shared social rejection rather than a way of life, the intrinsic worth of which is founded upon independent values held in common.

Communities that survive (and sometimes even transcend) their minority situation have the social resources for self-exclusion and an ideology of exclusiveness. They are, in a word, middle class, with institutions that can be enclosed. Such an institutionalized community makes possible individualized identity and the consequent autonomous choice of alternative affiliations. If the minority community is not able to provide an escape from the invidious social identity of negatively evaluated ethnic birth, its members may seek the nonidentity of social invisibility. That is, they may try to pass as members of the dominant group, if they can, rather than endure the continual consequences of their categorical status.

Along with its sacred ideology, the minority community may also lose its self-sufficiency (and its occupational specialization) with the economic decline of small business in the American social structure. To maintain the community then requires institutionalized links to its livelihood in the larger society. Otherwise new sources of livelihood, as we will see, may mean new sources of identity involving a shift from ethnic birth to occupational status. The forces of communality found in shared experience and expression may nonetheless outweigh the forces of dissolution that emerge out of acculturating contacts in the educational and economic areas. This is most likely to occur when social change is incorporated into the structure and style of life of the minority community to suit the changing status of each generation.

The first generation followed its dream of opportunity, and its children found the better life. In so doing, they lost much of the local color of ethnic existence. Increasingly committed to dominant values, members of the second generation sometimes seem more American than Americans, especially in their concern with the material values that are more accessible to them. In the critical eyes of their children, they are nothing if not dull as a result. And it is true that the second generation, insecure in its success and unsure of its acceptance, can afford to take few social risks. This may account for what appears to be a case of over-conformity, even within the confines of the minority community. It is a community replete with the excesses of respectability. Not only is its structure highly organized, but the content of its norms is entirely conventional, perhaps to counteract the lingering sense of the slums from which its members escaped.

The second generation took the only chance it was going to take in pursuing success. In a chronic state of social insecurity, it is not about to risk what it has achieved by taking any more chances. Although members of the prototypical minority community are more relaxed with each other than with outsiders, they lead very regulated lives. They continue to conform to constrictive conventions in large part because they are afraid of the reaction of others. (A recurrent theme in minority fiction is the concern about what the neighbors will think.) Much energy is invested in maintaining appearances since social acceptance within the community is contingent upon propriety. Propriety may assume such importance that it is elevated to the level of morality. Perhaps, too, the lower-middle-class mentality characteristic of the minority community still aspires for the good opinion of the dominant group. It is assumed that this can be gained through the social control of individual impulse, and sanctions are accordingly stringent. Hence, those who appear to embarrass the minority within the purview of the dominant group are publicly disavowed.

Ironically, the sociological literature provides more details about the organizational structure of the prototypical minority community than about its internal conflicts and consequent changes. Since its critical social characteristics are usually overlooked (often out of commitment to the community), the literature is likely to make the community seem duller than it is. The community is taken at face value, which is, of course, what it wants, and public attitudes rather than private motives are documented sociologically. As the ghetto is sentimentalized, so the gilded ghetto is conventionalized. Consequently both tend to be flattened out in the sociological literature as if there were no life left in the minority community at all. Yet there are real people living in real communities with real problems. They are rarely treated as such by sociologists, who are inclined to single them out for special treatment as minority members rather than study them as social persons in the full context of their communal being. To render people even duller than they are is perhaps its own kind of discrimination.

Let us now look at what happens in the third generation, and beyond, in and out of the sociological literature.

Chapter 7

The Third Generation— and Beyond

T H E community forms of succeeding generations represent, above all, a change from the traditional values of the minority group to the incorporation of dominant values, first of class, then of status. Presumably, when dominant values were acquired, they would undermine the basis for a separate community. However, they could do so only if the achievements of the minority were accorded social recognition by the dominant group. The community persists in large part because of continued differential treatment by the larger society, albeit in more subdued and less restrictive fashion. It is true that acculturation eliminates national origins as the cornerstone of the minority community. Nevertheless, the separate identity of religious groups, and even more, the physical visibility of racial groups still serve as sources of categorical status. The consequences of categorical status are somewhat different for religious and racial groups, and so, of course, are the communities that develop out of them. In neither case does the acceptance of dominant values eliminate the social exclusion inherent in the minority situation.

The increasing level of acculturation leads to greater conflict with the dominant group as more claims are made by minority members now qualified to participate in the institutions of the larger society. Their continued exclusion is resolved by appropriate adjustments in the accepted patterns of accommodation. These adjustments are embodied in the changing social forms of the minority community, which becomes increasingly like the communities of the dominant group. The ghetto of the first generation, as we have already seen, was organized around the ethnic values of its traditional society; the gilded ghetto of the second generation gave priority to the material values of American society. It is for the third generation to discover the nonmaterial values and to establish a community that encompasses all the elements of prestige enjoyed by the dominant group. Some of the third generation draw closer to the dominant group as it becomes possible for members of minority groups to be incorporated into the larger society by means of its specialized occupational communities.

The type of education and employment becomes the shaping, indeed the defining, characteristic of the third generation and of those to follow. This is the first generation whose shared experience has not been a traumatic one, and its tensions may therefore be less critical than those of earlier generations who sought survival and then success. The third generation has grown up in relative economic and social security that has freed it from much conflict (and that, according to some observers, has also diminished its creativity). Its acculturation has been secured by a college education; it is thereby qualified for social acceptance in the larger society. The third generation begins to aspire for such acceptance, whatever the probability of attainment. It is perhaps for this reason that the complacency engendered by comfort is disturbed by some seemingly unspecified discontent.

College education opens up a wider choice of careers to members of the third generation, who are impelled by the same desires for status and security as members of the dominant group. In occupations as organization men they escape from any ethnic visibility fostered by the traditional economic specialization of the minority group. Through greater participation in the larger society, they are sometimes eased out of the minority community entirely. Status tensions emerge out of the closer contact with the dominant group and the attempted escape from enclosure by the minority group. Since the social behavior of the third generation is no longer different from that of the dominant group, there is the risk of attenuated ethnic ties. Indeed, members of this generation avoid the imposed distinctiveness of social differences, sharing the style of life of the larger society. Some of them therefore grow ambivalent about participating in the minority community.

The dominant group constitutes a new status audience for the minority, and its judgments become more significant as the third generation grows more sensitive to the social subtleties of the status game. As interaction with the dominant group increases, class relations change to status relations. Increasingly there is one set of values for both dominant and minority groups, so there is less and less justification for social separateness.

However, most members of the third generation still associate only with each other in their primary relations, thereby retaining their minority identity. They continue to live in separate communities, whose stratification is increasingly differentiated by occupational distinctions and the incumbent styles of life.

As the structural components of personality grow more disparate for members of the minority group, a new distinction develops between individual identity and the sources of community. There are renewed questions of belonging when the members no longer assign priority to their ethnic origins. Ethnicity may be one of their characteristics, but it is not their only one, nor even their primary one; educational and occupational differences within the third generation begin to take precedence over ethnic similarities (insofar as such similarities still exist). The accident of ethnic birth may be confirmed by religious conviction, but such minority identity does not necessarily support a community. As occupation begins to determine the way of life, the influence of ethnicity is increasingly delimited.

The salient question is, of course, whether it is possible to retain a separate religious affiliation without invidious social consequence. As long as minority status of any sort leads to differential treatment at any level, there are grounds for a separate community, whether or not there are sufficient institutional resources. The third generation of the earlier nationality groups tries to eliminate the ethnic characteristics that make a difference in the way they are treated socially. This reduction of social visibility, however, creates a communal dilemma. Some members of the third generation reject the social enclosure of the minority community before achieving the qualifications for acceptance in another kind of status community. The resulting marginality remains unresolved by a new form of community.

Those who are not qualified to participate in the occupational communities of the larger society are at least able to move their residence from the areas populated by the second generation. Although they retain their social and economic ties to the established minority community, they find in the suburbs the makings of a more sophisticated communal life. This may represent a transition to a status community of the future where religious identity has no invidious social consequence, but that is not the case now. In suburban communities members of the dominant and minority groups, both having been socially and geographically mobile, live in close physical proximity. Obviously some patterns of exclusion break down when they are no longer protected by distance. Since the communal institu-

tions of this new social setting encompass members of both the dominant
and the minority groups, the more formal patterns of interaction among
them have changed. Their shared interests as suburbanites have led to
greater intergroup participation.

Differential intragroup association, however, continues to characterize
intimate interpersonal relations. It is difficult to assess the extent of exclusion by the dominant group since few members of the minority group
have yet acquired the social characteristics that transcend their categorical
status. At this point their changed residence has transformed some of the
categories of interaction, but not all the underlying patterns. These new
status communities are founded more upon the taste patterns of the
educated (who are most often found in expert occupations) than upon
the consumption patterns of the moneyed. It is for this reason that social
fate is now decided at college rather than at home. The consequent changes
in the sources of identity undermine the cohesion of the minority community. Acquisition of dominant status values requires recognition from
the larger society rather than the minority community.

When the minority community becomes too small a world, the third
generation may begin to try to resolve its tensions by eliminating the
status that gives rise to them. The consequences for community are not
yet crystallized. As always, the occupations that constitute an escape from
the minority community do not necessarily guarantee social acceptance in
the dominant society. Prestige may inhere in the achievement of occupational position, but it is not necessarily accompanied by any acknowledgment in interpersonal relations. Not all members of the third generation,
or even many, seek such escape. It is usually those of the lower class in the
minority community who look for a way out in the status community of
organization men. By contrast to higher-status members in the minority
community, who may be bound to it through family-based businesses,
lower-status members have little at stake in it. They therefore have less to
lose and more to gain in social mobility. We will now look at how these
factors operate in the lives of young Jews and Catholics.

The Changing Jewish Community

In a study of one hundred second-generation and one hundred third-
generation Jews, Kramer and Leventman find an increase in salaried
employment among the latter. There is a new social type emerging, the

Jewish organization man who has no family business to inherit or who does not want to go into the small retail store owned by his father. Specialized training now qualifies some of the third generation to enter occupations that are traditionally non-Jewish. There are not many who fall into this category yet, due to the extensive economic discrimination found in the city in which this study was done. There are enough of them, however, to suggest that the style of life of the third generation is increasingly influenced by occupation rather than ethnicity.[1]

There are few religious differences between the second and third generation, except for a further decline in orthodoxy.[2] The critical changes in religious observance had already occurred between the first and second generation. The social consequences of a more normal occupational distribution begin to reveal themselves in the third generation. Most members of this sample still have as their close friends other Jews. An increasing number however, include non-Jews among their intimates. Living in mixed suburbs, they even begin to disclaim a preference for Jewish friends.[3]

Although most of them remain closest with Jewish friends from childhood, they seek shared interests rather than shared birth in their social life. Many members of the third generation seem defensive about the personal attachments that they do have in the Jewish community. They are quick to explain that the basis for their in-group friendships is not necessarily ethnic; they feel more comfortable and have more in common in relationships of long standing. The non-Jewish friendships they may have formed in college or at work are of more recent and less informal origin and are thus regarded as less intimate. In addition to these changing interpersonal relations, there is also an increasing tendency to belong to non-Jewish organizations as well as Jewish ones.[4]

It thus becomes apparent that behavior that is class-linked in the second generation is more widely dispersed in the third generation. The Jewish community is thereby increasingly stratified by the same criteria of status that differentiate the general community. "Social variation within the third generation is produced by occupational differentiation."[5] Most of the third generation, nevertheless, continue to prefer endogamy for themselves and their children, although they might accept intermarriage in the next

[1] Judith R. Kramer and Seymour Leventman, *Children of the Gilded Ghetto* (New Haven: Yale University Press, 1961), pp. 134, 136, 170, 200.

[2] *Ibid.*, p. 151.

[3] *Ibid.*, pp. 171, 175–76.

[4] *Ibid.*, pp. 178–79, 183.

[5] *Ibid.*, pp. 196, 200.

generation if they were faced with it. Those in traditional Jewish occupations in particular maintain close social ties to the established community on whose good will their business or profession depends. In retaining their old friendships, they remain subject to the social control of the community and susceptible to its pressures for participation.[6]

Second-generation Jews were prototypically marginal, seeking access to dominant values within minority institutions.

> The "Jewishness" of the second generation hinged on a way of life founded on self-employment in traditionally Jewish occupations, commitment to such Jewish institutions as the synagogue and philanthropy, and exclusive association with other Jews.[7]

The scope of Jewishness in the third generation begins to be confined to religious affiliation (whose institutional sphere has already been narrowed). With occupation an increasing determinant of life style, those with nonethnic occupations have further reduced the social and cultural differences between Jews and non-Jews. They are committed to careers as organization men rather than to the vested interests of the minority community, and their social detachment is reinforced by geographic mobility.[8]

The new organization men of religious minorities are subject to the interpersonal influences of colleagues, who form a status community with a shared style of life. Since career commitment takes precedence over other considerations, social structures emerge that cut across ethnic boundaries. Young Jews begin to interact in integrated social circles based on occupational interests. Similarly their organizational memberships are a function of such shared values.[9] We will examine the potential consequences of these social patterns for assimilation later in this chapter. Since such changes are not yet characteristic of even a majority of the third generation, let us first establish the prevailing patterns. There is another study of 1420 Jews in Providence, Rhode Island, 40 percent of whom are the native-born children of native-born parents. Again, the observers find a secularization process, but also they find that it takes place largely within the Jewish context.[10]

Although traditional values have been abandoned, there has been little

---

[6] *Ibid.,* pp. 180–81, 200.
[7] *Ibid.,* pp. 206–7.
[8] *Ibid.,* pp. 207–8, 200.
[9] *Ibid.,* p. 201.
[10] Sidney Goldstein and Calvin Goldscheider, *Jewish Americans: Three Generations in a Jewish Community* (Englewood Cliffs, N.J.: Prentice-Hall, 1968), pp. 40, 231.

absorption into the dominant group. Some forms of Jewish affiliation are preserved to prevent any loss of formal identity in the third generation. Synagogue membership continues, and religious rituals are retained that have some familial or social orientation. Concomitantly there is a decline in the segregated pattern of organizational memberships. There is an increase in affiliation with non-Jewish associations such that the third generation tends to hold both Jewish and non-Jewish memberships in more equal proportion. In sum, this generation is completely acculturated, if not structurally assimilated. Young Jews are now no different from members of the dominant group, but to a large extent the Jewish community remains an identifiable separate entity.[11]

Even in this study, however, there is the beginning of some breaking away from the established communal life. Suburban Jews, who are less concentrated residentially and therefore less self-segregated socially, are already assimilating. They not only have a lower rate of affiliation with synagogues and Jewish organizations, they have a higher rate of intermarriage.[12] Although such patterns are not yet typical, even in the third generation, they may become sufficiently extensive to create problems for the community; group survival appears to be at stake, along with individual identity.

With the increasing incorporation of dominant values, there is a growing status consciousness within the Jewish community. The concern with the social acceptance of the dominant group is still less than the interest in inclusion in Jewish country clubs and social groups. Jews prefer to participate in leisuretime activities characteristic of wealthy non-Jews, but they choose to do so with other Jews. (Not that they can be said to have a choice as long as the dominant group engages in restrictive exclusion.) Their diversified social and cultural life reflects an attempt to establish themselves within the general values of the larger community, while at the same time maintaining some distinctive identity as Jews. Considerations other than interest thus operate among Jews in their leisuretime pursuits. In the minority community there is great pressure to conform, if social acceptance is desired.[13]

Jews, like most minority members, have had less time and tradition to cultivate an abiding commitment to any specific set of activities. They are

[11] *Ibid.,* pp. 228–29, 240.
[12] *Ibid.,* p. 230.
[13] Benjamin B. Ringer, *The Edge of Friendliness: A Study of Jewish-Gentile Relations* (New York: Basic Books, 1967), pp. 96, 109, 112–13.

therefore interested in such extrinsic functions of leisure as sociability and status. Their activities represent an adoption of a style of life, but one that does not presuppose assimilation. The country club, for instance, which is critical for elite status, is still segregated along ethnic lines. This segregation certainly applies to more informal arrangements, and even extends into other formal associations. Jews belong to many organizations, but most of them are still sectarian ones, albeit nonreligious ones. They also join nonsectarian organizations, reflecting their desire to belong to both the dominant and minority communities, but even these groups are not often integrated.[14]

Community organizations oriented toward public institutions are the least likely to be segregated, but neighborhoods, like social groups, remain disproportionately Jewish or non-Jewish. Sixty percent of the Jews in Lakeville live in neighborhoods in which they are in the majority. Their residence notwithstanding, 50 percent express a preference for an equally mixed neighborhood. Most of them explain their preference in terms of its potential for social learning.[15] Apparently such residence is recognized as an opportunity for further acculturation, if not actual assimilation. They do not yet feel socially secure enough for any more integration than a mixed neighborhood allows. But they would like to observe others in order to learn how they behave.

Interestingly enough, the value of integration is uniformly accepted, but there is considerable conflict about its upper limits. Jews agree, that is, that they should interact with non-Jews as long as they do not lose their special identity as Jews. No one is certain any more, however, of what constitutes the social core of that identity. There is therefore no consensus defining the extent to which Jews should participate in civic affairs, foster intergroup relations, and adopt the dominant style of life. The celebration of Christmas has become the focus of such conflict since it marks the boundary of acceptable accommodation to the mores of the larger society.[16] Again, the issue is identity.

The discussion of Jewish identity may, in fact, constitute for the modern Jew a kind of pious act of the type which he is not capable of performing in respect to certain more traditional manifestations of his identity. From this perspective talking about Jewish identity is an act of affirmation, and

---

[14] *Ibid.,* pp. 114–15, 118–19.
[15] *Ibid.,* pp. 123, 125–26.
[16] *Ibid.,* pp. 132, 134.

Jewishness remains alive as long as the individual is troubled by the problem of identity.[17]

The Lakeville study, which is a relatively recent and extensive one, is of a suburban setting in which Jews have constituted one third of the population since World War II. Before the considerable migration to the suburbs, Jews made up an insignificant minority with a separate social life that did not disturb the dominant tone of the surrounding community. They have now developed a visible and variegated communal structure with a highly prosperous and educated membership. Of the 432 Jews interviewed, 52 percent are managers, officials, and proprietors, and 61 percent are self-employed or the owner or part-owner of a business; 89 percent have had a year or more of higher education, and 34 percent have been in graduate or professional school. It is of particular interest to note for our purposes that 31 percent are third generation and 19 percent are already fourth generation.[18] This is to say that fully half of the respondents are completely removed from their immigrant origins. One would expect, therefore, to uncover little marginality among them.

Although they are relative newcomers to the suburbs, their community portends future developments for the Jews to follow. Lakeville Jews may still be regarded as somewhat elite; they exceed by a wide margin the national average in respect to generational position, level of education, occupation status, and income.[19] It may be for that reason, however, that they constitute a sociologically significant vanguard that enables us to trace communal trends; they are establishing patterns of behavior that set a social precedent eventually to prevail as normative. A new kind of community is emerging that should be examined for what it reveals about the institutional dynamics of social change.

These Jews see themselves increasingly as a religious group, which means they must somehow come to terms with a tradition that was elaborated under very different conditions than those that now obtain. In their religious definition of themselves, young Jews continue a process of personal selection initiated by their fathers, who also sought to eschew traditional prescription. The focus of their sacramental observance is now in the home, and even that is much reduced; of eleven practices surveyed,

[17] Marshall Sklare and Joseph Greenblum, *Jewish Identity on the Suburban Frontier: A Study of Group Survival in the Open Society* (New York: Basic Books, 1967), p. xii.

[18] *Ibid.*, pp. 14, 24, 27, 31.

[19] *Ibid.*, pp. 39, 44.

a mean of 2.8 were observed by the respondents (which is even less than the 5.2 observed by their parents).[20] The rituals that are selected for retention (such as the Passover seder and Hanukkah festival, and often some acknowledgment of the Sabbath) are, of course, capable of redefinition in modern terms since they do not require social isolation. Infrequent and child-centered, these rituals are in accord with the dominant religion, providing "Jewish" alternatives to its practices.[21]

Such secularization not only narrows the scope of the religion, it shifts its source entirely to the synagogue, again in accordance with acculturation. Seventy-four percent attend services irregularly, that is, for the High Holidays some years or just on Yom Kippur. Although this represents a decrease in regular attendance from their fathers, the decline began with the earlier generation, few of whom attended Sabbath services weekly. Sixty-six percent of the respondents, nevertheless, belong to a synagogue, and almost everyone will join at some point in his lifetime. The synagogue has taken on the character of a voluntary association and thus vies with other associations in and out of the community for active affiliation. Four of the five synagogues in Lakeville are Reform.[22]

"To remain Jewish, there must be an element of uniqueness—even in a pluralist America where structural uniqueness far exceeds cultural uniqueness."[23] There is considerable ambiguity, however, among these synagogues about their uniqueness. Although they are increasingly responsible for the inculcation of a separate and special identity in the next generation, the synagogues themselves may lack sufficient ethnic distinctiveness to do so. The religious education of children has become nonetheless their pre-eminent function. People join a synagogue when their children are of school age to provide for the formal transmission of Jewish identity. There is, of course, interaction among the members, but it emerges out of the synagogue's social and recreational activities rather than out of worship and study. The synagogue thus becomes a secular ethnic institution, contributing to group survival by encouraging in-group interaction. However infrequent their religious attendance, 33 percent spend some time each week in other synagogue activities.[24]

Organizational affiliation then becomes the salient form of belonging

---

[20] *Ibid.,* pp. 45–48, 51–52.
[21] *Ibid.,* p. 59.
[22] *Ibid.,* pp. 61–63, 97–98, 179.
[23] *Ibid.,* p. 151.
[24] *Ibid.,* pp. 180–81, 200–1.

to the Jewish community, a way of affirming identity as well as validating status. Nevertheless, mixed memberships are now common, as multiple ones have always been. Seventy-eight percent belong to Jewish organizations, including synagogue-related ones, and ninety-one percent belong to nonsectarian organizations. The fact that the level of organizational affiliation is not affected by the degree of religious commitment suggests that associational ties to the Jewish community afford a secular alternative for the expression of identity. Even integrationist sentiment can be channeled within the framework of the Jewish community. Those with such an orientation are attracted to the elite country and city clubs as an exclusive form of ethnic association. These clubs embody life styles that are characteristic of the upper strata of the dominant group, while still enforcing the separateness of Jewish identity.[25]

What Jewish organizations appear to offer, above all, is an opportunity for informal sociability, regardless of their expressed goals. Jewish friendship patterns are a significant (if not the sole) source of communal sentiment; they provide the most personalized mode of ethnic association, shoring up identity in an individualized manner. More time is spent with friends than family in this generation, but most of these friends are Jewish. Eighty-nine percent of the respondents (like 87 percent of their parents) have most or all of their close friendships with Jews. This remains the one area of continuity between the generations, and this is so in spite of the fact that younger Jews have had more informal contact with the dominant group. They have spent long periods detached from traditional communal relationships in the mixed settings of college and the army, enjoying shared experiences with non-Jews. Yet their earlier ties do not become attenuated.[26]

Non-Jewish friends, for those who have them, are often married to members of the Jewish social circle. Those who are not attached by marriage do not become part of the clique. Intergroup friendships are maintained apart from the in-group network, in which participation continues unchanged, and undiminished. Such relationships may dissolve with the termination of the situation in which they occur. Lacking a social context, they lack the stability of Jewish friendships, which are strengthened by the institutional reinforcement of the community. It is other Jews to whom Jews are given the easiest access through neighborhoods, organizations, and synagogues. Although only 40 percent claim a preference for Jewish

[25] *Ibid.,* pp. 252–53, 261, 263, 265.
[26] *Ibid.,* pp. 265, 270–72.

friends, most put themselves in a position where only Jews are readily available. There is still some unstated desire for in-group association; consequently they seek out other Jews, thus supporting the sense of solidarity that in turn leads to the primary relations.[27]

This sense of solidarity seems to exist independently of any commitment to religion or organizations. Those who are otherwise uninvolved in communal life have almost as many Jewish friends as those who are involved. Although respondents claim to be as comfortable with non-Jews as with Jews, this may be true only in less intimate social relations. They are still sufficiently self-conscious with non-Jews to be aware of being Jewish. They fear the continued categorical response others have known in the past; they know the stereotypes only too well, and they are afraid that they will not be seen as individuals, let alone treated as such. Their in-group friendships, therefore, may well represent a residual form of Jewishness for them, their last shelter against minority status. By the same token, such friendships may not serve as adequate stay against the assimilation of the next generation.[28]

Almost all of the respondents are to some extent concerned that their children have some background in Judaism. They rely primarily, if not exclusively, on the religious school of the synagogue for such socialization. It is at best a formal identity that is instilled in this fashion. To preserve the continuity of tradition, there must be endogamy, and only 36 percent feel certain that their children would not marry a non-Jew. Forty-three percent admitted that they would be somewhat unhappy over an intermarriage, but most felt constrained to be reasonable about it. Such a modification of traditional attitudes toward intermarriage itself represents a significant change, which may precede a change in behavior.[29]

Even their moderately negative reactions are not justified by a concern for group survival, but by a concern for marital adjustment. Since they approve of integration, they must eschew ethnocentrism in seeking a reason for their disapproval of the ultimate in social acceptance. When faced with a hypothetical choice in behalf of their children, however, fully 85 percent opt for the American concept of romantic love over the traditional norm of endogamy. Personal choice has become the preferred basis for marriage, even when it conflicts with communal restrictions on social eligibility. Hence 93 percent are prepared to accept

[27] *Ibid.,* pp. 274, 276–77, 279–81.
[28] *Ibid.,* pp. 284, 287–89.
[29] *Ibid.,* pp. 295, 298, 307, 309.

an intermarriage, if they must; their identification with their children now takes precedence over their commitment to the community.[30] It is perhaps for this reason more than any other that Jewish identity is regarded as imperiled; to the ideologues of the minority community such attitudes presage assimilation.

Many regard being a good Jew as a matter of accepting and acknowledging one's identity, but it is no longer clear to them how to affirm that identity in action. The behavior that is held in highest esteem by the third generation Jew is that of the dominant culture. "The lack of distinctiveness inherent in his model of the good Jew is capable of eroding away group boundaries."[31] This may well be the case since cultural similarity is a sound, and perhaps inevitable, source of social integration. Jews, however, hold back; they are not yet sure of themselves. They are still not aware of how much they resemble the dominant group by now, and they are unwilling to test the limits of its acceptance. Feeling they have more in common with Jews than with non-Jews, they remain, in some ways, more Jewish in action than in attitude. There is no telling how long this disparity between action and attitude will last.

There is no longer a supporting ideology for sectarianism. The only remaining justification for exclusive ethnic association is identity itself, and this becomes circular, with one supporting the other, without cultural content. It is the endogamous friendship circles that account for the continued cohesion of the Jewish community. Group survival has thus become a function of social relationships that are not necessarily self-perpetuating.

> The threat to such survival is that the Lakeville Jew lacks ideological commitment to his present pattern of friendship ties; he tends also to feel that a mixed neighborhood is desirable, that he should cultivate the friendship and esteem of Christian neighbors, and that he should not be parochial in his social attachments.[32]

With an identity already diluted by advanced acculturation, the next generation is less likely to maintain strong ties to the Jewish community. Its social life, as we will see, will be increasingly influenced by its choice of occupation.

[30] *Ibid.*, pp. 309, 311, 313–16.
[31] *Ibid.*, p. 329.
[32] *Ibid.*, p. 330.

The Emerging Catholic Community

By the third generation, the previously separate Catholic nationality groups are beginning to merge into a pan-Catholic community. Italians, for example, have achieved some mobility into the middle class. Since they are educated, they now have occupational opportunities offering job security. Many find white collar jobs; some enter the professions.

> New occupational and educational attainments are likely to have repercussions on the structure of the family, and on the peer group society generally. For one thing, they will create more social and cultural differences between people. This, in turn, will affect the family circle, for relatives who have responded to the widening opportunities may begin to find they have less in common, and are no longer compatible in their interests. At the same time, since people have fewer children than in previous generations, the number of potential family circle members will be reduced. Consequently, the family circle may be somewhat harder to maintain than in the second generation.[33]

As with Jews, less time is spent with relatives, and friends play an increasingly important role in social life. With this, the very structure of the family becomes acculturated.

Although many more are now in the middle class, they do not yet participate fully in the larger society. Italians do, however, become incorporated into American Catholicism as they move to the suburbs and send their children in growing numbers to parochial schools. Interestingly enough, the church becomes more significant in the suburban setting than it was among the village institutions of the urban neighborhood. It is now an ethnically mixed church that serves as a social expression of the newly achieved middle-class status of Italians. As a result of mobility, separate ethnic identities are gradually muted in the common identity of American Catholicism.[34]

The national parish of the immigrant groups declined in favor of the regular territorial parish, and the church is no longer oriented toward the ethnic community as such. Mobility notwithstanding, Catholics are still mostly upper lower and lower middle class. Nevertheless, with an increase in the number of college graduates now in business and the pro-

[33] Herbert J. Gans, *The Urban Villagers* (New York: Free Press, 1962), p. 214.

[34] Nathan Glazer and Daniel P. Moynihan, *Beyond the Melting Pot* (Cambridge, Mass.: The M. I. T. and Harvard University Press, 1963), pp. 202–4.

fessions, there is a growing adherence to the upper-middle-class style of life characteristic of the dominant group. There is thus a development of institutional life at the higher-status levels that protects the continuity of the Catholic world as its members begin to participate in the larger society.[35]

Catholic solidarity is supported not only by the church, but by a multiplicity of religious and secular organizations supplementing the core institution. It is therefore possible to engage in sociability entirely within the confines of the community, but its members are most likely to associate as Catholics only in their parochial activities. As social status rises, religiosity declines, and high-status Catholics are less susceptible to the influence of the church in their secular life.[36] In a study of 9,052 Catholics, Fichter found about one-fifth of them to be marginal to the church as an institution. It still exerts some influences over them as they continue to accept, at least partially, its religious values. They are increasingly drawn, however, to other institutionalized values, especially those of the dominant group, which frequently conflict with Catholic doctrine. The secularism of the surrounding society has impeded the functioning of the parish as a community. Many of its functions have been absorbed by dominant institutions.[37]

In another study of three urban parishes, only 5.7 percent of 8,363 Catholics were nuclear parishioners, that is, faithful believers and active participants, and most of these were teenagers. The mainstay of the church is still the lower middle class, wage workers who do not belong to upwardly mobile groups or exclusive social clubs; they tend to associate with each other as Catholics in supraparochial activities. About 70 percent, by contrast, are only moderately observant; they are modal Catholics who attend mass and send their children to parochial school. The church, however, is not pivotal in their lives. The parish as a communal group is held together more by shared religious values than by much institutionalized structure; few members share any functions or participate socially.[38]

[35] Milton M. Gordon, *Assimilation in American Life* (New York: Oxford, 1964), pp. 198–99, 208–9, 212–13.

[36] John Sirjamaki, *The Sociology of the Cities* (New York: Random House, 1964), p. 240.

[37] Joseph H. Fichter, S.J., "The Marginal Catholic: An Institutional Approach," *Social Forces,* Vol. 32, No. 2 (December 1953), pp. 169, 172.

[38] Joseph H. Fichter, S.J., *Social Relations in the Urban Parish* (Chicago: University of Chicago Press, 1954), pp. 24–25, 28–29, 40–42.

These modal Catholics associate with non-Catholics in their occupational and recreational activities. Since they are stratified by the same socioeconomic characteristics as members of the dominant group, Catholic business and professional people have close, multiple social relations with non-Catholics in the same general occupational category. This is also true to some extent of skilled and semiskilled workers. "Similar occupational and class status appears to constitute a more effective social bond between Catholics and non-Catholics than the same religion constitutes between Catholic and Catholic of different classes."[39] Perhaps even more than among Jews, higher status leads to greater interaction with the dominant group, and acculturation may indeed be followed by assimilation.

Only social participation within the Catholic community declines with status; religious observance may actually increase with education, perhaps because it is the only remaining source of identity. Fichter suggests that the concept of community as an integrated entity no longer applies to the whole urban parish as a social aggregate, although members of the parish still have primary relations with each other.[40] Lenski's analysis of survey data obtained from 2,374 Detroit Catholics reveals similar patterns of behavior. Over 70 percent attend mass at least once a week, and only 5 percent do not attend at all. Catholics are more inclined than Jews, however, to establish intimate interpersonal relationships outside their own group. Their rate of intermarriage is therefore higher; 30 percent are married to someone who was raised as a non-Catholic. By contrast to the high proportion of Jews, only 44 percent of the Catholics have Catholics as all or nearly all their close friends.[41]

Similarly, Lenski also finds that a high degree of communal involvement among Catholics is consistently linked with a low rate of vertical mobility. There are fewer Catholics than Protestants in the upper middle class, and they seem to favor less demanding, and hence less rewarding, positions. They do not advance as far on the job as Protestants, but when mobility does occur, it causes a weakening of communal ties.[42] Church and family are more likely to be mutually reinforcing for Catholics than for Protestants; a high degree of involvement with one is positively correlated with a high degree of involvement with the other. Churchgoers

[39] *Ibid.,* pp. 47, 49.
[40] *Ibid.,* pp. 50, 188.
[41] Gerhard Lenski, *The Religious Factor* (Garden City, N.Y.: Doubleday, 1961), pp. 34–35.
[42] *Ibid.,* pp. 74, 80, 86, 110–11.

are more likely to be active in other voluntary associations than non-churchgoers, but the proportions are not particularly high for either group (34 percent and 18 percent respectively). Parochial education strengthens ties to the Catholic church and community.[43]

> Catholics and Protestants alike have assimilated the materialistic values of contemporary society to the point where they equally value a good job with high income, and are equally likely to aspire to such a position. However, Catholics are at a disadvantage in the competition because of a series of values to which they become committed as a result of their involvement in the Catholic Church and subcommunity. For example, they become more strongly attached to the kin group than Protestants, and therefore less able to make the break with home and family that is required in many of the more demanding, and hence better-paid positions in contemporary American society. Also, involvement in the Catholic group apparently fosters a heteronomic intellectual orientation which is ill-adapted to the more creative and responsible positions in our rapidly changing social order.[44]

It would seem then that most Catholics are not yet as mobile as Jews; for all their acculturation, they are still attached to family circles, if not as much so to the church and community as such. The mobile Catholic, however, is even more likely to be assimilated than the Jew, who remains involved in friendships that tie him to his community. The underlying pattern of social relations is similar, the differences a function of class. The Jewish community, already completely middle class, has a greater capacity to absorb its more mobile members; its highly differentiated structure can encompass further achievement. The lower-middle-class core of the Catholic community may be strained by rapid social advance; mobility thus requires some break with the community, even if it doesn't lead to total assimilation. In any case, the middle-class Catholic is not much different from the middle-class non-Catholic. His social and economic status is therefore a better index to his behavior and attitudes than is his religion.[45]

American Catholicism has been largely determined by the cultural origins of the immigrants, impoverished peasants cut off from the intellectual traditions of their European origins. It was further influenced by the strength of the anti-Catholic prejudice prevalent in American society at the time of their arrival. "The result was that immigrant Catholicism

---

[43] *Ibid.,* pp. 223, 225, 243–44.

[44] *Ibid.,* p. 311.

[45] John Leo, "The American Catholic Is Changing," in Milton L. Barron, ed., *Minorities in a Changing World* (New York: Alfred A. Knopf, 1967), p. 306.

turned in on itself, developing deep defensive traits, and devoting its energies to parochial affairs."[46] Indeed, it was the cost of building a separate educational system that helped to impede Catholics in the acquisition of middle-class status. The schools, in turn, more than any other institution, reinforced their isolation within their own community. Catholics, therefore, have been under-represented in intellectual spheres and less likely than non-Catholics to excel in the academic world, particularly in the sciences.[47]

Since World War II, there has been an increase in Catholic mobility, and a concomitant increase in business and social relations with the dominant group. In addition, the Catholics now in graduate school are proportionate to their numbers. There is, as a result, a younger generation as much committed to the secular values of the larger society as to the Catholic religion, if not more so. This new breed of Catholic is increasingly indifferent to the institutional claims of the minority community. Like the young Jew who rejects the traditional concept of the "chosen people," this Catholic resists the idea that he is an agent of the church operating in society. Anxious to end Catholic separatism and to enter the mainstream of American life, he may cut through his social enclosure by passing up Catholic organizations in favor of secular service groups.[48]

> Many of the younger Catholic intellectuals, however, are involved neither in the intramural problems of the Church nor in the problems of the "official" Church and American culture. They are getting their degrees or are teaching in the whole spectrum of academic studies, are entering political life or the professions, are active in urban renewal or journalism or the arts. They have little or no interest in ecclesiastical matters, they often resent the ecclesiastical establishment as vaguely stupid, or narrow, or merely professional. . . . They often remain practicing Catholics, faithful to the sacraments. But the world of the spirit in which they live is that of the general secular world rather than that of the Catholic community.[49]

Ironically, sensitive young Catholics find the spiritual values of secularism more compelling than those of the church. In this respect they are no different from those gifted Jewish youngsters who find little to attract them in a gilded ghetto that has lost its relevance in their lives. Both chafe at the social enclosure of the minority community; for them its limited

---

[46] *Ibid.*, p. 307.
[47] *Ibid.*
[48] *Ibid.*, pp. 308, 313.
[49] Michael Novak, "American Catholicism After the Council," *Commentary*, Vol. 40, No. 2 (August 1965), p. 57.

horizons lack the vitality of the larger society.[50] In their changing occupational choices, they begin to leave the shelter of their small world to seek the satisfactions of a different style of life. In so doing, they come into closer contact with the dominant group and experience a shift in the source of their identity; it is then that occupational status takes precedence over religious affiliation. As ethnic origins grow more remote and irrelevant, the ties to the minority community become attenuated and the potential for assimilation increases.

The communities created by religious minorities represent complex forms of social organization that have emerged out of the ethnic enclaves of the immigrant groups. They provide a transition to greater participation in the larger society. As a way station in the minority situation, a shelter against discrimination and a stay against assimilation, the religious community remains essentially endogamous, if no longer entirely so. The family, its basic social unit, is all the more able to reinforce communal norms for being religiously homogeneous. And so, of course, are friendship cliques. The system of social relationships supporting the religious community is thus made up of intimate interpersonal ones, supplemented by an array of formal associations. In his analysis of 1958 survey data from Detroit, Lenski finds only a limited relationship in the degree to which individuals are involved in the religious institution and the degree to which they are involved in informal relations.[51]

The religious institution is not necessarily the core of the minority community any more. The social circle of family and friends sustains communal life. Its informal influence extends beyond that of the church or synagogue and tends to foster a provincial view of the world. The informal relations and the organized institutions, therefore, are not always mutually reinforcing.[52]

> To the degree that such primary groups form segregated communications networks limited to the adherents of the same faith, they facilitate the development and transmission of distinctive political and economic norms.[53]

They do, that is, until the third generation, and beyond, when distinctive norms begin to disappear under the impact of social mobility.

---

[50] *Ibid.*, p. 58; Glazer and Moynihan, *op. cit.*, pp. 150, 180.
[51] *Ibid.*, pp. 17–19, 296.
[52] *Ibid.*, pp. 296, 302.
[53] *Ibid.*, p. 303.

Occupational Changes and Consequences

A restudy of survey data gathered over twenty years reveals a change in the relative standing of Protestants and Catholics. In 1943, Protestants were well above Catholics in economic status; by 1964, Catholics were clearly above Protestants. The number of Protestants decreased and the number of Catholics increased in nonmanual work. There were also slightly more Catholics than Protestants in upper-nonmanual positions. Catholics thus have shown more net upward mobility than Protestants in the post-war period, thereby overcoming the initial disadvantage of their more recent immigration. They are now pulling ahead of Protestants in spite of the past influence of ethnic values impeding mobility. Young Jews similarly rank far above young Protestants in educational attainment. Although Catholics are still underrepresented in college, Protestants are losing their educational advantage. With the increased influence of college on the younger generation of minority members, religious influences are less likely to have a differential impact on worldly success.[54]

A National Opinion Research Center survey of college graduates in 1961 based on a 10 percent national subsample found Catholics as likely as Protestants to go to graduate school and to choose an academic career. Those Catholics who do not choose academic careers are more likely to go into business, seeking employment in large corporations. Jews, by contrast, choose self-employment or small companies. There are no such differences in aspiration among those Catholics, Protestants, and Jews who are planning a career in the arts and sciences. More than twice as large a proportion of low-status Jewish men, however, choose an academic profession than do high-status Jews (who are less likely to choose it than Catholics or Protestants). Almost two-fifths of the affluent young Jews plan to go into the traditional professions of law and business by contrast to one-tenth of those from low-status backgrounds.[55] This supports our suggestion that it is low status that serves as a spur to mobility among minorities.

[54] Norval D. Glenn and Ruth Hyland, "Religious Preference and Worldly Success: Some Evidence from National Surveys," *American Sociological Review*, Vol. 32, No. 1 (February 1967), pp. 75–77, 83–84.

[55] Andrew M. Greeley, "Influence of the 'Religious Factor' on Career Plans and Occupational Values of College Graduates," *American Journal of Sociology*, Vol. 68, No. 6 (May 1963), pp. 658, 662–64, 671.

The education they receive and the occupations they enter in turn change the life style of members of the younger generation. Their status as organization men then serves as the basis for a new kind of community. Patterns of formal affiliation and informal association change as occupation acquires priority over ethnicity.

> Third-generation Jews in the salaried professions and semiprofessions are in every way less affiliated with the Jewish community than those in traditional occupations. Fewer Jewish organization men belong to a synagogue or observe religious ritual. More of them include gentiles among their four closest friends. Fewer of these men in non-Jewish occupations belong only to Jewish organizations, and even fewer feel that Jews *should* belong to specifically Jewish organizations. The majority of both types of occupational groups live in mixed suburban neighborhoods and have some gentile friends.[56]

For all the social changes in this instance, these Jews still regard themselves as Jews, by which they mean the religious affiliation into which they were born. It is no longer, however, a primary determinant of identity as occupation becomes a more critical source of influence in their lives.

The Potential for Assimilation

There is as yet only one study that confirms the significance of occupation in the process of assimilation. Wilensky and Ladinsky investigated patterns of participation in communities of work and religion, anticipating that there is a point at which involvement in the occupational community may be incompatible with commitment to the religious community. The network of cliques, clubs, and voluntary associations that characterize religious communities function to enforce endogamy. Informal social life is centered in these self-contained worlds that set the limits for marital eligibility. Work roles vary in the degree to which they are segregated from other roles. Some are not related to the behavior that is expected in other contexts. Others, the more integrated work roles, are so elaborated as to encompass the expectations of other roles. It is these occupational roles, accentuating achievement rather than ascription, that begin to subvert

[56] Kramer and Leventman, *op. cit.,* p. 202.

religious endogamy. The contexts in which they are enacted mix ethnic groups in occupational communities undermining the primary relations of minority groups.[57]

It was expected that successful minority members in majority contexts, that is, occupations dominated by the Protestant establishment, would epitomize the process of structural assimilation. These "deviant ethnics," as they are called in this study, are escaping from the religious community of their origin and moving into an occupational community of their destination. The collegial relationship represents a principle of organization conflicting with that of the religious orientation; and the ties to family, friends, and formal associations in the minority community are increasingly attenuated. Four hundred and ninety employed, married (previously or currently) white males were interviewed in 1960. The solo lawyers and Church University professors were heavily Jewish and Catholic, members of the second generation of low-status ethnic background. The firm lawyers and engineers were overwhelmingly Protestant, of high-status ethnic background. Urban University professors fell somewhere in between the other occupational categories in ethnic status.[58]

The nature of their friendship circles and formal affiliations shows that more men are still strongly involved in the religious community than in the occupational community. This is least likely to be the case, however, for professors, who have the highest mean occupational community score and the strongest professional identification; they thus have a higher rate of association with each other than do members of other occupations. Their long training requires a heavy investment of self that promotes community. As a result, one-third have other professors for all three of their closest friends. The solo professional, by contrast, is oriented toward clients rather than colleagues. This is expressed in an appropriate pattern of participation. As Jewish and Catholic lawyers with minority clients, they manifest moderate contact with their shared religious community and relatively weak involvement with the work community; they have a stronger religious identification than firm lawyers. As "dominant ethnics" surrounded by minority men, the solo lawyers are free to express whatever identity they acquired in the family within the religious community.[59]

---

[57] Harold L. Wilensky and Jack Ladinsky, "From Religious Community to Occupational Group: Structural Assimilation Among Professors, Lawyers, and Engineers," *American Sociological Review*, Vol. 32, No. 4 (August 1967), p. 545.

[58] *Ibid.*, pp. 543, 545.

[59] *Ibid.*, pp. 548–50.

Work is most at odds with religion among "deviant ethnics." The requirements of their career lead to their incorporation into the occupational community, which in turn implies assimilation into the dominant group. They avoid the religious community and participate in the occupational community in their informal relations. Such "deviant ethnics" embody structural assimilation, manifesting its social processes in the fact that they have the lowest religious community score; they are less likely to associate with other members of their ethnic group than with colleagues. "Indeed, occupational community surpasses religious community *only* among deviant ethnics."[60] It is these professionals who display the weakest involvement in the religious community and the strongest involvement in the occupational community. Work and religion are not strongly in conflict in other contexts.

> *Work overcomes religion through the assimilation of deviant ethnics.* In varying degrees, whatever their religious or professional identification, minority men in majority contexts avoid the religious community and seek out one or another community of work.[61]

For these men, occupation and religion represent separate ways of life, and they have chosen the one over the other. Otherwise, for everyone else, religion remains far stronger than occupation as the basis for social ties. Indeed, the religious community seems to be the core of the church, independent of rites and beliefs (by contrast to the past when the church was the core of the community). As in previously cited studies, involvement in communal life is unrelated to such indicators of religiosity as ritual observance, prayer, church attendance, and contributions.[62] There isn't even much religious identification, only social commitment to the minority community. Under these circumstances there is increased interaction with the dominant group even for those who are not in assimilating occupations.

Young Jews, for example, are increasingly likely to be in occupations that crosscut ethnic lines, but they don't have to be salaried experts to live, as they do, in the suburbs. The neighborhood and the workplace thus bring them into contact with non-Jews, whom they now resemble more than their immigrant forebears. There is still, however, more communal association than personal relations, and the interaction is of a cordial rather than an intimate nature. Intergroup relations remain sufficiently superficial so that the participants do not know the actual content of each

[60] *Ibid.,* p. 550.
[61] *Ibid.,* p. 553.
[62] *Ibid.,* p. 557.

other's feelings. In the Lakeville study, both Jews and non-Jews agree that there is little or no intergroup strain, yet they are each uncertain of the other's private sentiments. Jews are afraid that these feelings might be at variance with the public behavior of non-Jews; they still fear the unstated disapproval of the dominant group.[63] Their ignorance of such feelings serves to disguise their apprehensiveness, and they do not risk the probing of intimacy, lest it uncover some underlying prejudice.

Consequently 50 percent of the Jewish respondents experience anxiety in their relations with non-Jews. They anticipate hostility, regardless of their past exposure to anti-Semitism, and they are self-consciously on their guard.[64] Fearful of prejudice and uncertain about perceptions, they are not yet aware of how much the same Jews and non-Jews have become. They have had so little opportunity to observe the similarities that they are unsure of themselves. Their lack of such knowledge exacerbates their anxiety, and they do not ascertain all the characteristics they have in common with the dominant group. They are sometimes afraid that they will not know how to behave so they do not try; they are worried about what the response will be so they don't find out. Such self-imposed limitations on social learning perpetuates in-group sociability.

As a result, most Jews still associate with non-Jews only in such structured situations as the occupational or organizational setting in which reciprocal behavior is clearly defined. They want these intergroup contacts, but their anxiety inhibits the development of more informal relationships. At this point, only one in five have extensive contacts with the dominant group. The relations that do develop among Jews and non-Jews are initially functional, limited to a situation requiring little personal involvement. These relations are separated from the private sphere, but they may in time become the basis for friendship just because they originate in natural social circumstances without undue emotional content.[65]

For those mixed friendships that do emerge, work is the most important context of occurrence. And it is, as we have already suggested, the large-scale organization that fosters such relationships; the majority of Jews who have non-Jewish friends have met them through their profession or business. Interpersonal relations that cross ethnic lines rarely occur in the contractual climate of the marketplace. They develop among occupational peers. Salaried Jews, most of whom work for firms employing a preponder-

---

[63] Ringer, *op. cit.*, pp. 4, 29, 36–37.
[64] *Ibid.*, pp. 139–40.
[65] *Ibid.*, pp. 145–47, 186.

ance of non-Jews, are, therefore, more likely to have mixed friendships. The most personalized relationships develop among professionals, for reasons already suggested. When these friendships are no longer relegated to the occupational context, they become more intimate as well as inclusive. The participants then perceive each as individuals rather than as representatives of their respective groups.[66] The occupational sphere has thus acquired sociological significance in its capacity to break through ethnic enclosure. New occupations for religious minorities are bringing about interaction with members of the dominant group as peers. It is in such peer relations that the achieved status of professional attainment takes precedence over the categorical status of ethnic birth.

Organizations, by contrast, are less likely to lead to such close personal relations; they do not provide as much opportunity for people to get to know one another. Organizations with an instrumental function may lead to some friendliness based on shared interests. Common experience may help to diminish the awareness of group difference. Expressive associations such as social clubs, however, are organized on the basis of status and remain exclusive; they are homogeneously constituted. Their restrictions on membership reinforce the social distance between the minority and the dominant group, protecting their respective ethnic enclosure.[67] It suggests once again the importance of shared interests in transcending ethnicity. Status-seeking alone is not effective; serious commitment to specific values is necessary.

The continued strength of ethnic enclosure is seen in evening sociability. A silken curtain is drawn after hours, and even casual intergroup neighboring stops. There is then only the established socializing of in-group intimacy. Most Jews consider these friendships closer than whatever mixed ones they maintain.[68] Obviously it takes more than usual effort to overcome the initial distrust they bring to intergroup relations. Few may consider it worth the effort (even when they are capable of it) since it is not required in in-group intimacy; such effort is not easy, and it may not be effective. Some special reason then is almost essential as motivation for the mixed relationship.

Yet sufficient intimacy is achieved for intermarriage to take place, and at an increasing rate. A survey of the Jewish community in Washington,

[66] *Ibid.*, pp. 187–88, 191–92, 197–98.
[67] *Ibid.*, pp. 205, 207–9, 220.
[68] *Ibid.*, pp. 225, 244.

D.C. as early as 1956 reveals some significant trends. The rate of inter-marriage is higher for each succeeding generation, and highest of all for the college-educated. Among third generation men, 17.9 percent were intermarried (by contrast to 10.2 percent of second generation men and 1.4 percent of first generation men). Thirty-seven percent of those who are college-educated are intermarried, while even in the third generation, those who are concentrated in traditional occupations tend to be endog-amous. Independent professionals have a lower rate of intermarriage than the national average for Jews, and self-employed businessmen have a negligible rate. These men remain rooted in the minority community, with economic ties reinforcing emotional bonds. Those who are now in the occupational category of "managers, officials, and proprietors" have an intermarriage rate of 34.9 percent;[69] these are men likely to be govern-ment employees, the kind of salaried experts who are undergoing the greatest change in social behavior.

Their assimilated patterns of interaction may thus find consummation in the ultimate form of social acceptance, intermarriage. Not only has the rate of intermarriage increased, its sociological characteristics appear to be different now; the nature of the partners involved is changing. Among second generation Jews, those who intermarried were mostly men, and usually successful men. They exchanged their economic achievement for the ascribed status of women of the dominant group, otherwise of lower socioeconomic background than the husbands. The dominant membership of the wives had symbolic significance in the social barter that went into their marital status. Such intermarriages did not necessarily lead to in-corporation into the larger community. On the contrary, the wives were more likely to become acculturated to Jews as members of the minority community in good standing (and even of high status).

In the third generation, Jewish women are as emancipated from tradi-tion by college education as men. They are available for acculturated mar-riages, thus protecting the endogamy of ambitious but conventional men. They are also, however, themselves beginning to enter into intermarriage. The greatest increase, of course, is still for men, and this has been brought about by a changing occupational structure that brings members of the minority and the dominant group into closer contact.

[69] "Jewish Intermarriage in the U.S.," *Council Woman,* National Council of Jewish Women, Vol. 25, No. 5 (November 1963), pp. 7–8.

Prognosis for the Future

As the changing economic structure of the larger society diminishes the importance of ethnicity, the prototypical minority community, if not religious identity itself, may well disappear. With acculturation, there is no longer any distinctive cultural content characterizing the minority community. There is still, of course, a separate set of institutions based on economic specialization as well as religious affiliation. Occupation, however, has become the basis for a new kind of status community as minority members increasingly find salaried employment in dominant contexts. The economic substructure of the minority community is thereby undermined, leaving it with only religious affiliation to serve as the source of its social life. The religious institution becomes a communal center for the enforcement of endogamy, but even the most intimate informal ties that grow out of a denominationally defined in-group are not sufficient to constitute a community.

The social circles that are presently maintained may not continue indefinitely without material reinforcement. In the absence of occupational support, the endogamous attitudes and homogeneous friendships of the minority community have already begun to change; and there is a concomitant increase in intermarriage. The very foundation of the minority community is shaken when there is neither cultural uniqueness nor economic specialization to shore up its ethnic segregation. These, after all, provided the institutional sources of the community that emerged out of the minority situation. When only categorical status remains, it leads to the informal ties of a shared social life. Such ties cannot be sustained, however, without communal institutions to socialize succeeding generations. The religious institution instills only a formal identity, and that may lack sufficient social content to determine life chances—independently of exclusion by the dominant group, that is.

If such exclusion declines, there is less need for the differential association of the minority group. It is the normalization of its occupational distribution that increases interaction with the dominant group. The hard core of the minority community is its lower middle class. Those of higher status become peripheral to the community by virtue of their closer contact with the dominant group. (Ironically, those of very low status may also become peripheral to the community. The impoverishment of chronic unemployment increases their dependency on the larger society. This may be compounded by personal disorganization and its ensuing social isolation.) The minority community is thus a middle-class phenomenon, all the more secure when it is less threatened by mobility.

That the institutional basis of the minority community is declining does not necessarily presage assimilation. Religious identity may survive, as it has in the past, in some new social form. The relevant sociological question is whether or not such identity can be sustained without some source in community. Jews and Catholics have always adapted their identity to their surroundings. They nevertheless continue to define themselves—and to be defined socially—as Jews and Catholics, whatever the changing cultural content of the social identity. The meaning changes with each generation, and by now, so does the priority given it.

The first generation, for example, defined its identity in terms of an ethnic way of life and an encompassing religious institution. Its marginal sons found their identity in the acculturated activities of the minority community. The second generation was secularized, but socially enclosed. As it found religious orthodoxy too confining as a way of life, so the third generation chafes at the social constraints of ethnic enclosure. Younger members of minority groups do not relinquish their religious identity, but they are disinclined to let it determine their way of life. Occupation becomes a more decisive influence, while religion is reduced to a denominational affiliation in the manner of the dominant group.

The focus of identity increasingly narrows as it loses its traditional communal base along with its characteristic cultural traditions. Religious identity is not yet without an institutional source, but the logic of denomination inheres in its acculturation. There is thus less social justification for more extensive and exclusive affiliation with the minority community—unless, of course, there is continued exclusion by the dominant group. If there is not, the result may be integration rather than assimilation; individuals, that is, may gain social acceptance as individuals—in spite of denominational differences—without any religious merging in a dominant melting pot. Religious identity is not lost, if most members of minority groups are still integrated into the larger society as Jews and Catholics. It simply becomes secondary socially when it is no longer a categorical determinant of life chances.

PART IV

THE RACIAL VARIATIONS ON THE MINORITY THEME

Chapter 8

Color, Class, and Culture

THE complex consequences of color and class compound the minority situation of the major racial groups in the United States. Their respective capacities to cope with the resulting complications are then functions of their cultural differences (or the absence thereof). Lower-class status leads to inadequate institutional resources for maintaining a separate way of life in modern society, however distinctive the values, and there are few of these values that survive intact today. The communal structure of these groups is, therefore, insufficiently organized to resolve the tensions of minority status. These tensions are rendered all the more severe by the physical visibility of race. Each such community thus represents an alternative to the prototypical minority pattern that is to some extent disorganized. In Part IV, we will examine the specific characteristics and consequences of four different racial situations, each one a somewhat unique variation on the minority theme.

The Impact of Poverty

The inadequately institutionalized community not only lacks the economic basis for maintaining itself, it is without the social resources necessary for solving its problems. In addition to being personally invisible as individuals, racial groups are socially inconsequential in their poverty. The interrelationship between the categorical status and the class situation may be tempered by the cultural content of the way of life. There is a difference in the kind of community that emerges out of lower-class situations of color, and that difference seems to be a matter of culture. None of the racial groups are economically qualified for integration into middle-class life, but neither are they all entirely disorganized. The Mexican and Puerto Rican communities, for example, are not structurally well organized, but most of their members may remain sufficiently integrated around their own values to function adequately. Their isolation, in so far as it continues, insulates them from marginality, protecting them from the consequences of relative deprivation, if not of real poverty.

By contrast, Indians and Negroes have been forcibly deculturated, and thereby disorganized. The cultural demoralization of Indians has been severe; their history has left them too removed from the dominant group to be readily Americanized. Negroes have had no access to dominant values, of course, but they have been acculturated to them in the physically close, but socially distant relationship Negroes have had with whites. These values were at least visible to Negroes, if not accessible. This has not been so for Indians. Deprived of their own values by the processes of deculturation that followed in the wake of their conquest, they had little opportunity to acquire the alternative values of American culture. The formal channels of official schooling did not provide the interpersonal learning that permits cultural options to take hold effectively. Hence there has been serious disorganization among Indians.

Each of the major racial groups is in some sense indigenous. Indians are, of course, the aboriginal Americans conquered by the early colonists; Mexicans had already settled in the southwestern borderlands of the United States long before the annexation of the area; Puerto Ricans arrive here as legal citizens, commuting between the island and the mainland; and Negroes had no choice but to become Americans after the deculturation systematically imposed by slavery. Each group thus has some legitimate claim to dominant values. Perhaps it is just this legitimacy that heightens the resistance of the larger society. They were, after all, here first, or they are already citizens, or they didn't choose to come here in the first place. For such reasons, they may be more entitled to dominant values than those groups who migrate voluntarily and must validate themselves before being accepted. This very fact appears to exacerbate the ambivalence of the dominant group (perhaps because there is guilt about such prejudice and discrimination), and racial minorities are denied access to the values of American society with particular vehemence. Race gains in importance as grounds for exclusion in part because there are so few other grounds.

Herbert Gans points out that a subculture is an organized set of related responses to both the opportunities and the deprivations created by the surrounding society. Such responses do not develop in a social vacuum, however; they are a function of the resources available to a given group. The resources of the racial minorities that we are about to examine are few, and the consequences critical. Deprivation is as endemic as it is extensive, and opportunity extremely limited.

> When these opportunity factors are lacking, the cultural responses made by people are frustrated. Should opportunities be deficient over a long enough period, downward mobility results. Should they disappear entirely, the subculture will be apt to disintegrate eventually.[1]

What Oscar Lewis calls the "culture of poverty" is little more than an adaptive reaction of the poor to their marginal position in modern society. To call it a culture may be a misnomer; it is really, as Hylan Lewis suggests, "a broad spectrum of pragmatic adjustments to external and internal stresses and deprivations."[2] In fact, part of the problem of poverty is that there may be no organized values representing a way of life. There are therefore few resources for coping with the feelings of hopelessness and despair engendered by the situation of the poor. Succeeding generations are not psychologically prepared to take advantage of changing conditions, and thus the situation is perpetuated.[3]

Poor people are aware of middle-class values; they may even prefer them. They simply cannot live by these values. Chronic unemployment and underemployment prevent effective participation in the institutions of the larger society. The characteristic marginal quality of the impoverished community is "above all a minimum of organization beyond the level of the nuclear and extended family."[4] And even the family is not always stable. Individuals are often inundated with feelings of helplessness, convinced of their own inferiority.[5] They are therefore unable to help each other as members of the family; they may well be as unavailable to each other for emotional support as they are for material assistance.

Although there are many who are poor in the United States, there is relatively little culture of poverty, according to Oscar Lewis. What there is

[1] Herbert J. Gans, *The Urban Villagers* (New York: Free Press, 1962), pp. 249–50.

[2] Hylan Lewis, *Culture, Class, and Poverty* (Washington, D.C.: CROSS-TELL, 1967), p. 11.

[3] Oscar Lewis, *La Vida* (New York: Random House, Vintage Books, 1968), pp. xliv–xlv.

[4] *Ibid.*, p. xlvi.

[5] *Ibid.*, p. xlvii.

is found among the lowest income members of the four major racial groups. There is something peculiarly demoralizing about their poverty in modern society. It is possible for preliterate people to be impoverished and still have an integrated and satisfying culture.[6] It is the function of the institutions and ideologies of traditional groups to provide a way of living with their particular human condition. Although this function was to some extent still fulfilled for earlier immigrants, it is less so for racial minorities. The problems of these poor are compounded by a sense of relative deprivation; their feelings of frustration are exacerbated by being surrounded by a middle-class style of life that they cannot hope to achieve. One of their adaptive mechanisms may be a low level of aspiration to reduce frustration, another the legitimization of short-range hedonism.

> However, on the whole it seems to me that it is a relatively thin culture. There is a great deal of pathos, suffering, and emptiness among those who live in the culture of poverty. It does not provide much support or long-range satisfaction and its encouragement of mistrust tends to magnify helplessness and isolation. Indeed, the poverty of culture is one of the crucial aspects of the culture of poverty.[7]

Oscar Handlin describes "the feebleness of internal communal institutions" among contemporary newcomers that deprives them of social control. This is not to say that they do not find outlets for sociability in family and neighborhood cliques; there is friendship, and even some mutual aid when possible. But there is no development of an integrated pattern of voluntary organizations that characterized the early ethnic enclaves.[8]

> As a result, they [the Negroes and Puerto Ricans of New York] could not find the help they needed within the context of the group; and the group lacked this means of giving its identity significant expression.[9]

These racial groups also lack much means of communicating among themselves, rendering them all the more susceptible to the mass media. There is thus no appropriate way of articulating their social identity, no unique form of expression reinforcing group consciousness.[10] And the images of general affluence conveyed by the mass media heighten their sense of relative deprivation.

[6] *Ibid.*, p. xlviii.
[7] *Ibid.*, p. lii.
[8] Oscar Handlin, *The Newcomers* (Cambridge, Mass.: Harvard University Press, 1959), pp. 98, 104.
[9] *Ibid.*, p. 105.
[10] *Ibid.*, p. 110.

Without a tradition for communal solidarity, the responsibility for philanthropic services is shifted from voluntary organizations to government agencies. Welfare needs are all the more pressing as economic opportunities in the larger society grow more limited. In the absence of adequate institutions within the community, the difficulties of establishing a social identity are increased.[11]

> In the context of poverty and slum life, the instability of the family becomes a pervasive source of personal disorder. The individual on the verge of trouble seeks in vain for support from the security of fixed relationships as child or parent, husband or wife. Deprived also of external control or discipline from strong ethnic institutions and prevented, by intruding fears of color, from accepting fully the standards of the broader American community, such an individual is likely to yield to a sense of isolation and through one form of delinquency or another to strike back at the hostile society to which he remains a stranger. At the crises, which an adverse life situation makes frequent, when a Negro or Puerto Rican feels adrift, without a clear sense of purpose or goals, he has no props to lean upon and is the easy victim of disaster. Any accident is a catastrophe to which the only possible reaction is collapse which among Puerto Ricans may take the form of an emotional *ataque,* among Negroes of a sullen desperation.[12]

The racial groups thus lack the institutional resources to fulfill the functions of the prototypical minority community. There are simply insufficient values available within these groups to make up a way of life independent of the dominant group, and they are denied access to the values of the larger society. They suffer in this insufficiency, and no resources are forthcoming in their poverty. The failure of the inadequately institutionalized community results in higher rates of personal disorganization and social pathology. Without a source of social honor to counteract dominant discrimination and derogation, self-esteem is lost to self-hatred. Apathy and ambivalence overwhelm ambition, and the possibility of mobility is minimized. Government agencies (particularly those of the federal poverty program) now attempt to serve as the source of social organization for racial communities. Externally enacted institutions are substituted for the indigenous institutions of the earlier ethnic communities, but this may well prove to be a contradiction in sociological terms.

[11] *Ibid.,* pp. 103, 110, 113.
[12] *Ibid.,* pp. 102–3.

Mexican-Americans

Mexican immigrants, a majority in some areas of the Southwest, have a unique relation to the land, culture, and institutions. With an indigenous Hispanic population already settled there, Mexicans have been drawn to the Southwest by a feeling of continuity, and they have usually remained within the protective confines of its familiar environment.

> Psychologically and culturally, Mexicans have never emigrated to the Southwest: they have returned. In many cases, they have returned for the second, third, fourth, or fifth time.[13]

Unlike most minorities, Mexicans have been rooted in a particular region for a long time. They were annexed by conquest, along with the territory. In effect, their culture is native to the area. Their proximity to the border permits them to commute between Mexico and the United States, crossing back and forth, legally and otherwise.[14]

Isolation is a critical, indeed defining, characteristic of their culture; the geographic isolation of the area has bred social isolation.[15] The Hispanic culture of the Southwest is therefore a homogeneous one that resists change, even when traditional values can no longer be enacted. There is little division of labor, and poverty is an integral part of the culture, compounding isolation with insufficiency. Historically, most members of the Mexican-American community have been lower class.[16] Immigrants remain within their *colonias,* segregated by both residence and occupation. There has been little opportunity for acculturation since large-scale employers have consistently isolated Mexicans as a way of restricting them to limited categories of work. A large proportion of immigrants were imported under contract by particular employers for particular jobs. Immigrants thus were to be found in dead-end jobs in undesirable locations, working on the railroads, in smelters, copper mines, sugar-beet refineries, farm-factories, and large fruit and vegetable exchanges.[17]

The work was seasonal or casual; the men lived in separate camps or

---

[13] Carey McWilliams, *North from Mexico* (Philadelphia: Lippincott Co., 1949), p. 58.

[14] *Ibid.,* pp. 207, 209.

[15] *Ibid.,* p. 63.

[16] *Ibid.,* p. 75.

[17] *Ibid.,* pp. 187–89, 215.

company towns. Much of it was (and still is) migratory employment; they traveled in groups with other Mexican workers. Not only were they common laborers in situations of mass employment, they were insulated from contact with others by their homogeneous work gangs. Not only was acculturation impeded, but so was any consequent mobility. Instability of employment and frequent migration reinforced the residential and institutional isolation of Mexicans. The language barrier became a persistent symbol and instrument of isolation. Their ethnic enclaves, whether rural or urban, are marginal neighborhoods detached from the economy as well as the life of the larger community, although dependent upon it for both jobs and services.[18]

The community that develops under such conditions is not likely to be institutionally adequate. Mexican-Americans, some of whom are citizens by default of the land accession of the nineteenth century, rank second only to American Indians in historical priority. Yet they also include the most recent of immigrants; there has been no end to the replacement of their population. Together old settlers and new immigrants remain largely unorganized—and mutually ambivalent about each other.[19] Until recently there has been virtually no middle class providing service functions. Those who have advanced educationally or economically have tended to lose their ethnic identity. They become "Spanish" rather than "Mexican," thereby shedding the social stigma of poverty along with its material problems.[20]

The Mexican-American community is thus made up of a relatively homogeneous population with a narrow status distribution. Its service facilities are rudimentary, its commercial enterprises marginal. Indigenous organization is inadequate to integrate the community and establish relations with the larger society.[21] In the absence of a middle class, what leadership there may be is equivocal, and political problems are thereby aggravated. By now, Mexican-Americans are predominantly urbanized, but the conditions of social isolation have changed little. The largest concentration of Mexican-Americans is now found in the Los Angeles area, where most of them still live in *colonias*. These peripheral communities of

[18] Leonard Broom and Eshref Shevky, "Mexicans in the United States: A Problem in Social Differentiation," *Sociology and Social Research,* Vol. 36, No. 3 (January–February 1952), pp. 152–53.
[19] Carey McWilliams, *Brothers Under the Skin* (Boston: Little, Brown & Co., rev. ed., 1951), pp. 113, 120.
[20] Broom and Shevky, *op. cit.,* p. 154.
[21] *Ibid.,* pp. 155, 157.

seasonal agricultural workers have become, by virtue of the process of urbanization, marginal neighborhoods of industrial workers.[22]

Some of these communities were originally labor camps. All of them, emerging with the arrival of the early immigrants, are located in unincorporated areas adjacent to the towns and cities of southern California. They are always on the other side of something; never intended to be part of the wider community, they remain apart, separated in every way. Social isolation is thus perpetuated, and psychological isolation is induced. The children of the immigrants, resentful of their segregation in inferior schools, tend to drop out after the eighth grade, only to find themselves working in the same jobs for which their fathers were imported. Even they leave the *colonias* only for shopping and recreation.[23]

Those whose migrations have taken them to the industrial centers of the Midwest have more contact with the dominant culture. Originally concentrated in the packing plants, tanneries, steel mills, foundries, and railroad yards of such cities as Chicago and Detroit, they have met members of other groups. They are now more widely distributed occupationally, and Mexican-American communities begin to resemble those of other nationalities in northern cities. There is, however, a high rate of intermarriage since so many of the migrants are single men.[24] Class divisions develop out of the adoption, and the achievement, of American standards. The successful constitute the leadership of these communities.[25]

Most Mexicans, however, still live in isolation in the five states of the Southwest: Arizona, California, Colorado, New Mexico, and Texas. Most of them arrived there after 1900 (some illegally) as part of a great wave of migration unrestricted by the federal legislation of 1921 and 1924. They have become the third largest minority in the United States, but they have remained the least Americanized. There is little acculturation and less mobility; they rank close to lowest in socioeconomic characteristics among all minorities. There is very little intergenerational change, whether economic or geographic. Mexican-Americans are the only group for which there is no rise in socioeconomic status when the census data for first and second generation are compared. By contrast to other groups, "they display a marked lack of internal differentiation, whether in terms of schooling,

---

[22] *Ibid.*, p. 155.

[23] McWilliams, *North from Mexico, op. cit.,* pp. 219–20, 242.

[24] *Ibid.*, p. 221.

[25] Don Martindale, *American Social Structure* (New York: Appleton-Century-Crofts, 1960), p. 413.

occupation, or income."[26] Although 85 percent are now native-born, 76 percent are still manual laborers; three-fourths of the Mexican-Americans live in *colonias,* albeit increasingly urban ones.[27]

There is an element of fatalism in Mexican culture that derives from the conviction that the environment cannot be controlled. Such resignation, in combination with isolation, accounts for much of what seems like passivity to the dominant society. The continuity of the group is nevertheless crucial, and its importance is reflected in the strength of family ties. These are large families (one-third of whom have four or more children under eighteen years of age), involved in large webs of extended kinship. The bonds of affection and respect imply obligations for mutual aid that spread through several generations. It is a patriarchal family with a sharply defined sexual division of labor. Its values, as we shall see, do not encourage mobility.[28]

> The most important role of the individual is his familial role and the family is the most valued institution in Mexican-American society. The individual owes his primary loyalties to the family, which is also the source of most affective relations.[29]

Familial solidarity has such significance that it is a very serious offense to violate an obligation to kin. As a sanctuary in a hostile world, the family is valued above any individual achievement; its needs are put before those of the self. Although it may be an obstacle to advancement, the family is not without its compensations; the man, subservient on the job, reigns supreme in his home. Few abilities are recognized and developed, however.[30] In the second generation the dominant role of the father declines; the wife remains subordinate, but the sons are more emancipated by virtue of their somewhat greater acculturation.[31] Traditional familial forms persist, but there is no longer an integrated system of kin relations.

Among lower-status Mexicans, children are regarded as working members of the family. Schooling is considered unimportant by a father who

---

[26] Celia Stopnicka Heller, *Mexican American Youth: Forgotten Youth at the Crossroads* (New York: Random House, 1966), pp. 4–5, 9.

[27] *Ibid.,* pp. 12, 13.

[28] *Ibid.,* pp. 19–20, 35.

[29] William Madsen, *Mexican-Americans of South Texas* (New York: Holt, Rinehart & Winston, 1964), p. 17.

[30] *Ibid.,* p. 48.

[31] John H. Burma, *Spanish-Speaking Groups in the United States* (Durham, N.C.: Duke University Press, 1954), pp. 85–86.

sees their future as a duplication of his own life.[32] A strong sense of honor is instilled, but education is not seen as a source of social mobility. In traditional socialization, independent achievement is not stressed. Although there is now a conflict of authority between father and son,[33] the family still serves as a center of social life. Although some of its traditional functions have atrophied, its continued vitality derives from the collective celebration of the rites of passage. Sociability in general follows the informal style of village life. "The proliferation of societies, clubs, and associations which distinguishes American life has not yet intruded upon the *colonia*."[34]

The majority of Mexicans are nominal Catholics, only a small proportion of whom (mostly women) attend church regularly. It is a Catholicism different from the American Catholicism so much influenced by the Irish; it is a blend of Spanish and Indian beliefs derived from Mexican folk Catholicism.[35] Although religion is a source of cultural conservatism among Mexican-Americans, reinforcing their separatism, the church has not played the critical role in the community that it has among other groups. It does not constitute the core of communal organization. Nor is there any other institution serving as the functional equivalent of the church in the social structure of the Mexican minority.

> In the small Catholic parish in the United States, the immigrant found nothing to replace the old community life. It would have been impossible to transplant—it was too closely tied to the activities and association of a region. But for many years, nothing which even remotely took its place existed in the Mexican-American parish. The instruction of the young in the catechism, the administration of sacraments, and the erection of a large, fine church structure were the goals of most parish priests. Few attempts were made to provide recreational outlets for the community under the sponsorship of the parish church, or to center the life of a Mexican colony around it.[36]

For all the problematic aspects of their communal institutions, Mexicans maintain a strong sense of social honor that survives in spite of their situation in the larger society. Whatever despised position the dominant group puts them in, they are still members of *la raza*, the race, united by

[32] Madsen, *op. cit.*, p. 31.
[33] Heller, *op. cit.*, p. 40.
[34] Ruth D. Tuck, *Not With the Fist* (New York: Harcourt, Brace & Co., 1946), pp. 157–59.
[35] *Ibid.*, p. 152; Heller, *op. cit.*, pp. 17–19; Madsen, *op. cit.*, p. 58.
[36] Tuck, *op. cit.*, p. 155.

cultural and spiritual bonds. In Mexico, it "carries the idea of a splendid and glorious destiny."[37] There is thus a fierce racial pride that exists independently of their minority status and remains intact in the face of exploitation and exclusion. Mexican-Americans therefore resent the economic dominance of the Anglo-Americans and their air of superiority. They are not convinced that American ways are necessarily better than Mexican ways, and they object to the intolerant pressure to conform to dominant standards. They are not without their own prejudice about Anglo-Americans; it helps them to retain their pride.

> Feelings of resentment stem from a mutual lack of understanding and stances of superiority. Each group finds the other lacking in propriety of behavior and each feels superior in some respects.[38]

It is this very pride that serves Mexicans so well as a source of social honor that exacerbates their sensitivities in intergroup relations. Their concept of manliness requires that they conduct themselves in a way that supports their public image; the categorical treatment to which they are subject not only violates their sense of propriety, it compromises their dignity (as it does to anybody). Among themselves, a proper relationship respects the individuality of the participants,[39] which is exactly what categorical treatment fails to do. They are thus understandably touchy about the exclusion they encounter and too proud to go where they are not wanted. Surrounded by social hostility, Mexicans protect themselves by avoiding painful situations; withdrawal is their most commonly used defense mechanism.

> Mexican-Americans, generally, would rather not try to reach a goal barred by serious obstacles than pursue a goal at the risk of failure. Not to try does not reflect negatively on their manliness and honor but to try and fail does.[40]

The values of *la raza* are strongest among the lower class, whose ranks continue to be replenished by immigration. Interestingly enough, and perhaps as a consequence, lower-class Mexicans do not experience the disabilities of their minority status as severely as do members of the middle class. No Mexican is unaware of American prejudice, but members of the lower class are so insulated from the world of Anglo-Americans that

[37] Madsen, *op. cit.,* p. 15.
[38] *Ibid.,* p. 11.
[39] *Ibid.,* pp. 18, 21.
[40] Heller, *op. cit.,* p. 100.

discrimination does not affect them directly. They do not regard participation in the larger society as necessary or desirable. Hence they maintain their isolation without ambivalence; they do not feel any need to improve their status by acquiring American ways.[41] The functions of the minority community are apparently most effectively fulfilled for those close to the core of its value system, in this case, the lower class. These Mexicans still embody the folk tradition—so long as their subsistence is not threatened.

There is also by now a small, but influential, middle class oriented toward mobility and experiencing all the consequent conflicts of marginality. The acculturation of the members of this class, however, permits them to serve as intermediaries in intergroup relations. For all their social aspirations, even they are ambivalent about incorporating the dominant life style at the cost of their own cultural identity. They favor a fusion of "the best of both worlds." Conceding the superiority of some American values, they accept patterns of behavior promoting achievement and advancement, while retaining other elements of their ethnic heritage.[42] Occupation, of course, is a major determinant of status, as is education, but a member of the middle class must be willing to use these social assets in the service of group interests. For all his Americanization, he cannot disclaim *la raza* without losing status in the Mexican community.[43]

A third generation has begun to make its appearance in the *colonias*. Most members of this generation are still too young to ascertain as yet what direction they will take. Although they are certainly more acculturated than their parents, their principal language, especially in interpersonal relationships, is still a form of American Spanish, a local dialect. This language of the in-group remains the symbol of loyalty to *la raza;* it is also a symptom of their continuing sense of foreignness.[44] School is still a frustrating experience for them. In addition to being subject to the ridicule of hostile peers, they are expected to behave in ways that contradict the values with which they are brought up. (They are particularly discomforted, for example, by individual competitiveness.)[45] Marginality is unabated, and the intergroup tension is accompanied by psychological conflict.

[41] Ozzie G. Simmons, "The Mutual Images and Expectations of Anglo-Americans and Mexican-Americans," in Milton L. Barron, ed., *Minorities in a Changing World* (New York: Alfred A. Knopf, 1967), p. 297.

[42] *Ibid.,* pp. 297–98.

[43] Tuck, *op. cit.,* pp. 132, 134, 137.

[44] Heller, *op. cit.,* p. 31.

[45] Madsen, *op. cit.,* p. 107.

Nevertheless, there is the beginning of assimilation in Los Angeles, where increasing internal differentiation has weakened the ascriptive bonds among Mexican-Americans. Up until now there has been a low rate of intermarriage. Mexican-Americans have maintained strong ethnic boundaries, in part due to the many isolating mechanisms associated with their initial contact with Anglo-Americans. This reinforced their almost exclusive reliance on kin as a source of emotional support; among kin they found both a shared outlook and style of life. With a decline in isolation and an increase in mobility, variations are introduced into the way of life. In-group relations, no longer maintained mechanically, lose some of their functional importance. The socializing structure of the ethnic group, the family, is weakened as growing dissimilarity among its members undermines their shared identity.[46]

In Los Angeles, where there are more opportunities for social advancement than elsewhere in the Southwest, 25 percent of Mexican-Americans are intermarried. Exogamy increases with the generation and the socioeconomic status of the male; occupation is even more significant than generation in explaining intermarriage. Women, however, intermarry more often than men, perhaps as a means of mobility.[47] There was a time when the ethnic culture of the minority group and the kinship relations of the family were closely interwoven. Obviously, by the third generation, other kinds of social relations and status distinctions emerge.

> Increased experience in the larger system—especially rewarding experience—decreases the saliency of the ethnic group as the prime source of identity, in turn weakening the control of the primary group over social relations of its members. Ascriptive identity decreases in salience.[48]

A new militancy is also evolving as Mexican-Americans begin to organize in protest against their minority situation. There are now regional spokesmen for *La Causa* expressing the contemporary struggle for ethnic identity—and social equality. The civil rights movement has given impetus to Mexican-Americans, whose *colonias* are often adjacent to the Negro ghettos and whose economic situation may be even worse. (The per capita income for Mexican-Americans in the Los Angeles area is $1380; for nonwhites it is $1437.) Until recently, there were no defense organizations

[46] Frank G. Mittelbach and Joan W. Moore, "Ethnic Endogamy—The Case of Mexican Americans," *American Journal of Sociology*, Vol. 74, No. 1 (July 1968), pp. 51–52, 61–62.
[47] *Ibid.*, pp. 52–55, 57.
[48] *Ibid.*, p. 62.

except the United Farm Workers Organizing Committee. Now there are the Mexican-American Legal Defense and Educational Fund and the Southwest Conference of *La Raza,* both supported by the Ford Foundation.[49]

A prime target for militants is the school system; strikes and boycotts are becoming frequent, and for reason. Schools have been a traumatic experience for Mexican-American children, who are often punished physically for speaking Spanish, even on the playground. The education that is provided fails to take into account in any way the cultural background and social experience of the students. Parents are resentful of the attempt to make their children over as Anglo-Americans, and the dropout rate continues to be high. (In Texas, 34 percent of the Mexican-American children in grades 7 to 12 leave school.)[50] The resistance against the institutionalized authority of the dominant group may help to strengthen the structure of the Mexican-American community, reinforcing its informal relations with organized resources. Such formal organization in turn implements the communal potential for improving the categorical condition of Mexican-Americans.

Puerto Ricans

Puerto Ricans arrive here as citizens from an American territory, and they continue to commute between the island and the mainland throughout their stay. Theirs is not a total uprooting; the migration has a tentative quality that is reflected in the travel agencies found in Puerto Rican neighborhoods. Dealing mainly in thrift tickets to Puerto Rico, these agencies are unique to *El Barrio.*[51] Mass migration began in the 1940's, and most of the new arrivals settled in New York City. Their departure was motivated by population pressure in Puerto Rico, low living standards and lack of jobs. Since they are seeking economic opportunity, the number of migrants varies with the volume of business activity in the city. Most of them lived and worked in the urban centers of Puerto Rico before migrating in search of a better job. They usually find only low-level jobs in

[49] Homer Bigart, "A New Mexican-American Militancy," *The New York Times,* April 20, 1969, p. 54.
[50] *Ibid.*
[51] Christopher Rand, *The Puerto Ricans* (New York: Oxford, 1958), p. 20.

factories, hotels, restaurants, and other service trades in New York, but the income is higher than on the island. Such unskilled work, however, is highly insecure.[52]

Although many of the new arrivals live in Spanish Harlem and still others on the Lower East Side, there is no concentration in any one part of New York City that can be called a community as such, at least not in ecological terms. Slum clearance and urban renewal further disperse them. In no area is everyone Puerto Rican, and nowhere is there a way of life transplanted intact. Puerto Ricans, however, regard Spanish Harlem as *El Barrio,* a center of informal social life; if they do not live there, they visit there.

There is probably no longer a distinctively Hispanic culture characteristic of Puerto Ricans. They come from an island that in its commonwealth status is part of the United States; its culture has already been affected by sixty years of contact with mainland values.[53] Their culture has been further Americanized by the impact of mass media, and the Spanish heritage is no longer strong.[54]

There are still some values shared with other Spanish-speaking groups such as the importance of *dignitad;* self-possession remains a source of pride, and masculinity is stressed among Puerto Ricans as among Mexicans. These values are embodied in their institutional patterns, of which the most significant configuration is the extended family. Even on the island, however, exposure to some of the key structures of the mainland has undermined indigenous patterns.[55] Marital conflict certainly increases with migration, but there were already familial problems on the island. Consensual unions, common among Puerto Ricans, prove less binding when placed under the stress of uprooting. The increasing independence of the wife, who can now find employment outside the home, threatens the authority of the husband; accustomed to superiority, he feels humiliated. "His world often falls apart—this is why there is so often a descent into incapacity and into mental or physical illness."[56]

[52] C. Wright Mills, Clarence Senior, and Rose K. Goldsen, *The Puerto Rican Journey* (New York: Harper & Bros., 1950), pp. 33, 43, 60, 68–69, 73–74.

[53] Joseph P. Fitzpatrick, "The Adjustment of Puerto Ricans to New York City," in Milton L. Barron, ed., *Minorities in a Changing World* (New York: Alfred A. Knopf, 1967), pp. 283–84.

[54] Nathan Glazer and Daniel P. Moynihan, *Beyond the Melting Pot* (Cambridge, Mass.: The M.I.T. & Harvard University Press, 1963), p. 129.

[55] Charles F. Marden and Gladys Meyer, *Minorities in American Society,* 2nd ed. (New York: American Book Co., 1962), pp. 151–52, 154.

[56] Glazer and Moynihan, *op. cit.,* pp. 126–27; O. Lewis, *op. cit.,* p. xlii.

When families in Puerto Rico dissolved, there were godparents and extended kin to care for the children. Such responsibilities are no longer clearly defined in the United States. There is still the expectation that relatives are obligated to help in time of need, but those who rely on close interpersonal relations as a source of mutual aid are frequently disappointed; such traditional obligations are not always honored—or reciprocated—any more.[57] Even when the family remains intact, there are problems causing conflict. Established patterns of socialization are breaking down with the changing roles of family members. Children chafe at the conservatism of their parents and refuse to respect their authority. Parents in despair often abdicate responsibility for disciplining children, believing that government agencies will assume formal authority over them.[58]

Since friends and relatives cannot be counted on to the extent necessary, there is a sense of emotional insecurity and social stability that is further exacerbated by the constant turnover among Puerto Ricans.

> The frequent complaints of recent migrants that the Hispano group is not a united front are expressions of the migrants' awareness that the group does not respond to their ideal of it as the bulwark of Hispano institutions, a way of life, and a set of cultural values.[59]

The feeling of belonging that Puerto Ricans do have is reinforced by maintaining ties with others from the same hometown. They visit each other regularly, although they are often scattered throughout different areas of New York. There is thus some continuity in social life, strengthened by the sentiments of holiday celebration. The family still constitutes the basic set of social relations and reciprocal expectations, but it is defined as much by residence as by blood; those who live together make up the household, and it is the household that is the center for most friendships.[60] Since Puerto Ricans do not live in geographic isolation the way Mexicans do, they do not have as easy access to each other.

It is questionable whether an organized Puerto Rican community exists in New York. There is no organizational tradition among Puerto Ricans accustomed to the informal relationships of village life. Their communal structure in the city is therefore relatively weak, lacking in leadership.

---

[57] Elena Padilla, *Up from Puerto Rico* (New York: Columbia University Press, 1958), pp. 58, 216.

[58] Rand, *op. cit.*, pp. 85–86; Glazer and Moynihan, *op. cit.*, pp. 123, 125; Mills, *et. al., op. cit.*, pp. 97–98.

[59] Padilla, *op. cit.*, p. 52.

[60] *Ibid.*, pp. 217–18; Mills, *et al., op. cit.*, pp. 95, 99, 101.

The successful migrants of an earlier period have moved out of the community to participate in the larger society.[61] They left behind neighborhoods that may be characterized more by their state of poverty than by their sense of community, Hispanic or otherwise. Describing one such area, an anthropologist observes:

> There is a high incidence of violation of norms because of their ineffectiveness in providing the individual with suitable personal and social adaptations. The slum has a culture of its own. It is a way of life whose consistency is partly determined by their position at the fringe of the larger society. Its code for living makes allowances for behavior not necessarily tolerated by other segments of the society.[62]

The life of the slum is thus to a large extent endemic; it exists independently of the cultural origins of its inhabitants. Solidarity is most pronounced when an individual has been (or is believed to have been) mistreated by an agency of the larger society. The threat to a neighborhood by urban renewal may also create a common interest in organizing against its destruction.[63]

There is, in a word, little indigenous organization among Puerto Ricans. Even the Spanish newspapers that serve the community are not its own creations. It may be that the paternalistic guidance of the island government (as well as the social services of New York) obviates the need for a grass-roots organizational response from the community. The Office of the Commonwealth of Puerto Rico serves as an orientation center for newcomers, employment agency, and defense organization. It is thus the official representative of the community, a government office supported by government funds, unwittingly stifling any indigenous impulse toward organization. It all but constitutes the entire organizational complex of the Puerto Rican community.[64] And it remains so in spite of the fact that members of the community do not like to turn to such social agencies in time of need.[65] There are none of the characteristic ethnic associations of mutual aid found in earlier groups; Puerto Ricans continue to depend upon friends and relatives, although personal services are no longer regarded as reciprocal obligations.

No formal institution has filled the gap left by the failure of informal

---

[61] Glazer and Moynihan, *op. cit.*, p. 101; Mills, *et al., op. cit.*, pp. 105–6.
[62] Padilla, *op. cit.*, p. 62.
[63] *Ibid.*, p. 52; Glazer and Moynihan, *op. cit.*, p. 108.
[64] Nathan Glazer, "The Puerto Ricans," *Commentary*, Vol. 36, No. 1 (July 1963), p. 5.
[65] Mills, *et al., op. cit.*, p. 114.

traditions. Although most Puerto Ricans are Catholic, the church plays little role in their lives. They are even less likely to attend church here than on the island; very few send their children to parochial schools. The church has not created a national parish among Puerto Ricans as it did among older Catholic groups. It is weakest as an institution where the needs of the immigrants are the greatest. The church does not constitute a supportive communal structure replacing the extended family; it does not even supply a social setting to sustain the community, as it has in the past. The traditional functions of the church have been usurped by welfare agencies and commercialized recreation. Perhaps the most vigorous religious institution is the Pentecostal church, small, store-front evangelical Protestant congregations, offering a sense of community.[66] There is also a small percentage who belong formally to the Spiritualist church, and many more who work with spirits at home in private sessions.

> There is no way to measure accurately the increase in spiritualist interest among the migrants, but the many *Botánica*-studded streets of Spanish Harlem, as well as the neighborhood legends and rumors, bear testimony to its great importance.[67]

Its importance signifies the rapid cultural change that has threatened the traditional way of life. As established values are undermined, there is greater commitment to spiritualist beliefs.

Because Puerto Ricans are relatively scattered, frequently dispersed by urban renewal, they are separated from each other as well as isolated from the dominant group. They are thus less available for mutual aid than are Mexicans. The impact of urban life accelerates the pace of social change, and the family suffers critical strains. It cannot provide even the emotional resources that the Mexican family does. As a result, Puerto Ricans experience disappointment with each other, compounding their disenchantment with the mainland. The reciprocal expectations of informal patterns are no longer met; the consequent frustration may find an outlet in spiritualism.

One strong social bond persists, that of language; speaking Spanish is a source of solidarity as well as a sign of differentiation between darker-skinned Puerto Ricans and Negroes. There is sufficient tension about color, perhaps acquired on the mainland, so that Puerto Ricans do not want to be confused with Negroes. Those with dark skin are particularly insecure

---

[66] Glazer and Moynihan, *op. cit.*, pp. 103–4, 106–7.

[67] Dan Wakefield, *Island in the City* (Boston: Houghton Mifflin Co., 1959), p. 69.

in their status, and thus strive to establish themselves as members of an ethnic group. Working in unskilled jobs and living in the same neighborhoods, Puerto Ricans can function without learning English. Nor is there much formal pressure from the larger society to do so; officials in New York try to acquaint themselves with the background and language of Puerto Ricans in order to work more effectively with them.[68] The immigrants expect, therefore, that Spanish will remain their major language.

> Some adults come up here without knowing English, and don't see the need for learning it—often they don't even see the possibility of learning it, for they are not experienced in the way education can dispel ignorance, stage by stage, if one sticks to it. They are also too proud to use bad broken English. So they get a job in some shop with a Spanish-speaking straw-boss, and in their spare time they consort with other Puerto Ricans and watch the Spanish movies or Spanish TV programs. They stay in their ghettos and think about going back to their island some day.[69]

There is, in fact, little social mobility among the immigrants. The men may advance from unskilled to semiskilled work, but rarely do they go any further. The women are even more restricted to semiskilled jobs, usually using the skills in needlework that they had already acquired on the island. Consequently they have a low level of aspiration for themselves and are pessimistic about achieving even that.[70] Most of the first generation, like so many immigrants of all times, place their hopes in their children. In a survey of 1113 Puerto Ricans in New York City in 1950, 61 percent said they would like their children to go to college, but only 25 percent expected them to do so. Similarly, 62 percent would like their children to be professionals, but 65 percent do not know what they are likely to do.[71]

Even the hopes for the next generation are uncertain of fulfillment, beclouded, in part, by ignorance of the possibilities (as well as by pessimism about the probabilities). School is a difficult experience for Puerto Ricans as for Mexicans, and there are many drop-outs. Nevertheless, an organization called Aspira was formed by Puerto Rican professionals to help students and parents to take advantage of available educational opportunities.[72] There is already some indication of an upward shift in the

[68] Glazer and Moynihan, *op. cit.*, p. 101; Fitzpatrick, *op. cit.*, p. 283.
[69] Rand, *op. cit.*, p. 72.
[70] Mills, *et al.*, *op. cit.*, pp. 69, 71, 89, 163.
[71] *Ibid.*, pp. 163, 165.
[72] Glazer, *op. cit.*, pp. 8–9.

occupational distribution of the second generation as early as the 1950 census. Native-born sons of Puerto Ricans under 24 years of age are still few in number, but 24 percent of them are in sales and clerical work by contrast to nine percent of their fathers. Thirty-seven percent of the first generation are semiskilled operators, and 28 percent are service workers; there is a decline in both these categories for the second generation.[73]

However, the median family income remains even lower for Puerto Ricans than for nonwhites in 1960, and the rate of unemployment is higher. About one-seventh of the Puerto Ricans in New York City receive public assistance from the Department of Welfare.[74] With so much to threaten their self-respect, some immigrants see small business as an escape that saves their dignity.[75] Puerto Ricans own around 4,000 small businesses in New York, which is more than the number owned by Negroes, who have been in the city thirty years longer. Much like the Jews before them, Puerto Ricans open stores in response to the special needs of their group, supplying such products as food, records, books, herbs, and so forth. The many *bodegas* in Spanish Harlem testify to the entrepreneurial tradition to be found on the island, if only in peddling.[76]

Although shopkeeping is familiar to Puerto Ricans as a source of status on the island, it is not a secure escape from economic instability on the mainland. The changing context in which business operates constitutes a greater impediment to success than does ethnicity. The present economic structure of the larger society is such that "the growing advantages of bigness put the small and new competitor at a disadvantage."[77] Entrepreneurial activity becomes a less effective source of mobility as more capital is required and it becomes more difficult to acquire. Nor are the special needs of the Puerto Rican market likely to survive another generation of acculturation. The next generation will have little alternative but to get an education to qualify for salaried employment. At this point there is still discrimination in large enterprise, but such economic barriers have already been erased by the availability of employment in the government.[78]

[73] *Ibid.*, p. 6.
[74] *Ibid.*
[75] Mills, *et al.*, *op. cit.*, p. 86.
[76] Glazer and Moynihan, *op. cit.*, pp. 112–13.
[77] Handlin, *op. cit.*, pp. 74–75.
[78] *Ibid.*, pp. 75–76.

Shared Characteristics of the
Spanish-Speaking Groups

The critical contemporary characteristics of these Spanish-speaking groups, the Mexicans and Puerto Ricans, derive from their color and their class. It is color and class that shape individual lives in such a way as to bring about some personal disorganization. Its source is in the social structure. The prejudice of the dominant group and the resulting poverty of the minority group are pervasive. Their socially disorganizing consequences account for the institutional insufficiency of the Spanish-speaking communities. Even their impoverishment is different from that of earlier immigrants. The larger society is such that poverty has become self-perpetuating, justifying its psychologically incumbent sense of despair. The near-hopelessness of the economic situation underlies the communal inadequacy, fostering fatalism about the future. Even the possibilities for the next generation no longer seem promising; they are neither clear nor certain.

> Poverty today has a new shape, one that did not exist sixty-five years ago. The older poverty was an adjunct to industrial expansion, and though as unpleasant as today's, it was nevertheless surrounded by hope. Growing industries were ready to absorb newcomers to America, and the economy's need for muscle power obviated the need for high educational attainment. Job opportunities were plentiful and the ladder of opportunity allowed a young man to gain experience in work. The American promise had some measure of reality.
>
> As the economy settled, those trapped in poverty found themselves in an unending cycle. Poverty became self-perpetuating. The poor had been trapped by being born to the wrong parents in the wrong part of the country in the wrong racial group.[79]

The quality of life for the poor suffers all the more from its stark contrast to the expectations generated by an affluent society. The sense of relative deprivation is endemic, exacerbating the suppression of living standards. Lost in their social invisibility, the poor risk losing their humanity in their personal insecurity.[80] Although the economic sources of their problematic situation may seem insoluble, their culture is not yet irrele-

[79] Ben B. Seligman, *Permanent Poverty: An American Syndrome* (Chicago: Quadrangle Books, 1968), p. 18.
[80] *Ibid.*, p. 16.

vant to the Spanish-speaking groups. Its values still help to define their minority situation and to determine their response as individuals.

Indeed, for both Mexicans and Puerto Ricans, the cultural impact of migration has been mitigated by the fact that they are not entirely uprooted. Mexicans have settled in an area of the United States that was already Hispanic, and Puerto Ricans come from an area that is already Americanized. For good reason then they feel less alien than earlier immigrants; they are in a land that is less strange to them. Furthermore, there is no sharp break with the place of origin for either group. Mexicans and Puerto Ricans are close enough to home to commute. They therefore do not have to sever their connections with the past; it remains vital, if not always viable for them, but at the cost of creating some social problems in the present. Not all of their values are transferable to American society (no more than any ethnic values are), but neither are traditions transplanted that might help to establish a community. In discussing Negroes (as internal migrants) and Puerto Ricans, Handlin describes the consequences of this as follows:

> By contrast, the Negroes and Puerto Ricans were American citizens; and that diminished the distance between Harlem on the one hand and Mississippi or the island on the other. Migration was not the decisive break it had been for the Europeans. The movement of individuals back and forth between the old home and the new never ceased, so that communications were close and the sense of connectedness was never broken. In this respect the Negroes and the Puerto Ricans were similar to the French Canadians of New England and the Mexicans of the Southwest who were also never altogether detached from the lands of their birth. Such newcomers did not feel the complete and total sense of foreignness that overwhelmed the European immigrants and, therefore, did not feel called upon to create the institutions which were the response to the shock of separation.[81]

There are structural difficulties in both Spanish-speaking communities that stem from lack of organization and leadership. The Catholic church does not attempt to play a critical communal role as it has for other groups. Neither is there a tradition for organized assistance among Mexicans and Puerto Ricans, who are accustomed to the mutual aid of relatives and friends. Such informal resources have proven inadequate in the United States. Although often too proud to ask for help, these groups are increasingly defined as the problem of the formal institutions of the larger society.

[81] Handlin, *op. cit.,* p. 109.

The impulse toward self-help is undermined by both the conditions of contract labor and the consequences of government paternalism that discourage indigenous organization. Mexicans and Puerto Ricans each have, however, something that is significant to group survival, an independent source of social honor. Their sense of pride, reinforced by shared language, stands them in good stead under the oppression of poverty. It helps to counteract the consequences of minority status; but so also does such pride heighten Mexican and Puerto Rican fear of intergroup contact since they are so sensitive to humiliation.

There is now for both Mexicans and Puerto Ricans the beginning of organized protest. In addition to attempts at unionization, there are territorial claims being made in the Southwest and rent strikes in the Northeast. Some community action is actually organized under the auspices of government agencies, but sometimes it is initiated by grass-roots leadership. It is, of course, always possible for protest to be at cross-purposes with government. Whatever the conflict of interests, however, the militancy does serve to structure the minority community. Whereas in the past such organized action emerged out of the communal structure, it now helps to create that structure. Minority institutions are thereby formally enacted that once grew out of an ethnic tradition; they may be a sociological substitute for the voluntary associations of other groups. If they are able to fulfill the equivalent functions, they will provide a social adequacy to the Spanish-speaking communities that they have been lacking.

Once their communities have achieved some institutional sufficiency, Mexicans and Puerto Ricans are likely to recapitulate the established ethnic patterns of earlier nationality groups. Their pace has been slowed by the characteristics of their situation in the changing structure of the larger society. More than their cultural values, their color is a complicating factor further impeding mobility. Yet in spite of the modern meaning of poverty and prejudice in American society, the Spanish-speaking groups are coping with the consequences of their minority status by emulating to some extent previous ethnic groups. In their acculturation, they are taking as role models Jews and other Catholics.[82] In following the example set by these groups, Mexicans and Puerto Ricans are modifying their traditional values in favor of individual achievement. There is less stress on the extended family as they begin to seek economic security. And if they succeed, there will be less need for such kinship.

[82] Glazer, *op. cit.*, p. 9.

It may not be possible to adhere to these ethnic patterns, at whatever pace, if the social process starts with deculturation. Indians as a conquered group and Negroes as an enslaved group were forcibly deprived of their original cultures. The consequences of such coercion are not the same as those of acculturation, the voluntary acceptance of another culture at some time after immigration. Indians and Negroes were given no choice; neither were they given any access to an alternative culture. They lost their own without gaining the dominant one. We will now look at the consequences of their deculturation.

Chapter 9

Consequences of Deculturation

THE conquest of the Indians and the enslavement of the Negroes constitute unique conditions in the origins of American minority groups. The deprivation inherent in their categorical status was compounded by the demoralization that accompanied their legal subordination. Bereft of the values that once served as a source of social honor and personal identity, neither Indians nor Negroes were left any communal resources with which to endure the circumstances of defeat or the state of servitude. If, indeed, there is anything that enables a group to cope with such a situation, it would be too threatening to the oppressors to be permitted to persist. It is for this reason that these two groups have been least able to live down their respective histories in their own eyes. Their past remains so pressing that the responses of others in the present seem irrelevant. In these instances, therefore, it is not what the dominant group attempts to do (one way or another), but what the minority group is able to do that is significant.

It is not a question of whether or not the racism directed at Indians and Negroes is worse than that directed at any other group of color. It probably is worse; it may even be a qualitatively different order of prejudice, one cast in the special mold of contempt reserved for the deculturated. The humiliation of a people without a culture is perhaps more exquisite than that of the man without a country, whatever his sensibility. The real issue is, nevertheless, the particular—and peculiar—history that impels each of these groups. As a result of their respective histories, Indians and Negroes feel the need to prove something to themselves, regardless of the reactions of the larger society; the need is independent of the prejudice and discrimination of the dominant group. The impulse toward self-validation exists not so much because of their categorical status, but because of the reason for that status.

Negroes may well be more driven by the past than Indians. The latter were at least conquered as free men, however humiliating their defeat and consequent dependency. They could, and did, feel that they had traded their land for their keep, much as later immigrants traded a vote for a job with the ward bosses of city politics. Indians, after all, did have something concrete to offer in the exchange, however inequitable the terms; they were not forced into hard labor. Unlike slaves, they had some claim on the larger society and were entitled to expect something in return. This expectation was never more than minimally fulfilled, and it was frequently violated flagrantly, if legally. Still, the legitimacy of the claim affected the attitudes not only of Indians toward themselves, but of others toward them.

Max Weber, on a visit to the United States, was convinced that the discrimination against Indians was of a quite different character than that against Negroes. It was his impression that the dominant attitude toward Indians was "friendlier" (if one can describe any categorical context in such a fashion). Informants explained their feelings by the fact that the Indians, in contrast to the Negroes, "did not submit to slavery."[1] This suggests the significance of the contemporary demand of black militants for reparations for historical enslavement. It would serve as payment for forced labor, as land grant claims make some compensation for the consequences of past defeat for Indians. Such restitution would help to restore the self-respect of Negroes, who would not then be put in a position of asking for charity from the dominant group. Their sense of manhood, so threatened by pity for the past, rests on the conviction that recompense has been earned. The Indians, unlike the Negroes, had an aboriginal communal structure that provided them with the basis for organized (if ultimately futile) resistance to conquest. This capacity for organization has since been undermined by the legal status of Indians as wards of the federal government; the very structure of their community has been rendered meaningless, as we will now see.

---

[1] Ernest M. Manasse, "Max Weber on Race," *Social Research,* Vol. 14 (June 1947), p. 198.

The Indians and the Reservation

Indian culture has never been one culture, but a variety of cultures developed for thousands of years before the white man's presence brought about drastic changes. In their subjugation, tribes remained separated from each other, and hence distinctive in their cultures. For a long time not only didn't the tribes adapt to the dominant society, they didn't acculturate to each other either. Their cultures were preliterate, and the tribes were small; relationships were almost entirely personal. Economies were primarily based on hunting and gathering, with some fishing; what agriculture there was was woman's work. Property belonged to extended kin or to tribal groups, although individuals did own items of personal adornment. There were few class distinctions, and the material standard of living didn't vary much with what status differences there were.[2] This was the world, a world without the written word, that was devastated by conquest.

The defeat of the Indians was so complete by 1871 that there was a government act ending the use of treaties in dealing with them. No longer recognized as sovereign nations, the tribes acquired the legal status of wards of the federal government. Indians were segregated on reservations, the conditions of which did more to decimate their number than military force. As self-sufficient nomads, Indians did not take to the settled life, and as proud warriors, they did not take to the surveillance of government guardianship.[3] They were put in a position of supplication to meet their needs. Tribal authorities were destroyed by the Indian Office, institutions shaken, and a way of life shattered. In their pauperized isolation, only some tribal traditions persisted in those areas of reservation life that were left relatively unstructured.[4]

Land was set aside for the exclusive use of Indians, but it was reduced by half in a relatively short time because white men wanted it. Most reservations were located west of the Mississippi, although there were also a few in the east. There was an agent in charge of each reservation, exer-

[2] Charles F. Marden and Gladys Meyer, *Minorities in American Society,* 2nd ed. (New York: American Book Co., 1962), pp. 330–32.

[3] *Ibid.,* p. 335; Brewton Berry, *Race and Ethnic Relations* (Boston: Houghton Mifflin Co., 1965), p. 234.

[4] Don Martindale, *American Social Structure* (New York: Appleton-Century-Crofts, 1960), pp. 399, 404.

cising complete power as representative of the government. Indians chafed at the absolute control of the federal government since they had no recourse for their grievances except through appeals that were so often ineffective. Indians were supplied with rations by private individuals contracted by the government. These rations were not only inadequate, they were frequently condemned stuff from which the children died. Indians were thus threatened with extermination on the reservations because of sickness. In addition to measles, diphtheria, and tuberculosis, many died of homesickness and despair; "a number of young men, seeing no desirable future, committed suicide."[5]

The agents were instructed to force Indians to give up their original forms of shelter and to live in wooden or log houses. They were to wear "citizen dress" and to begin farming at once. Above all, "every Indian must cut his hair short and give up braids." Nothing aroused more resentment than this rule, and it was generally ignored except by those who were regularly employed by the agent. The regulation was nevertheless given much importance by whites.

> It would humiliate the Indian and give him pain, for he took pride in his hair; and to the white man long hair was the symbol of Indian ways, so he wanted to blot out the symbol and then believe that he had civilized the Indian.[6]

This was not the only insult added to the injury done to Indians; it was simply the most gratuitous. Farming was a more complex problem since raising crops was not considered a proper activity for a man.

In 1887, the Dawes Severalty Act permitted the division of tribal lands, giving allotted portions to family heads and other individuals (as well as full citizenship). The ostensible object of this allotment policy was to make each Indian breadwinner self-supporting by having him work his own land. The land was to be held in trust for twenty-five years, during which it could not be taxed or sold; in the meantime, the Indians were to be supported directly by the government. Most leased their lands to whites since they lacked both the technology and the credit to farm efficiently. In effect, the allotment policy undermined the economic and social organization of the tribes by destroying communal ownership of land. The backbone of the culture of the Indians was broken, at the same time that there was an attempt to coerce their assimilation as individuals.[7]

[5] Clark Wissler, *Indians of the United States* (New York: Doubleday Anchor Books, 1967 ed., rev. by Lucy W. Kluckhohn), pp. 310–14, 317.

[6] *Ibid.,* pp. 315–16.

[7] Berry, *op. cit.,* pp. 234–35; Marden and Meyer, *op. cit.,* p. 335.

Part of the difficulty lay in putting Indian farmers on the same independent basis as white farmers.

> The Indian had lived under a different kind of economic and social system, one in which there was no capital, no permanent ownership of land, but in which hospitality and free giving were the rule. Between these ideals and the rugged individualism of white society there could be no compromise.[8]

Indians were fearful of offending nature by plowing up the land. Crop failure further discouraged them, confirming their fears. They lacked the accumulated experience to sustain them with the hope of a more successful season; they had no reason to believe there would be one. Without tradition or training, it was easier for Indians to turn their land over to whites to farm. In the process, their initiative and self-confidence were destroyed. "By shattering the foundation of his culture it robbed the Indian of the drive that comes from believing in the future of one's society and nation."[9] It was an irreparable blow to the spirit. So bitter was their physical and moral defeat that Indians lost interest in their own values. The demoralization was so severe that some simply lost their will to live.

These were terrible times. A sympathetic journalist writing of contemporary Indians sums up their past as follows.

> From the end of the Indian Wars to just before World War II the tribes were thought of as defeated nations, and were so treated and so held captive. The stringent military occupation did not end until little more than a generation ago. On one Western reservation the U.S. Army was not withdrawn until the 1920's. Neither side, during that time, had a great deal to say to the other. It would have been conversation between prisoner and jailer.
>
> The tribes were not, however, merely defeated nations. Unique in modern history, they were wholly surrounded by the nation of their conquerors, who because of this untenable blot on their geographic map and because of their Puritan ethics, set out zealously to "convert the heathen" and to "civilize the savage." Henceforth, the Indians were "wards," and the government was their "guardian." Psychologically this "ward of the government" status was more injurious to the tribes than had been their military defeat. It further inhibited any truthful communication.
>
> * * *
>
> To the reservation Indian this meant an assault on his dignity, his self-respect, and his belief in his tribal integrity. He was reduced, if not to supplication, then to self-abnegation, in order to receive the handouts that

[8] Wissler, *op. cit.*, p. 318.
[9] Carey McWilliams, *Brothers Under the Skin* (Boston: Little, Brown & Co., rev. ed., 1951), p. 75.

enabled him to stay alive. For he had been denied his ancient way of living, but had as yet learned no other.[10]

In the depths of despair there sprung up among the defeated Indians messianic movements based on the belief in an imminent change. These religious cults revived the symbols of the past in anticipation of a return to the time before conquest. The resurrection of an idealized past helped to alleviate the frustrations of the present; Indians once again adhered to the traditional ways of their aboriginal life, expecting the intervention of the Great Spirit in their behalf. Young men, who no longer could achieve status through hunting and warfare, were especially attracted to the Ghost Dance as an escape for the ridicule they endured.[11] This revivalistic movement propagated the belief that the plains would once again be populated by buffalo and the whites would disappear. By 1890, thousands of Indians had given themselves over to the prescribed ceremony of preparation.

> As the animals upon which their whole way of life had been based disappeared, as they were alternatively threatened and cajoled to exchange the excitement of buffalo hunts and horse-stealing expeditions for the drudgery of the plow and the hoe, the warriors grasped at straws. When their religious leaders reported revelations in which the Great Spirit was critical of men plowing instead of hunting, the Indians eagerly believed them.[12]

But this, too, was a disillusioning experience like all of defeat. The magical methods of the Ghost Dance failed to bring on the millennium. The ensuing desperation persisted; with each crop of children it was perpetrated anew by the off-reservation boarding schools that prevailed in the latter part of the nineteenth century. The educational policy aimed at nothing less than the destruction of Indian culture and family life. Children were taken away from their homes; their language, ceremonies, and traditions suppressed; not even their arts and crafts were encouraged in these schools. Compulsory assimilation inhered in this coercive break with the native environment. The curriculum was that of any white school, with no adaptation to the particular needs of the Indians. The result was a marginality that unfitted the youngsters for Indian life without equipping them for the larger society.[13]

[10] Stan Steiner, *The New Indians* (New York: Harper & Row, 1968), p. 83.

[11] Michael Banton, *Race Relations* (New York: Basic Books, 1967), pp. 91, 93; Tamotsu Shibutani and Kian M. Kwan, with contributions by Robert H. Billigmeier, *Ethnic Stratification* (New York: Macmillan, 1965), p. 309.

[12] William T. Hagan, *American Indians* (Chicago: University of Chicago Press, 1961), p. 131.

[13] Marden and Meyer, *op. cit.*, p. 336; McWilliams, *op. cit.*, p. 76.

These crowded institutions trained girls in the operation of laundries and the mass production of food. Boys were schooled in the handling of farm machinery and the adjusting of furnaces. None of these skills had any application to the activities on the reservation, where such work was not available. Students who succeeded in adapting to school routine were miserable when they went home. "By 1900 every reservation had its quota of returned students who at the same time felt superior to their fellow tribesman and yet resented being regarded as outsiders by their fellows."[14] Eventually there were day schools on the reservations, and when possible Indian children attended public schools.

Between 1887 and 1934 Indians were separated from about 86,000,000 of their 138,000,000 acres. Most of what remained was desert or semi-desert, worthless to whites. Still, administrators found it difficult to believe that Indians had been better off with their tribal culture. Their way of life was therefore undermined, but Indians were still not permitted to participate in the larger society. Although tribal identity became blurred, Indians had not become like the dominant group. Instead there was the beginning of pan-Indianism. As the unique characteristics of each tribe disappeared, they borrowed practices from other Indians. "Intertribal contacts in the boarding schools and the crowding together of tribes into smaller areas led to a considerable cultural exchange and standardization."[15]

There was a change in policy with the New Deal. It included an attempt to make Indian groups self-sustaining, while permitting them to retain what was left of their tribal culture. The reforms were to encompass considerable economic rehabilitation and increased self-government for the tribes. The physical resources, however, remained inadequate for a now growing Indian population, and their material culture lagged in modernization.[16] Nevertheless, the Indian Reorganization Act of 1934 allowed the organization and incorporation of tribes for the political and economic management of their resources and affairs. Allotted lands could be consolidated for tribal use. These changes were not imposed upon the Indians; they could choose to incorporate or not, as they wished, and this option itself was indicative of a change in government policy. Corporate ownership was regarded as a means of preserving Indian societies. Over one hundred tribes chose to draw up constitutions, and twice as many economic organizations were chartered.[17]

[14] Hagan, *op. cit.*, p. 135.
[15] *Ibid.*, pp. 147–48, 150.
[16] Marden and Meyer, *op. cit.*, pp. 337–38, 349.
[17] Hagan, *op. cit.*, p. 155.

Unfamiliarity with dominant practices and the structure of formal associations nullified some of these efforts. And so did the paucity of land, which was insufficient to support the residents of the reservations. In 1946 the Indian Claims Commission was established to consider claims against the government for past usurpation of Indian lands without adequate compensation.[18] Some of these claims have since been granted. In addition, there have been attempts to locate industry on reservations and to relocate Indians off reservations.[19] Still, poverty and its incumbent despair are endemic among Indians.

The economic basis of their life is now wage work, largely periodic and seasonal; it is used to supplement the uneconomic system of land utilization. Sixty-five percent of the Indian labor force is in farming, farm labor, and unskilled industrial work with low-paid jobs. The 1950 Census reported a median family income of $983 for reservation Indians. Although it has risen since then, it is still not sufficient to maintain an adequate standard of living. Most of these Indians cannot improve their economic position since the reservations are isolated from centers of industry and trade. They are untrained, with little formal education, and there are not enough resources on the reservation to afford more than mere subsistence; productivity is insufficient and employment unavailable.[20]

Indians do not fare much better off the reservations. Since the 1950's the Bureau of Indian Affairs has encouraged them to resettle in urban centers with offers of financial assistance. They go to the city because they cannot support themselves on the reservation, and there they encounter other difficulties. The burden of change is on the Indians; they are expected to integrate into the dominant cultural patterns. Yet their past geographic and social isolation has inflicted deep damage on the morale of the group. White paternalism and Indian dependency have been so demoralizing that there is a psychological problem in forsaking the pseudo-security of government wardship on the reservation. Many do not succeed in making the transition from a protected status to independent responsibility.[21]

The process of deculturation imposed upon Indians by their defeat bore

[18] Wissler, *op. cit.,* p. 324.

[19] Hagan, *op. cit.,* p. 165.

[20] William H. Kelly, "The Economic Basis of Indian Life." *The Annals of the American Academy of Political and Social Science,* Vol. 311 (May 1957), pp. 71, 75.

[21] Daisuke Kitagawa, "The American Indian," in Arnold M. Rose and Caroline B. Rose, eds., *Minority Problems* (New York: Harper & Row, 1965), pp. 27–28.

no resemblance to the eventual acculturation of European immigrants, which was, after all, as voluntary a social change as their original migration. By contrast, everything about the Indian situation was coercive, from conquest to deculturation. Perhaps because Indians were left so little choice, they felt compelled to retain the refuge of the reservation, even at the cost of accepting federal charity. There they could maintain some of their "Indian-ness," a remnant of the life in which they once knew dignity. In isolation they were able to build psychological barriers to protect themselves from the ultimate consequences of deculturation. They thus refuse to relinquish what is left of their Indian culture to gain dominant acceptance; it is the source of what personality integration is possible under such strained circumstances.[22]

The deprivation of Indian life remains so severe, however, that it must be tempered by something transcendental. The peyote cult has been organized as the Native American Church, in which eating peyote is a sacred ritual. The hallucinatory drug permits the participants to claim direct communication with God. The religion blends fundamentalist Christian theology with pan-Indian moral principles and religious ceremonials, stressing such values as brotherly love, honesty, family commitment, and self-reliance.[23] The Navajos, for example, are the largest of 300 tribes, with 120,000 members. It is estimated that anywhere from one-third to four-fifths of them belong to the Native American Church. It has become a significant crutch in a troubled time. Lacking any satisfying guide for their drifting cultural identities, Indians find spiritual fulfillment in this hybrid religion during a shattering social transition in which they are no longer of a tribal world and not yet of the dominant society.

> The hunger for spiritual succor arises from the mutely desperate atmosphere of the Navajo reservation. Despite recent gains in obtaining reservation industry and upgrading living standards, $700 is the average annual family income. Such facts as a life expectancy of 45 years, unemployment rates of 80 percent in remote settlements, high infant mortality and an inordinate incidence of trachoma, pneumonia, and impetigo suggest the daily reality of Navajo existence.[24]

Along with economic depression, there has been the erosion of Navajo religion, leaving them without a viable tradition to serve as a source of

[22] *Ibid.,* pp. 29–31.
[23] Shibutani, *et al., op. cit.,* p. 310.
[24] Peter Nabokov, "The Peyote Road," *The New York Times Magazine,* (March 9, 1969), p. 129.

community. Indians thus suffer spiritually as well as structurally, and the peyote cult is a bridge between ancient worship and Christian religion. There is a sense of insecurity about the old ways, and Navajos have learned to doubt the psychological and physical healing powers of their traditional religion. The Navajo way offers no cure for new problems; peyote supplies an interim solution. Up until recently the cultural vacuum had been escaped only through bouts with the bottle. About 80 percent of the Navajos have had drinking problems. The proportion has declined with the increase in membership in the Native American Church. Peyote has given the participants something to which they can cling in stress.[25]

The acceptance, if not active encouragement, of native religions, ceremonials, and crafts was part of the new Indian policy, the better received part. Cultural repression had been in effect for so long, however, that some of the practices were beyond revival.

> What frequently appeared was a blend of tribal remnants and borrowings from other Indians. The results helped further the Pan-Indian movement and had an incalculable effect in raising Indian morale by removing the stigma previously associated with tribal cultures.[26]

Although many Indians have been sufficiently educated by dominant standards to remove them from their aboriginal way of life, they have not been integrated into the larger society. Basic Indian systems of social structure and culture persist even though little meaning is attributed to particular tribal ways anymore. The pan-Indianism that has emerged includes customs synthesized from diverse tribal cultures; it even encompasses some dominant patterns.[27]

Ironically, pan-Indianism "includes those elements that are central features of white stereotypes of Indian culture."[28] It may be because of this that pan-Indianism is able to counteract the categorical consequences of subordinate status; it replaces derogation with dignity by substituting a positive evaluation for the negative one of the dominant group. For this reason, the movement offers a social framework in which Indian groups can maintain a sense of identity and integrity. Community is thereby restored to some extent. As a result, most of the present identifiable groups on reservations continue as distinct social units. They preserve the basic

[25] *Ibid.*, pp. 129–30.
[26] Hagan, *op. cit.*, pp. 157–58.
[27] Evon Z. Vogt, "The Acculturation of American Indians," *The Annals of the American Academy of Political and Social Science,* Vol. 311 (May 1957), pp. 138–39, 145–46.
[28] *Ibid.*, p. 146.

values of a now conglomerate culture. While adjusting to the economic and political demands of the larger society, Indians have not fully accepted American ways. Although few of their institutions remain intact, the kinship system and its lines of descent still function. Indians still play roles as clansmen and members of ritualistic societies, and half of the original one hundred and fifty languages are still in use; Indian children may, for example, start school without knowing English.[29]

Because the gap between the Indian and the dominant culture is so great, the strain of accommodation between them has been unusually severe. Under conditions of tribal insularity, even the sense of solidarity among Indians was weakened. Pan-Indianism has succeeded in bringing about sufficient cohesion among the various tribes, no longer so culturally different from each other, that there is now the beginning of organized protest against the dominant group. A new generation of college-educated Indians constitutes its indigenous leadership. As youthful advocates of "Red Power," they defend the ideological superiority of the Indian way.[30]

There is the emergence of a minority consciousness with this restoration of an independent source of social honor. Often this consciousness is self-consciously achieved since many of the young Indians are students of sociology. They are not only marginal, they know they are marginal, and they gather together in groups fully aware of the characteristics of their hybrid culture. The new tribalism does not look to the past in a desperate attempt to hold on to a disappearing heritage. No longer driven by defeat and impelled by the necessity of its nothingness, these college graduates foresee a future once more. And they are determined to create a modernized version of their Indian way of life for the twentieth century. The new Indians thus reject assimilation. In their tribal nationalism, they press for self-determination and political independence.[31]

The relationship between the generations is more than an individual matter; it has tribal implications. The mutual commitment and reciprocal communication are such that young Indians with their bolder approach to the dominant group can exercise considerable influence on their communities. "It was uniquely Indian: the respect for the elders by the youth; the recognition of the youth by the elders."[32] Members of the younger generation have thus become the spokesmen for the long unspoken thoughts

[29] D'Arcy McNickle, *The Indian Tribes of the United States* (London: Oxford University Press, 1962), pp. 4–5.

[30] Steiner, *op. cit.*, p. x.

[31] *Ibid.*, pp. 30, 44, 283.

[32] *Ibid.*, pp. 60–61.

of their fathers. Of all the cultural conflicts that remain unresolved for the older generation, the most immediate is the attitude toward work. Work for the tribal Indian was, and is, secondary to living. Human needs and desires take precedence over commercial needs and demands, and this wreaks havoc with industrial work schedules and production quotas. Indians may work hard at economic survival, but not in the labor market. Many take odd jobs and seasonal work as much by choice as necessity.[33]

The relocation of industry on the reservations has proven to be relatively ineffective. One-third of the businesses have failed, with Indians losing tribal money on them. They financed these businesses, but didn't own or control them. There are now several tribal enterprises combining traditional patterns of communal organization with the commercial demands of a market economy. These have particular appeal to the younger generation, educated in modern technology and dreaming of a new tribalism.[34] These undertakings, however, are still few and far between. Many still have to leave the reservations in search of jobs. About half the Indians now live in cities, struggling with problems of urban poverty. Some try to supplement the reservation economy with part of their earnings. But the kinship system is stretched over great distances now, and it is frequently overwhelmed by the new tensions it experiences. It often reaches the breaking point.

> Poverty is not the worst enemy of the kinship family. The way of life of the dominant society, with its enticements and pressures, and the competitiveness of urban living, make the tribal way of sharing difficult.[35]

And yet poverty is still the enemy; there is too little for the family to share, and too many problems to solve without sufficient resources. Congregated together in cities, Indians may establish some form of ethnic community to fulfill the traditional functions of tribal life, but the old ways fail them out of their social context. Lost in the city and yearning for the land to which they are deeply attached, some return to the reservations. The emotional ties to their life and land are as intense as the economic problems are endemic. Such ties may be binding for generations to come, in spite of the pervasive and self-perpetuating poverty.

[33] *Ibid.,* pp. 127–28.
[34] *Ibid.,* pp. 128, 131–32.
[35] *Ibid.,* pp. 148, 171.

Negro Identity and Black Nationalism

Slavery stripped the Negro of his identity, and along with it, his sense of humanity. His deculturation was so systematic and so sweeping that it left him nothing but the pattern of enslavement that prevailed on the plantation. Coerced into adjustment as a slave, he had no choice but to accept his situation and thereby to become the most extreme case of *déraciné,* as Stonequist describes it, found in American society.[36] Slavery was so shattering an institution that the traditional culture of Afro-Americans was completely lost. Although they constituted 20 percent of the population of the early republic, Negroes were too geographically isolated and socially atomized for concerted collective action.[37] Rebellion, if it occurred, was effectively squelched.

Negroes came from a wide variety of ethnic groups in Africa, each speaking a different language. They were thus strange even to each other, which contributed to their deculturation. More critical, however, was the trauma of the "Middle Passage," the months in transit in slave depots, their final dispersion and mingling with American-born slaves. There was nothing slow about this process in its onset, and it was forcibly accelerated by the destruction of the family. Baptism and marriage were not encouraged for slaves; even common law unions were broken up by the sale of the partners. Children past infancy were often separated from their mothers.[38] Neither familial stability nor socialization to alternative values was possible under such conditions. Without any separate existence, let alone an independent one, Negroes adapted to a large degree the values and attitudes of the whites for whom they worked.

They internalized the dominant culture to the extent of acquiring a sense of their own inferiority. Why else would they be enslaved? The deculturation of the slaves was so ruthless that it robbed many of their self-respect, and they felt the inescapability of their status. Ultimately the social system of the antebellum South rested not only on the coercion of physical force, but also on the sullen acquiescence that accompanies ex-

---

[36] Everett V. Stonequist, "The Marginal Man: A Study in Personality and Culture Conflict," in Ernest W. Burgess and Donald J. Bogue, eds., *Contributions to Urban Sociology* (Chicago: University of Chicago Press, 1964), p. 336.

[37] Pierre L. van den Berghe, *Race and Racism* (New York: Wiley, 1967), p. 83.

[38] *Ibid.,* pp. 82–83.

treme degradation. And there is no greater degradation than slavery. Slaves were deculturated more quickly and completely even than Indians. Living within close proximity to their masters, they were forced to take on the alien culture of the oppressor.[39]

Such total detachment from the prior culture was accomplished in part through shock. Trauma inhered in the fact of enslavement itself as well as in the experiences that inducted Negroes into it. So severe was the mode of procurement and the type of authority to which they had to adjust for physical and psychic survival that two-thirds died during captivity and passage alone. For the remaining third, "the new adjustment, to absolute power in a closed system, involved infantilization, and the detachment was so complete that little trace of prior (and thus alternative) cultural sanctions for behavior and personality remained. . . ."[40]

With every connection to the past severed, the African culture of the Negro was in effect annihilated. None of it had much meaning any more, neither language nor kinship nor religion. Traditional values became unreal, and tribal patterns could not exist without anyone with whom to enact them.[41] Slavery was an extreme situation which, by definition, was unprecedented in the life of the individual; there was thus nothing that could guide the slave's conduct, except, of course, his master's orders. The only reciprocal role of relevance was that of master and slave, and that was a relationship of total subjugation for the Negro. Torn out of his original social context, he was forced to rely for his survival entirely on the white man who oppressed him. With his very existence at stake in the system of slavery, the Negro had no choice but to take his cultural cues from his master. The slave survived, in a word, by taking on those same norms that subjugated him.

So drastic a change in social conditions compelled an alteration of personality as well. Those who could not perform such a feat of adjustment died; some pined away, others got sick, and still others were killed in hopeless revolt. The experience was critically different from that of the European immigrant who remodeled his personality under the stress of ambition and the hope of advancement.

> The immediate goal of the slave system was to teach the Negro labor routines and to make effective aggression from his side impossible. . . . The

[39] *Ibid.*, pp. 83–84, 124.
[40] Stanley M. Elkins, *Slavery* (Chicago: University of Chicago Press, 1959), p. 88.
[41] *Ibid.*, p. 101.

slavery system was not a benign device for inducting the Negro into full participation in American life, but obviously a device for getting work done without regard to its effect on Negro personality. "Breaking in" was the term used . . . , and it was recognized as a separate and difficult process.[42]

The consequences of deculturation were rendered all the more inevitable by the futility of resistance. Each Negro encountered the condition of his enslavement alone, one by one facing the full force of white domination. Slaves could find little social support among themselves since few even spoke the same language, let alone shared the same values. Their culture was as remote as their country, and all continuity was disrupted. Only despair remained.

John Dollard suggests the contrast with the case of the Indians, where the conflict initially occurred between societies rather than between the individual and overwhelming social forces. The odds may have been against the Indian, but he had the support of an organized social structure. He had a culture, and he knew the land. His philosophy of life was integrally related to his physical setting, and he fought for his values as much as for his land—and as bitterly. Under these circumstances, Indians could face extermination rather than yield to slavery. It was the Negro, alone and alien, who was enslaved, and it was his isolation that helped to perpetuate and protect the indefinite tenure of his involuntary servitude.

> The other possible alternatives were an isolated death—which had no significance in the eyes of others, as did the death of an Indian fighting with his own group—flight, or accommodation. Flight was in the main impossible until Negroes were actively and illegally aided by Northern white people. It is suggested that these were the circumstances under which African Negroes accepted the inevitable and submitted to personality reorganization and accommodation to slave status in America.[43]

Slavery left indelible scars, for in becoming slaves, Negroes became more white than black. Even with emancipation, they were not free of the past any more than they were free from oppression. Segregation and subordination continue in the present; segregation is, in fact, a systematic way of enforcing subordination, a calculated and invidious device in race relations that makes use of legal means to maintain the second-class citizenship of Negroes. The deculturation of the Indians was a long, drawn-out

[42] John Dollard, *Caste and Class in a Southern Town* (Garden City, N.Y.: Doubleday Anchor Books, 1957), pp. 417.

[43] *Ibid.*, p. 420.

process that in the end was not entirely successful. That of the Negroes was quick and all too effective. The consequences are still to be seen in their identity and community (or the lack thereof). It is through segregation, as Kenneth Clark points out, that victims can be made to accommodate to their victimized status. They even learn to prefer to be set apart, thinking it beneficial rather than detrimental. "The fact remains that exclusion, rejection, and a stigmatized status are not desired and are not voluntary states."[44] Segregation simply compounds the problems of identity.

Even the protection such segregation affords may be debilitating. Those so enclosed already doubt their own worth; their cumulative experience with others has led to a negative self-image. They therefore seek psychological safety among each other, refusing to risk rejection by strangers. Someone who has been forced to be ashamed of his identity does not easily accept himself as a human being. Neither does he readily surrender his group identification nor his intergroup hostility.[45] Unfortunately the group identification of the Negro is not always sufficiently supportive. Members of the group are not often able to help each other; they may not even want to do so. Part of the social pathology of the ghetto, as we will see in the next chapter, is an unwillingness to make any personal sacrifice beyond those already required by the ghetto itself. *"The ghetto fails to prepare one for voluntary sacrifices precisely because it demands so many involuntary ones."*[46]

"For what if there is nothing," asks Erik Erikson, "in the generations past nor in the accessible resources of the contemporary community which would help to overcome the negative image held up to a minority?"[47] What indeed? This is the crux of the identity problem for the Negro. It is difficult to achieve a positive identity when there is a past to live down; and worse still, it is difficult to prevent the future from being premised on that past. With no access to the dominant values they have long since accepted, Negroes are likely to acquire a negative identity that is no different from the stereotyped images held up to them in the larger society.[48] Surrounded by scorn, with slavery still its source, Negroes may well come to despise themselves. Even in childhood games, the subject crops up.

[44] Kenneth B. Clark, *Dark Ghetto* (New York: Harper Torchbooks, 1965), p. 63.

[45] *Ibid.,* pp. 19–20.

[46] *Ibid.,* p. 189.

[47] Erik H. Erikson, *Identity: Youth and Crisis* (New York: Norton, 1968), p. 25.

[48] *Ibid.,* p. 303.

Piri Thomas reports that in a game of "dozens," an exchange of insults, he thought twice about becoming seriously offensive with a Negro friend with whom he has been joking:

> Was I trying to tell Brew that I'm better than he is 'cause he's only black and I'm a Puerto Rican dark-skin? Like his people copped trees on a white man's whim, and who ever heard of Puerto Ricans getting hung like that?[49]

For all the Negroes who have migrated north, there is still an occasional Negro who makes a southern pilgrimage as, for example, the artist in search of himself. He goes south not only to sorrow, but for identity. Claude Brown reveals the thinking behind such a trip:

> "Well, here's one place you *really* find out if you're Negro. If I go down there, am I gonna be a Negro to them or not?" But you never know if you don't go.[50]

Much is involved in this symbolic return to black roots. It is, above all, a way of coming to terms with the past in a present that most signifies slavery, a present whose history still shows in its social structure. The south provided more than the physical setting of slavery; it established institutionalized patterns of segregation. Ralph Ellison explains that in the south the Negro, like the white, also sees in terms of race. He doesn't exist in his own right because he doesn't exist as a person for others. The values of the southern Negro community have been pre-individual, "stressing the survival of the group rather than the assertion of individuality."[51]

The artist, seeking a self-achieved humanity, strives to transcend social categories. He thereby comes into conflict with his own community, a community that has defensively erected categories that enforce those of the dominant group. When all thinking is in terms of race, the conflict is as much with one's own as with the oppressor. Nowhere is this more so than in the south. For this reason the artist goes home again, to free himself from the categorical terms of color so that he can find his individual self. He cannot escape the past until he accepts it. The reality discovered,

[49] Piri Thomas, *Down These Mean Streets* (New York: New American Library, Signet Books, 1968), p. 123.

[50] Interview with Piri Thomas and Claude Brown, *The New York Times Book Review,* May 21, 1967, p. 46. Perhaps the most beautiful fictional portrayal of such a pilgrimage can be found in Jean Toomer, *Cane* (New York: Harper & Row, A Perennial Classic, 1923, 1969).

[51] Ralph Ellison, *Shadow and Act* (New York: Random House, 1953), pp. 83–84.

or recovered, by such a seeker has its own quality, a richness born of "its own insights into the human condition, its own strategies of survival." It is, after all, no mere sociological abstraction, but a human existence, however inhuman its conditions.[52]

In the south the Negro confronts "the obscene absurdity of his predicament" with the greatest immediacy. But nowhere is he really removed from the brutality within which he is formed. The artist may be as much a product of his reading as of his experience, but what all Negroes have in common is their shared suffering, "an identity of passions" that comes out of their imposed alienation.[53] It is questionable whether the "concord of sensibilities" that results from their painful history constitutes a subculture. Ellison, in criticizing Myrdal's conceptualizaion of Negro life, argues that it is more than a secondary reaction to the primary pressures exerted by the dominant group. No group can survive only by reacting, and Negro culture is not simply the product of social pathology.[54] There is even an occasional sociologist to claim that the following is *not* true.

> Whatever is different or distinct in his [the Negro's] life style represents a kind of negative reaction to exclusion from the white society. The Negro is the creation of the white. Like the criminal he is a pathology, a reaction-formation to the problems of inadequate opportunities to achieve and to compete in the American system.[55]

It is indeed true that the Negro artist may achieve a separate and self-determined identity, in part by accepting reality at its worst and thus transcending it. There is scarcely a black novel that does not portray the plunge into the depths of despair that precedes coming to terms with the socially imposed negative images of the self. It is difficult, however, to ascertain such cultural affirmation in the average Negro. E. Franklin Frazier agrees that it is possible to turn to the group experience for materials for artistic creation, and even for a source of some tradition. There is, however, he contends, no unique Negro culture, and thus no independent basis for building a community. Negroes had no choice but to take over the dominant cultural forms, although they lived by these patterns in social isolation. They are, therefore, in a different position than any other minority group. "The Negro has no source to draw on outside of America

[52] *Ibid.*, p. 112.
[53] *Ibid.*, pp. 116–17, 131, 263, 298–99.
[54] *Ibid.*, pp. 315–16.
[55] John Horton, "Order and Conflict Theories of Social Problems as Competing Ideologies," *American Journal of Sociology,* Vol. 71, No. 6 (May 1966), p. 711.

and only an inadequately assimilated American tradition from his past in this country."[56]

There is now talk of "soul" suggestive of a subculture. Until recently there have been lower-class adaptations to the fact that the dominant goals that are accepted cannot be attained. There can be no consistent commitment to values to which there is no access, but that doesn't mean that the social patterns of the black masses are preferred, least of all by them. Their circumstances are ascribed without choice and therefore cannot be said to be determined by values. What lower-class Negroes do have, however, is a shared social reason for not achieving accepted goals. There is less sense of personal failure when there is categorical exclusion, and they know that no one of their status is allowed to succeed. Lower-class Negroes, nevertheless, have grown more ambivalent about their chances; they are now less certain of the impermeability of the group boundaries that have debarred them in the past from social participation. It is in this context that the vocabulary of soul has emerged in response to a new uncertainty in the black situation.[57]

Young men especially are feeling the pressures. They have had even less chance than their female counterparts in the lower class to become competent in the dominant culture. This exacerbates their doubts about their own worth at a time when they cannot easily explain lack of achievement. If, as it is said, the social structure is changing, then failure might reflect inability rather than absence of opportunity. The function of soul then is to idealize the accomplishments of the lower-class and to proclaim the superiority of its way of life. Self-doubts are eased as the soul brothers reassure themselves of their success since having "soul" is by shared definition superior to having anything else. Once more convinced of their own worth, they thereby belong to a select group rather than to a residual category. There is one difficulty, however. For all the emotional commitment to the concept of soul, there is little intellectual clarity about its content.[58]

The rhetoric of soul is reinforced by such symbols as food and music to express the ideals and avoid the realities of lower-class life in the black

---

[56] E. Franklin Frazier, "The Ambivalence of Negro Intellectuals," in Francis L. Broderick and August Meier, eds., *Negro Protest Thought in the Twentieth Century* (Indianapolis, Ind.: Bobbs-Merrill, 1965), p. 99.

[57] Ulf Hannerz, "What Negroes Mean by 'Soul,'" *Trans-Action*, Vol. 5, No. 8 (July–August 1968), pp. 59–60.

[58] *Ibid.*, pp. 60–61.

ghetto. It does not add up to a culture, yet there is something in it that serves as a source of self-respect. Soul is a social style, a way of presenting the self to others, rather than a way of life, but a style that is black, not white. As such, it has sufficient meaning that any action program, even a job-training program, that attempts to change the style by modifying the manner of speech and dress is experienced as threatening and treated accordingly. Any such white threat to black self-respect is subtly subverted. Women are inclined to have a different orientation toward the dominant society and to share the value it places on respect and respectability. "For the men, on the other hand, becoming a Negro (as opposed to a 'nigger') meant giving up much that they considered positive." The style of lower-class men has developed around their estrangement from the larger society, and it is essentially antagonistic to the dominant culture.[59]

Perhaps soul is a black antidote to having become sociologically white, even if it does not constitute an encompassing cultural answer. The social background of Negroes is not Africa, but slavery; their values evolved out of the master-slave relationship. No prior loyalty to an independent African culture survived to provide resistance to new patterns of behavior. The very nature of slavery contributed to the prestige of all that attached to the master class.[60] Soul is a way of deflating the status of everything white that smacks of slavery without solving the problem of being black. "The Negro's central problem is to discover his identity, or to create an identity."[61] He must invent himself more than most, and he has neither the social nor psychological resources for such invention; only the exceptional are capable of so much creativity.

Since Negroes were formed by American society, they must find their identity within it. It is one thing to recapture an African past, to reestablish a history prior to slavery; it is something else to solve the problem of identification in the present. In so doing, slavery cannot be overlooked. It must be accepted

as an experience that explains a large part of their present predicament. Only if they understand *why* they are what they are, can Negroes change

[59] David Wellman, "The *Wrong* Way to Find Jobs for Negroes," *Trans-Action,* Vol. 5, No. 5 (April 1968), pp. 10, 14–15.
[60] Hortense Powdermaker, *After Freedom* (New York: Atheneum, 1968), p. 358.
[61] Charles E. Silberman, *Crisis in Black and White* (New York: Random House, Vintage Books, 1965), p. 166.

what they are. Identity is not something that can be found; it must be created.[62]

Soul is not sufficient. The Negro is an American, but Americans define the Negro as inferior. Hence the Negro disavows the dominant culture that demeans his humanity. Soul may help the Negro to reject those who reject him, but it does not establish a cultural alternative; it lacks sufficient concrete content. This is, nevertheless, what the Negro needs in his increasing sense of relative deprivation. With the recent independence of African nations, his expectations are higher and his tolerance is lower. He sets a dearer price on his pride and will no longer accept the old terms of a subordinate relationship.[63] Such group pride has considerable sociological significance.

> It is hard for a group to build an organization and a common loyalty on shared misfortune without a counterbalancing faith in its own value. If, instead, the idea of being Negro could be made elevating and positive, then the dilemma could be solved.[64]

Black nationalism is a powerful source of social honor with potential for building a strong community. By asserting that Negroes constitute a distinctive nation, it permits them to claim to be a group of the same order as the dominant group. This legitimates the demand to control their own social, economic, and political institutions. Whether or not the concept of national autonomy is applicable to Negroes, black nationalism succeeds in overcoming feelings of racial inferiority. It thus fulfills a psychological function even without achieving the political goal of self-rule.[65] In fact, black nationalism fulfills many of the traditional functions of the ethnic community of religious minorities.

The search for identity is a quest for dignity, a meaning that gives life purpose. Nationalist leaders attempt to arouse group consciousness as a source of identity and to strive by collective effort to redeem black communities. They appeal in particular to lower-class, urban Negroes, who are compelled to remain on the periphery of the larger society, enclosed within their own ghetto. It is these Negroes who are most alienated from the dominant group that demands that they conform to its material and moral standards while denying them the economic and social resources

---

[62] *Ibid.*, pp. 184–85.
[63] Michael Banton, *Race Relations* (New York: Basic Books, 1967), p. 162.
[64] *Ibid.*, p. 357.
[65] *Ibid.*, pp. 359, 361.

for doing so.[66] There is little internal cohesion and communal involvement among the black masses, in large part because they have no significant say in their communities; they do not determine the outcome of social decisions nor the norms by which decisions are made.

> Furthermore, the Negro community provides few or no criteria by which its members can meaningfully interpret and relate the dominant white culture and the realities of American society to their specific experiences. The Negro masses cannot participate fully and responsibly in their communities.[67]

The realities of the lower-class situation reinforce a sense of separateness. There is a feeling of dual alienation that is not always articulated; lower-class Negroes are estranged from middle-class Negroes as well as from whites. They are, as a result, without any sense of belonging in society, and they are without identity. Resentful of the incomparably better position of the middle class, they are themselves often rootless and restless. There is no one with whom they can identify. The lower class is necessarily preoccupied with survival. Their needs are so pressing that they resort to opportunism or seek some addictive escape. The Black Muslims provide a social context in which shaken pride can be restored. Confidence is regained in the pursuit of a meaningful goal.[68]

Upwardly mobile, lower-class Negroes join the Muslims out of a desire for self-improvement and a need for identity. As members they acquire self-esteem and social recognition in their practice of middle-class habits. In their quest for respect and respectability, Black Muslims "strive for traditional American middle-class values while maintaining their identity with the Negro community."[69] Dominant stereotypes are repudiated and human dignity asserted in the idealized images of racial pride. Yet there is an anomaly even in this nationalism; its way of life is not ethnically distinct. The cultural values it embodies are derived from the American mainstream. Only their common suffering unites Negroes and separates them from the rest of society, and that unity has its source in slavery.[70]

> The "nationalism" of the American Negro is not voluntary, prompted by a desire to set himself apart in order to preserve some cultural values.

---

[66] E. U. Essien-Udom, *Black Nationalism* (New York: Dell, 1962), pp. 17, 23.
[67] *Ibid.*, p. 26.
[68] *Ibid.*, pp. 27–28, 353–56.
[69] *Ibid.*, pp. 95, 120, 362.
[70] C. Eric Lincoln, *The Black Muslims in America* (Boston: Beacon Press, 1961), pp. 43–45.

It is, rather, a defensive response to external forces—hostile forces which threaten his creative existence. It is a unity born of the wish not to conserve but to *escape* a set of conditions.[71]

It is the unresolved dilemma of the Negro to have adopted the cultural heritage of the dominant group that excludes him. Black nationalism reconstructs history and provides the glorious ancestry that shores up self-respect. Even more essential, it establishes the certainty of a brilliant future in which the inherent superiority of the race will triumph.[72] It may still be difficult to be proud of the past, but the slogan "Black Power" creates pride in the future. It is not really relevant that Negroes cannot create a parallel economy or an autonomous government in the context of American society. Any significant gain in economic and political power of Negroes increases the viability of the black community and enhances its bargaining power with the dominant group. In the ensuing social conflict, a sense of peoplehood is forged and a genuine group pride emerges.[73]

Deculturation and Acculturation

The Indians, much deculturated, have restructured a pan-Indianism out of a variety of tribal values. Negroes have been and remain entirely deculturated. Many have therefore attempted to resurrect an Afro-Americanism as the basis for the black nationalism that serves as a source of identity, if not culture. The common social impulse of both movements is separatism. It may be a necessary first step toward future integration. Since ethnic status and the minority situation are not synonymous, a deculturated group strives to reacquire the ethnicity it lost in subjugation. In this way, it becomes, among other things, an ethnic group in its own right and a minority in the established sense. By reestablishing its past, the deculturated group is able to justify its present minority situation, and perhaps to follow the precedent of previous ethnic minorities.

A social paradox may inhere in this two-step process. Groups that were forcibly deculturated may become ethnic only to acculturate again, this

---

[71] *Ibid.*, p. 45.
[72] *Ibid.*, pp. 44, 231.
[73] Lewis M. Killian, *The Impossible Revolution?* (New York: Random House, Studies in Sociology, 1968), pp. 138–39, 157.

time voluntarily. Having once more affirmed their ethnicity, they may then be able to afford to acculturate and to follow the pattern of social pluralism already established by the religious minorities. There is, of course, no guarantee that any kind of integration will eventually emerge. It is, however, unlikely to emerge unless there is first renewed ethnicity as its necessary (but not sufficient) condition. Culture is, after all, the pre-requisite of acculturation. A group not only acculturates to something, it acculturates from something. Acculturation thus encompasses two cultures in its conceptualization.

What the deculturated groups are trying to do then is to create a culture for themselves. They are trying to fill in that which is missing in the process of acculturation, what they bring to acculturation rather than what they take from the dominant group. All culture is an artifact; these cultures are simply more obviously so in the social visibility of their con-scious creation. Such enacted cultures may be artificial to a large extent, but they help to resolve the crisis of identity for deculturated groups. If ethnicity can be affirmed, then acculturation can be affirmative; in the absence of the original culture, acculturation is imposed without consent.

This crisis of identity is even more severe for Negroes than for Indians. The black ghetto in which most of them are enclosed by and large lacks any compensatory characteristics. There are no values defining social desirability other than those of the dominant group. What Negroes want is what they don't have due to categorical exclusion. Without the possi-bility of achievement, there is not the hope of aspiration.

> It may be argued that a meaningful and satisfying Negro culture can come into existence in a pluralistic American society only through an antecedent state of black nationalism. In turn, it is through the myth of Black Power that the new radicals are attempting to create this black nationalism.[74]

Until it succeeds in doing so, the problems of community reflect those of identity. We will turn now to look at the contemporary Negro community and the problems that develop from its lack of both structure and suf-ficiency.

---

[74] *Ibid.*, p. 160.

Chapter 10

The Community without Community

THE impact of the minority situation is intensified in the absence of a viable ethnic tradition and the social alternatives it makes possible. Culture is at the core of community. Negroes, having experienced the most extreme deculturation, suffer the most severe structural consequences in their communal life. Left only with the cultural remnants acquired in a history of slavery, Negroes, unique among minorities, lack any independent source of status. This renders them more than usually susceptible to the derogation of the dominant group. Their American heritage rests on a relationship with whites in which they have been subjected to the utmost degradation, and they continue to endure its psychological effects. Such effects can be seen not only in a sometimes unsuccessful struggle for identity, but also in a community that is not always a community.

The functions of a minority community are rarely fulfilled by the black ghettos found in the big cities. There are few indigenous institutions, and those are controlled by outsiders, who are not concerned about meeting the needs of members of the community. The traditional ethnic community was built around the family and the church. Among Negroes, as we will see in this chapter, the church has little influence where, and with whom, it would be most critical. And the family, with fewer resources than are available to other minorities, is even more strained. The community is thus weak at the core; its other institutions are secondary, too peripheral to fulfill the special requirements of a minority group. Voluntary associations are usually social in orientation, and such formal organizations as defense agencies are frequently, and of necessity, geared to the dominant group, whose interests remain vested in the inferiority of Negroes. There are simply too few social and psychological resources within the community for self-help (which is why the need for it is stressed by black nationalists).

Socialization into Nonidentity

The problems of living in such a community set in at the start of each new life, and they are rarely solved during its course. They are imposed from the outside by the dominant group, but it is the members of the minority community who must live with these problems, whatever their capacity to cope with them. Because of this, their children must be socialized into subordinate status. They learn very young that they are different and disprivileged. "Sooner or later each child in a minority group learns how human beings are classified and where he is located within this scheme." They learn from the way they are treated and from what they are told.[1] Parents must somehow explain the facts of minority life to their children. In so doing, they may transmit a communal ideology that counteracts categorical treatment by providing an alternative basis for self-esteem.

Presumably the family and its community constitute "a protective capsule for its young," although there comes a time when the young can no longer be protected. The point at which they encounter the prejudice and discrimination of the dominant group is a learning experience that often leads to a moral crisis.[2] The discovery by children of their minority status in the larger society may be traumatic, particularly if the anticipatory socialization has been inadequate. Proper, and protective, preparation for members of the disadvantaged minority can only be provided by a community with sufficient resources and supporting institutions. No group has a more serious problem in socialization than Negroes, nor more severe difficulties in personality development as a result.

Without a communal ideology to define an independent identity there can only be socialization into the nonidentity of personal invisibility and

[1] Tamotsu Shibutani and Kian M. Kwan, with contributions by Robert H. Billigmeier, *Ethnic Stratification* (New York: Macmillan, 1965), p. 296.
[2] Erving Goffman, *Stigma: Notes on the Management of Spoiled Identity* (Englewood Cliffs, N.J.: Prentice-Hall, A Spectrum Book, 1963), pp. 32–33.

racial visibility. Frequently the family feels that it must suppress individuality rather than encourage its emergence lest its assertion endanger their collective safety. In the absence of sufficient support from other institutions, there is a chronic awareness within the family of the dominant group and its dangers for the Negro. Horace Cayton points out that, "Fear and insecurity of the parents is transmitted to the child long before he realizes that he is a Negro and what that implies in our culture." Children so conditioned are not given the protection and security they need. They do, however, learn to adapt to fear, an unhappily necessary prerequisite for their future survival. The constant presence of fear in their lives prepares them by providing them with some immunity to it. It may not function protectively, but without such conditioning, they would be paralyzed by anxiety, as would anyone else faced with their categorical circumstances for the first time. No member of the dominant group would be likely to survive it.[3]

Socialization into subordination is a difficult, not to say heartbreaking, task undertaken with some trepidation by any parent of sense and sensibility. An awareness of their situation takes hold very early among Negro children. Since so little protection can be provided, they know about their status by the time they are six years old. In fact, many of them identify themselves by their color by age two or three. Much of their first knowledge comes in subtle, indirect ways such as hearing their parents discuss their hard lot; some of it is acquired gradually through observation that permits them to see what difference color makes. Parents are at a loss for explanations, and most often they simply say, "That's the way it is"—and offer cautions for living with it.[4] Even so articulate a parent as J. Saunders Redding cannot find words adequate for the occasion of his child's first experience with prejudice.

> This was the deeper infection, and I didn't know how to deal with it. Words were poultices to seal the infection in. I could recall them from my own childhood in answer to a "why?" For children are not born with answers. Words spoken by my parents, my teachers, my friends. Words could seal in the infection and seal in also the self that might never break

[3] Horace R. Cayton, "The Psychology of the Negro Under Discrimination," in Arnold M. Rose and Caroline B. Rose, eds., *Minority Problems* (New York: Harper & Row, 1965), pp. 211–12.

[4] Hortense Powdermaker, *After Freedom* (New York: Atheneum, 1968), pp. 215–16; John Dollard, *Caste and Class in a Southern Town* (Garden City, N.Y.: Doubleday Anchor Books, 1957), pp. 68, 255.

through again except with extreme luck. But I had no choice save to use them. I told him about prejudice. No one has ever made the anatomy of prejudice simple enough for children.[5]

Only the exceptional can invent an identity out of the Negro condition. Sometimes it is the arts that serve as a source of alternative socialization so that some do succeed in shaping the beautiful out of being black. Ralph Ellison writes, for example, that he was formed "by composers, novelists, and poets who spoke to me of more interesting and freer ways of life."[6] Without such esthetic options for establishing an identity, there is only socialization into the problem of being black without any solution inhering in the process itself. (This may well be the special significance of the arts for all minorities, the potential for the formation of individual identity as well as the discovery of beauty in being—being anything, whatever it is, in the face of categorical treatment.) What is transmitted then are strategies for survival.

The focus is on how to get by with the dominant group rather than on how to get ahead, perhaps because there is no conviction that there can be any achievement. The content of socialization varies, of course, with class and with region, but there is a sense of shared fate among all Negroes that is expressed in the common frustrations of their minority situation. To some extent, the ways of dealing with their suffering have developed into cultural forms, if not communal institutions, that are passed on from one generation to the next within the segregated group.[7] It is socialization to segregation that in turn perpetuates segregation. And if culture has sometimes been created by the emergence of artistic forms (as it certainly has in the instance of Negro music), a community has not yet been built that is based upon it. Alone, esthetic expression is not enough to constitute a community; it encompasses too little of the lives of most minority members.

Instilling fear in their children follows naturally from the parents' own fears. Especially in the southern family, children must be instructed in the roles they will have to assume in their relations with the dominant group. They are taught defensive and compensatory behavior lest they make mistakes and thereby risk endangering their families. Many are

[5] J. Saunders Redding, *On Being Negro in America* (Indianapolis, Ind.: Bobbs-Merrill, Charter Books, 1962), p. 110.
[6] Ralph Ellison, *Shadow and Act* (New York: Random House, 1953), p. 117.
[7] J. Milton Yinger, *A Minority Group in American Society* (New York: McGraw-Hill, 1965), p. 92.

afraid of reprisals for the misdeeds of children, however unintentional. "Accordingly, great care is taken by parents in teaching children 'to stay in their places' in order to shield them from the humiliating experiences of the caste system."[8] Individuality is thus discouraged for the sake of communal self-defense; someone who asserts himself as a person may bring disaster down upon the whole community. Negroes have a variety of interpersonal methods for controlling in-group behavior and preventing possible violations of caste. "The primary technique in its enforcement is to impress the Negro child with the omniscience and omnipotence of the whites to the point that whites appear as ahuman. . . ." Since the impulse toward individual assertion and aggression must be annihilated by the family and community, however, it is they who may be regarded as the oppressors. Their protective intention about the safety of the children (and themselves) may not be perceived.[9]

The impact of such socialization is pervasive, and no area of the Negro child's life, whether in the north or in the south, is unaffected. Robert Coles, in studying children in the desegregation of schools, observed the process:

> The task, then, is one of making sure the child is afraid: of whites, and of the punishment his parents fearfully inflict upon him whenever he fails to follow their suit. The child's bravado or outrage must be curbed. In my experience even two- and three-year-old Negro children have already learned the indirection, the guile needed for survival. They have also learned their relative weakness, their need to be ready to run fast, to be alert and watchful. They have learned that white children, as well as adults, are big, strong, and powerful; and that such power is specifically related to the colored man's defenselessness.[10]

In this sense being Negro serves to organize the experiences of childhood; it renders them coherent with shared racial interpretations, which are in turn reinforced by the sanction of parental punishment. It is through this process of socialization that children acquire all the feelings appropriate to a subordinate status, the feelings of inferiority and worthlessness and their accompanying anger and resentment. In this way, they are prepared, long and painfully, for being black in a white world.[11]

[8] Mozell C. Hill, "A Comparative Analysis of the Social Organization of the All-Negro Society in Oklahoma," *Social Forces,* Vol. 25, No. 1 (October 1946), p. 74.
[9] Ellison, *op. cit.,* pp. 84, 90–91.
[10] Robert Coles, *Children of Crisis* (Boston: Little, Brown & Co., 1964), p. 67.
[11] *Ibid.,* pp. 336–37.

There is no confusion, at least among southern children, about the meaning of being Negro. It has its coherence as well as its chaos, and children acquire a rather rigid and fearful certainty of their social position, both present and future. They have had it beaten into them more often than not, and they know the score, at least about their own situation. They have a shrewd, calculating awareness of the rules of the racial game.[12] Socialization, like all his life, does more than toughen the child, it conditions him to its problems. There may be a burden to bear, but so also is there a discipline for doing so.[13] The child not only learns his fate, he knows what he needs to survive, and how to make use of this knowledge. This process of socialization is a conscious one, whose effects are intended. Coles quotes at length one mother expressing feelings common to many:

> I guess we all don't like white people too much deep inside. You could hardly expect us to, after what's happened all these years. It's in our bones to be afraid of them, and bones have a way of staying around even when everything else is gone. . . . White people are a real danger to us until we learn how to live with them. So if you want your kids to live long, they have to grow up scared of whites; and the way they get scared is through us. . . . So I make them store it in the bones, way inside, and then no one sees it. Maybe in a joke we'll have once in a while, or something like that, you can see what we feel inside, but mostly it's buried. . . . The colored man, he has to hide what he really feels even from himself. Otherwise there would be too much pain—too much.[14]

That the price of such socialization is inordinately high is confirmed by Negro psychiatrists in their clinical experiences. Grier and Cobbs point out that while the Negro mother gives her child life, she must also wound him deeply so that he may survive. She hurts her child to inoculate him against the cruelty to come; in response to that hurt there may be hatred.[15] Lee Rainwater suggests that one of the effects of segregation is to mask the ultimate enemy. The process of victimization operates within the family; an understanding of its source comes later. It may come too late to change the conceptions of self (and other Negroes) acquired in familial intimacy. Much of this knowledge about the victimized status of the Negro is derived from experience within the ghetto rather than with the dominant

---

[12] *Ibid.*, p. 339.

[13] Ellison, *op. cit.*, p. 112.

[14] Coles, *op. cit.*, pp. 66–67.

[15] William H. Grier and Price M. Cobbs, *Black Rage* (New York: Basic Books, 1968), pp. 174–75.

group, experience that may be all the more traumatic for the child because of the closeness of its source.[16] The resulting hostility is then turned on the group itself, if not also the immediate family, while the dominant group remains at a safe social distance, too far removed from the perception of a child to be seen as relevant in his victimization.

Although such experience toughens the young Negro sufficiently so he can function in the ghetto, it impedes his ability to function in any other context. Growing up in the lower class requires an acute awareness of the impossibility of finding a self-sufficient and satisfying way of life. As the child learns this lesson, most devastatingly in his own family, he also learns to defend himself as best he can. With mounting frustration at his social entrapment, he strikes out at others around him, often unmasking their self-protective pretensions. His prime target may be his parents, whose rationalizations for failure he knowingly and effectively attacks. Members of the family may therefore feel least secure with each other.

> The result is a peculiar strength and a pervasive weakness. The strength involves the ability to tolerate and defend against degrading verbal and physical aggressions from others and not to give up completely. The weakness involves the inability to embark hopefully on any course of action that might make things better, particularly action which involves cooperating and trusting attitudes toward others.[17]

Children in the slum are exposed not only to experience, but to a rhetoric that conceptualizes them in a way that communicates to them their essential weakness. It conveys the understanding that they can expect little gratification of their needs, and even this must be sought by less than straightforward means.[18] It is small wonder that they begin to feel debased at so young an age. Because lower-class children are so often left on their own to find company on the street corner, the cut-off point in parental control and emotional support comes early. By the time children are five or six years old, parents begin to lose confidence in their ability to control them. Consequently there is also diminished willingness to give children their attention. Influences outside the family are thus more important (and start sooner) in the socialization of the lower class than

[16] Lee Rainwater, "Crucible of Identity: The Negro Lower-Class Family," *Daedalus*, Winter, 1966, pp. 204–5.
[17] *Ibid.*, pp. 203–4.
[18] *Ibid.*, pp. 205–6.

of the middle class.[19] On the streets they learn such strategies of survival as manipulation and coercion, whatever it takes to get others to give them what they want.[20] The categorical condition of Negroes is such that they cannot expect to get what they want by asking for it; hence they acquire the deviousness associated with their subordination.

Children, at least in the lower class, are thus taught not only to act the subordinate role, but to think and feel it.[21] Parents may have relatively high educational aspirations for their children, but they lack knowledge about how to achieve these goals. Nor do they know what to do to motivate their children.[22] Mostly they are concerned that their children stay out of trouble and be able to earn a living. The greatest anxiety of the youth of Kent themselves, for example, is about getting a job.[23]

"Learning that one is Negro is one thing; knowing what to do about it is another." The patterns of adjustment to minority status are standardized among Negro youth, passed on to them by parents and peers.[24] They learn that reserve, to say the least, is required in any relationship with whites; no white is to be trusted since his loyalty is to his own kind. Without the possibility of intimacy between individuals of the two races, there are stringent limits on permissible behavior with the dominant group, and the young rapidly learn the necessary restrictions. This is how they learn to "get along"—without getting into trouble. This is also how they learn to accept segregation as if it were a social inevitability. "The typical family is no organ of frontal attack on discrimination." Its satisfactions are sought in terms of the status quo.[25]

Although lower-class youth appear to accommodate to their subordinate status, they do not always withdraw into passivity. Their conflicts about their social inferiority and consequent conceptions of themselves are expressed in resentment toward the dominant group and in sporadic out-

---

[19] Hylan Lewis, *Culture, Class and Poverty* (Washington, D.C.: CROSS-TELL, 1967), p. 3.

[20] Rainwater, *op. cit.,* p. 207.

[21] Jessie Bernard, *Marriage and Family Among Negroes* (Englewood Cliffs, N.J.: Prentice-Hall, A Spectrum Book, 1966), p. 147.

[22] Lewis, *op. cit.,* p. 5.

[23] Hylan Lewis, *Blackways of Kent* (New Haven, Conn.: College & University Press, 1964), pp. 24–25.

[24] Robert L. Sutherland, *Color, Class, and Personality* (Washington, D.C.: American Council on Education, 1942), p. 42.

[25] Lewis, *Blackways, op. cit.,* pp. 109–10, 112.

bursts of aggression among themselves.[26] They try to get away with as much as they can. Frazier quotes one boy as follows:

> If you know how to flatter and "jive" white people, you can get farther than they expect "niggers" to go. I usually make a big joke of it and act the part of a clown. I generally get just what I'm after. After all, I think that's all white people want anyway. They just want "niggers" to recognize them as superior, and I'm the man to play their game. I don't care what he says or does as long as he kicks in.[27]

Middle-class youngsters are not as accommodated to a subordinate status. Ambitious for mobility, they resent the discrimination of the dominant group. They learn to behave "properly" in interracial situations, but they do not believe they are inferior. Critical of lower-class improprieties, their motivation to maintain respectability is high. The upper class tries to protect its young by avoiding interracial situations and thereby preventing even the pretense of inferiority.[28]

The avoidance of accommodation, whether in appearance or actuality, is a luxury few can afford, however. "Few individuals escape some variety of social or personal insecurity." This is all the more so because the members of any Negro community are disproportionately lower class, living in a socially isolated world that is economically dependent on the dominant group.[29] In such isolation, youngsters have few approved avenues of self-expression. Cultural alternatives are limited, and there are not many patterns for emulation. In some areas, such as the Black Belt, there is so little contact with the outside world that children don't know about other Negroes and their achievements. They are uninformed about those in whom they could take pride and whose precedent they might follow.[30] For themselves, they have such grave misgivings about obtaining employment they even doubt the utility of education.[31]

It is their economic suppression, and not their social segregation, that is the source of greatest resentment for all Negro youngsters. The injustices of whites—and the insults—are disturbing even to those who are other-

[26] E. Franklin Frazier, *Negro Youth at the Crossways* (Washington, D.C.: American Council on Education, 1940), p. 41.

[27] *Ibid.,* p. 51.

[28] *Ibid.,* pp. 55–57, 63.

[29] Charles S. Johnson, *Growing Up in the Black Belt* (Washington, D.C.: American Council on Education, 1941), p. 72.

[30] *Ibid.,* pp. 228, 255.

[31] Frazier, *op. cit.,* pp. 134, 267.

wise indifferent to their isolation.[32] The incumbent insecurity is so great that the structure of the family is affected as much as the substance and style of its socialization. Half of the families in Johnson's study of Black Belt youngsters were of various types other than nuclear.

> The effects of these irregular structures upon youth at the very beginning of socialization are inescapable. They appear in the family, the frustrations, timidity, overcompensations, and various antisocial activities.[33]

Adaptations of Family Life

Social disorganization is not necessarily characteristic of Negro families, not even in the lower class, although stabilization certainly increases with status.[34] It is nevertheless difficult for them to provide the nurturing their children need. Most particularly in the lower class "the black family is prevented from performing its most essential function—its *raison d'être*—protection of its members." Living in the social isolation of their categorical status, men and women are often unable to make a whole life for themselves, and the consequences are perpetrated upon their children, whom they cannot shelter sufficiently.[35] There is, of course, considerable diversity in the child-rearing practices of low-income families, ranging from concerned behavior to extreme neglect. There are those whose conduct of life is conspicuously disorganized in terms of their own immediate needs as well as in terms of dominant standards, but most families express middle-class values of stability and security, at least verbally. They are simply not able to live up to them.[36]

> Parents, with few exceptions, do not prefer or approve the circumstances in which they now live and in which their children are being brought up.

[32] Johnson, *op. cit.,* p. 288.

[33] *Ibid.,* p. 78.

[34] E. Franklin Frazier, "The Negro Family in Chicago," in Ernest W. Burgess and Donald J. Bogue, eds., *Contributions to Urban Sociology* (Chicago: University of Chicago Press, 1964), pp. 405, 410.

[35] Grier and Cobbs, *op. cit.,* pp. 81–83.

[36] Hylan Lewis, "Culture, Class, and Family Life Among Low-Income Urban Negroes," in Arthur M. Ross and Herbert Hill, eds., *Employment, Race, and Poverty* (New York: Harcourt, Brace & World, A Harbinger Book, 1967), pp. 155, 157, 169.

Even in the case of the most neglectful parents, the evidence points to the fact that they ascribe no virtue to neglectful behavior in themselves or in others or to the neighborhood disorganization and poor housing.[37]

Most behavior in the lower class is a pragmatic response to material circumstances; it is not a function of any distinctive ethnic values of marriage and family. The values of marriage and family are no different from those of the larger society. Low-income mothers, like all mothers, "want and prefer their men to be strong and supportive in marriage, family, and community relationships." Their husbands, however, cannot fulfill their economic expectations. Even with employment, there is little reward for hard work, and the families lead necessarily circumscribed lives.[38] The economic and social roles expected of lower-class men as husbands and fathers are the same as those played by members of the middle class, but their capacity to enact them is different. The relatively frequent dissolution of lower-class marriages is a result of the disadvantaged economic position of the men. Their status in the family is undermined, and their self-esteem suffers to the point where they are not willing to struggle with the incumbent responsibilities. Marriage, however, (neither its lack nor its loss) is by no means a matter of indifference.[39]

Quite clearly these patterns of behavior represent fragmentary (and not always functional) adaptations to economic necessity rather than an integrated way of life. There is no distinctive ethnic culture, but an acceptance of dominant values to which lower-class Negroes are all too frequently unable to adhere. The consequences for family life are severe. They know they live differently than others, and they are likely to think that their patterns of behavior are the only possible ones under their circumstances. But lower-class Negroes do consider the more stable family forms more desirable. The fact that they do so aggravates the tension within the family.

The existence of such ideas about normal family life represents a recurrent source of stress within families as individuals become aware that they are failing to measure up to the ideals, or as others within the family and

[37] *Ibid.*, p. 157.

[38] *Ibid.*, pp. 158, 169.

[39] Hylan Lewis, "Agenda Paper No. V: The Family: Resources for Change—Planning Sessions for the White House Conference 'To Fulfill These Rights,' November 16–18, 1965," in Lee Rainwater and William L. Yancey, *The Moynihan Report and the Politics of Controversy* (Cambridge, Mass.: M.I.T. Press, 1967), pp. 325–26, 333–34.

outside it use the ideas as an aggressive weapon for criticizing each other's performance.[40]

Because dominant norms are accepted, members of these families have a chronic sense of failing and being failed. It is for this reason that even adults are likely to blame the family (and thus each other) for their frustrations, whose source in the structured patterns of their minority situation they do not always understand. "The effect of the caste system . . . is to bring home through a chain of cause and effect all of the victimization processes." Unlike earlier ethnic enclaves, the black ghetto affords little comfort and security to counteract categorical status; it thereby exacerbates the difficulties of its members rather than alleviates them, for as much frustration is experienced within its confines as in the larger society.[41] When a husband cannot support his family, he has a sense of shame that intensifies his feeling of failure. To avoid hating himself any more than he already does, he may well turn his hatred against his family, or simply eliminate all feeling for them in order to protect his ego. When his wife goes to work, as she usually does since she has an easier time finding a job, the reversal of roles may strain the marital relationship to the breaking point.[42]

> The result, all too frequently, is more than just psychic withdrawal. Unable to play the usual male role, the husband all too often tries to demonstrate his potency through a display of sexual prowess. But the effort fails as it must, and so he begins to wander and ultimately leaves for good.[43]

Financial support is the principal obligation that is not met by the lower-class husband. It is the pressure of the wife's expectation about money that usually leads him to leave her. The wife wants her husband to be a full-time member of the family with a public commitment to it. "Most important of all, perhaps, she wants him to be *head of the family,* not only to take an interest and demonstrate concern but to take responsibility and to make decisions." And the men themselves want marriage; they recognize it as a passage into adult responsibility. It also has higher status and greater respectability than consensual unions. In their experience, however, marriage doesn't work. The very fact that its rights and duties are clearly

[40] Rainwater, *op. cit.,* pp. 182–83.

[41] *Ibid.,* p. 200.

[42] Charles E. Silberman, *Crisis in Black and White* (New York: Random House, Vintage Books, 1965), pp. 117–18.

[43] *Ibid.,* p. 119.

defined intensifies their sense of failure when they are unable to fulfill its role expectations. Nevertheless, they do marry, and thus when they fail, they do so in an area that they themselves consider critical to their manhood.[44] To stay married would be to live with failure.

> In self-defense, the husband retreats to the streetcorner. Here, where the measure of man is considerably smaller, and weaknesses are somehow turned upside down and almost magically transformed into strengths, he can be, once again, a man among men.[45]

Public fictions help to sustain the respective egos of the men, but their succession of mates constitutes repeated failures rather than a cultural pattern or even a personal preference. Their relationship to their children (or those of other men by the women with whom they share a household) varies. Affection may appear to be absent in the enactment of the paternal role at home; it tempers the sense of failure. Men want children as further confirmation of their masculinity, but children are a financial liability. Fathers feel they ought to support their children, but they cannot do so. Once they have left their families and are free of its institutional obligations, they may show greater warmth toward their children in the infrequent and irregular contacts that are sometimes maintained.[46]

Not all men, even in the lower class, leave home, of course. Nevertheless, in 1960, only 76.1 percent of all Negro men over fourteen years of age who were ever married were living with their wives, and only 58.5 percent were living with their first wives. A large segment of poor Negroes live in households headed by women. Almost 39 percent of all nonwhite families have an income under $2000, and 59.9 percent of the female-headed families have incomes of less than $2000. Since 1951, the proportion of nonwhite women who are separated from their husbands has been significantly correlated with the unemployment rate of the preceding year. (The explanatory value of this correlation is limited by the fact that the number of separated women is many times the number of unemployed men from whom they could be separated.) In 1960 thus 27.1 percent of all Negro heads of households were women.[47]

In a study of Negroes in New Orleans, Rohrer and Edmonson find that the matriarchal family remains prevalent in the lower class. It is held

[44] Elliott Liebow, *Tally's Corner* (Boston: Little, Brown & Co., 1967), pp. 108, 114, 132.

[45] *Ibid.*, p. 136.

[46] *Ibid.*, pp. 75, 78–80, 86–87, 90–92, 221–22.

[47] Bernard, *op. cit.*, pp. vii, 14, 21–23.

together by the economic interdependence of mothers and daughters and the emotional ties forged by recurrent personal and family crises. "Among the cardinal mores in Negro society is the guarantee that mothers will always provide for and protect their children, and that daughters will care for their aged mothers." Even when the men remain on the scene, the bond between mother and daughter is stronger than that between husband and wife.[48] Children, particularly daughters, are a form of old-age insurance. Economic aspiration usually invested in the husband in the larger society is centered in the children among Negroes. They are a source of familial cohesion; because of the mother's emotional involvement in her children, the household is less disrupted by marital separations. A series of temporary mates may come and go, but the mother and grandmother remain to care for the children.[49]

Many of these lower-class family patterns originated in slavery and the greater economic value it gave to women. They were permitted to care for the children they produced as property, unlike the men, who were frequently separated from their offspring.[50] Even when the husband is present now, the wife is frequently the chief economic support and, hence, the more important source of authority (which is one reason that the household remains stable, although there is little permanence in marriage).[51] It is true that the middle-class Negro family, by contrast, approximates that of the dominant group, "a nuclear kinship unit held together by a relatively stable marriage and rarely including other relatives." With greater economic security, the Negro male assumes greater authority in the family. This middle-class family is a stable one with an explicit ideology supporting its permanence.[52] The respectability of the members is a source of pride as they struggle to dissociate themselves from lower-class behavior with the cultivation of conventional morals. Consequently their morality about sexual behavior, for example, approaches the puritanical. Family stability is thus a distinguishing characteristic of the middle class and a critical symbol of status for those oriented toward mobility.[53]

Middle-class status, however, does not necessarily solve the problems of marital role playing. There is some indication that wives assume a greater

[48] John H. Rohrer and Munro S. Edmonson, *The Eighth Generation Grows Up* (New York: Harper Torchbooks, 1960), pp. 30–31.

[49] Powdermaker, *op cit.,* pp. 199, 219.

[50] Bernard, *op. cit.,* p. 73.

[51] Powdermaker, *op. cit.,* pp. 145, 156.

[52] Rohrer and Edmonson, *op. cit.,* p. 31.

[53] Lewis, *Blackways, op. cit.,* p. 87; Bernard, *op. cit.,* pp. 27–28.

role in family decision-making even in families with a higher income. They may not demand or desire such authority, but it falls to them by default. They may dominate their husbands by virtue of their greater social skill in the ways of the black bourgeoisie, if not by virtue of their greater economic contribution to the family's welfare.[54] Such studies of the Negro family as there are have thus far been so "problem" oriented that they rarely investigate the internal workings of stability. They focus on the problems that emerge with the absence of the father and ignore the problems that develop in his presence. As it happens, there are a variety of family forms among Negroes,[55] and none of them are free of the difficulties of being Negro. The result is that the father's presence may be as problematic as his absence. His social emasculation leads to such serious role strain that he cannot fulfill his paternal functions.

It is, to be sure, important to have a stable father in the home, but the denigrated position in which he so often finds himself may cancel his contribution to his children's socialization. They may perceive him as emasculated by the surrounding white society and be so disillusioned about his effectiveness that it undermines his authority in their eyes.[56] They learn all too quickly that their father can do nothing about his categorical status and their consequent situation, and that fact of black life is embedded in the family structure. In Lewis's study of the Negroes in Kent, half of the children are raised for major portions of their lives by the mothers and maternal relatives without significant help from the father. The mother is also more important in disciplining and dispensing rewards when the father is present. When there is the total or frequent absence of one or both parents, children may have to compete for care in a large extended family situation. Even when the nuclear family remains intact, the lesser part played by the father often leads to a lack of appreciation and an implicit rejection of him.[57]

Underlying the dominant position of Negro women is a history of actual or potential sexual relations with men of both races that is a constant threat to the self-esteem of Negro men. Not only must Negro men themselves play a subordinate role to whites, they cannot protect their

[54] *Ibid.,* pp. 91–92.
[55] For a typological description of the different family patterns, see Andrew Billingsley, *Black Families in White America* (Englewood Cliffs, N.J.: Prentice-Hall, A Spectrum Book, 1968).
[56] Bernard, *op. cit.,* p. 129.
[57] Lewis, *Blackways, op. cit.,* pp. 100, 102–3.

women from sexual exploitation by whites. Their own sexual relationships, restricted to Negro women, are thereby weakened, and their frustrations may be expressed in violence within their own group.[58] Psychologically the Negro male cannot support his desire for dominance in the family with a subservient status in the larger society. And the compensatory strength of the Negro female, who has had to hold the family together as a result, perpetuates his weaker role.[59] The tensions that inevitably develop in their marriages and liaisons are compounded in the lower class by the relative independence (both economically and sexually) of the female and the inclination toward dalliance of the male, who asserts himself in the only way he can, by displaying his sexual prowess with other women. This contributes greatly to marital bickering, and even to physical aggression.[60]

In effect, being black in a white world is so erosive an experience that it can debilitate the very core of the family. No area of its life is left unaffected.

> But, for most people, wearing their dark skin is like living with a chronic disease. One learns to "take it" and not to let it unduly cramp one's style of life. And anodynes are always present: religion, the social ritual, whiskey, dope—and for those who can afford it, an occasional trip.[61]

There is, of course, nothing inherently problematic about a matriarchal family, particularly when it is the prevailing form in a society. Its problem among Negroes is that it is not preferred. They do not deem it desirable as such; they simply accept it as necessary due to the economic deprivation of Negro men. Matriarchy is not the norm in the dominant group, and its prevalence among Negroes contributes to their sense of difference, a difference that they do not likewise choose. The very disparity between Negro family forms and dominant patterns helps to make the matriarchy problematic. Having adopted the alternative norms of the larger society, Negroes may disparage the ways imposed upon them by social necessity. The fact that the style of family life is not a matter of personal preference

[58] Hortense Powdermaker, *Stranger and Friend: The Way of an Anthropologist* (New York: The Norton Library, 1967), pp. 156, 164; Maurice R. Stein, *The Eclipse of Community* (Princeton, N.J.: Princeton University Press, 1960), p. 163.

[59] Kenneth B. Clark, *Dark Ghetto* (New York: Harper & Row, Harper Torchbooks, 1965), p. 70.

[60] Lewis, *Blackways, op. cit.,* p. 84.

[61] St. Clair Drake and Horace R. Cayton, *Black Metropolis: A Study of Negro Life in a Northern City,* Vol. 2 (New York: Harper Torchbooks, 1962), p. xxvii.

exacerbates the role strains manifest in the matriarchal tradition, often responsible for serious problems in mental health. (Sons, for example, may suffer severe difficulties in establishing their sexual identity.) These structural adaptations in the Negro family sometimes fail in their effectiveness (they are less successful in the north than in the south, as we will see), and then its stability is as much undermined as the status of men.

Southern Origins

Many of these social patterns have their origins in the south, along with the history of slavery. They persist there in their original form, or close to it, in part because nowhere in the United States is the color line drawn with more rigidity. The racial situation arouses great status anxieties in southern whites, and Negroes there pay even greater social penalties than elsewhere.

> Scorned by the aristocrats, and without a respected middle-class tradition, the individual and group identities of the middle- and lower-class whites are apparently tied to their feelings of alleged superiority over Negroes. The identity of these white men is meshed with their status in a caste-like social system. The civil rights struggle threatens the system and the traditional status positions.[62]

This caste-like social system has replaced slavery as a means of maintaining the old order of status. Social inferiority and superiority are still defined in racial terms, and these definitions in turn regulate the behavior of the races.

As a result, Negroes in the south live in relative isolation, and their personal development is as blocked as their social advancement. Whites and whiteness inevitably form an inseparable part of the Negro's life and imagery. "He has a white employer, often white ancestors, sometimes white playmates, and he lives by a set of rules which are imposed by white society."[63] The focus of dominant institutions is on keeping Negroes subordinate; there is a repressive system of social control that pervades every community.[64] Under such extreme segregation, Negro communities

[62] Powdermaker, *Stranger and Friend, op. cit.,* p. 205.
[63] Dollard, *op. cit.,* pp. 1, 62–63.
[64] Stein, *op. cit.,* pp. 154–55.

are entirely separate, and their organization is distinctive. There are some parallel social institutions, but no independent economic institutions.[65]

The sociological studies of the deep south in the late 1930's found that the plantation system still controlled the lives of those families existing within it. Under the conditions which it imposed, tenants lived by costly credit advances and low returns on the labor invested.

> The plantation tenant families have no stake in the land and no voice in determining what or how much they shall plant, when or where the crop will be sold. Since they keep no books and have no interests beyond the daily routine, they have no strong incentives to self-improvement. . . . Actually fewer make a net profit than "break even." As recent studies show, a third or more of the families usually go into debt.[66]

There was thus a state of dependency upon the landlord from which few tenant farmers escaped. Perpetual indebtedness bred chronic insecurity and served as a safeguard against separation from the soil as a source of income. Few ended the year with enough money to begin the next, and so they had to borrow all over again from the landlord. So great has been the isolation of these families that the social attitudes, and many of the patterns of behavior, set in the economy of slavery have continued to prevail.[67]

Powdermaker suggests that the sharecropping system had a certain function after the Civil War when white planters had land but no capital and Negroes had neither. It might have continued to have some advantage for Negroes had it operated in a social milieu where they had legal rights. But the economic system functioned in an unstructured fashion calculated to deprive Negroes of any profit. Whether or not a sharecropper received an honest settlement depended completely on the character of the individual landlord; no more than 25 to 30 percent of the Negroes got an honest settlement, and whites took for granted the acceptability of their fiscal irresponsibility. Whatever regulations inhered in the system were honored more in the breach than in their enforcement since Negroes had neither political nor economic rights. They were without legal protection and thus unable to defend themselves.[68] It is this unique vulnerability that constitutes the ultimate heritage of slavery, the disavowal of black human-

---

[65] Charles F. Marden and Gladys Meyer, *Minorities in American Society,* 2nd ed. (New York: American Book Co., 1962), p. 242.

[66] Johnson, *op. cit.,* pp. 46–47.

[67] *Ibid.,* p. 47.

[68] Powdermaker, *Stranger and Friend, op. cit.,* pp. 161–62, 184.

ity that allows Negroes no legitimate expectations in their social existence. It is indeed a deprivation beyond all sociological definition.

The younger generation was less likely to fit into the pattern of the plantation. Many moved to towns and cities, or even went north, having gained at least a little of the education for which their parents aspired in their behalf.[69] And with the increasing industrialization and urbanization of the south in recent decades, the color line is no longer part of a fixed and comprehensive system. Racial barriers remain, but the encompassing social framework has expanded. The color line is still most inflexible in interpersonal relations, but it exercises its greatest influence in smaller communities.[70] Although the paternalistic patterns of the plantation system no longer obtain, the status quo in race relations is nonetheless maintained with relative rigidity. When legal sanctions fail, there is the threat of physical violence,[71] and Negroes who do not accept the traditional modes of accommodation (as many now do not) must struggle against their subordinate status at great cost—and continued risk of penalty. The odds are still very much against their succeeding.

It remains true that those areas having high proportions of Negroes tend to be those with a history of the greatest discrimination. And the greater the discrimination, the more marked the social and economic differences between Negroes and whites.

> The greater the proportion of Negroes, the more important separate Negro institutions tend to be. And the greater the segregation, the greater the sense of separateness. Given the institutionalized dominance of the whites in such areas, political and economic controls are systematically used to perpetuate Negro-white disparities in education, wealth, income, power, and prestige. Any proposed alteration in the control system tends to be reacted to as a threat.[72]

The Negro church is a significant institution in the context of southern segregation; it symbolizes the social separateness of the black community. Membership in it is, among other things, a symbol of respectability, and respectability is an important criterion of status where there are few other class differences.[73]

[69] Johnson, *op. cit.,* p. 49.
[70] Michael Banton, *Race Relations* (New York: Basic Books, 1967), p. 152.
[71] Johnson, *op. cit.,* p. 327.
[72] Robin M. Williams, Jr., *Stranger Next Door* (Englewood Cliffs, N.J.: Prentice-Hall, 1964), p. 377.
[73] Marden and Meyer, *op. cit.,* p. 244.

The church is the only institution completely controlled by Negroes since their economic life is regulated by whites, and this affects most other areas of their existence, whether directly or indirectly. More women than men participate actively in church life, although men officiate as its functionaries. In fact, women are dominant in all the institutions of the Negro community in Mississippi studied by Powdermaker; it is an extension of their family role. The religious emphasis is on the rewards of the hereafter. Although such an otherworldly orientation serves as an escape from an unrewarding mundane life, it also helps to sustain self-respect in a racial situation geared to destroying the sources of selfhood. There is also emotional release from the frustrations of categorical status. Within the church, the Negro functions as a whole human being; there are no whites to make him feel less than human and thereby to undermine his sense of self. The secular activities of the church provide, therefore, major leisure-time pursuits.[74]

As the pivot of Negro communal life and social activity, the church is an avenue for abilities, administrative and otherwise, that have little, if any, other outlet. It thus provides its members with the social respect that is essential to their self-esteem, a social respect deliberately refused them by the dominant group. The church is nonetheless a palliative in the racial situation. Although it affords Negroes their one institutionalized arena of public expression, it supports the status quo. The church does not function to change the social facts, but to make them more bearable; it is in that sense a conservative institution that channels discontents.[75] Yet it produces leaders who strive for change through social action and who have been nationally acknowledged in their civil rights role. In so far as the younger generation attends church, however, it is out of social interests rather than religious convictions. And lower-class youth find little appeal in the church at all; it is too otherworldly to give them a sense of worth.[76] They are inclined to seek it in earthier terms.

The south may be changing now to a limited extent, but it is clear that until recently the Negro community had been accurately described by Ellison as "pre-individual." As a consequence of slavery and a continuing caste-like situation, southern Negroes have not been able to establish the kind of minority community characteristic of ethnic groups. Their community has been premised on an acceptance of the status quo, and there is consequently no confusion about the status of its members. Categorical

[74] Powdermaker, *Stranger and Friend, op. cit.,* pp. 156, 171–72, 174–77.
[75] Powdermaker, *After Freedom, op. cit.,* pp. 243, 274, 285.
[76] Frazier, *Negro Youth, op. cit.,* pp. 266–67.

status is so much incorporated into the communal structure that insufficient individuation occurs even within its confines. For this reason some of the traditional functions of the minority community are not fulfilled. There is certainly social stability, but there is little personal security. The accepted modes of accommodation are adaptations to the exigencies of the racial situation, coerced by its circumstances; they do not always serve the needs of the individual. Because of such structural inadequacy, some of the stability of the southern Negro community may be spurious; it is sometimes dysfunctional for its members.

The same matriarchal family, for example, that maintains the continuity of the household also contributes to the social emasculation of the male by further undermining his status. The same church that shores up self-respect is too conservative to serve as an agent of change in the conditions that deprive its congregants. And these institutional adaptations, whatever their effectiveness, then acquire a vested interest in perpetuating themselves. What social autonomy exists within the confines of southern segregation, and that is little enough, is likely to be self-interested. As Negroes move north, there is somewhat greater opportunity and therefore less clarity of status. Considerable confusion may set in when there is not sufficient community to cope with change. The institutional adaptations that constituted an adequate accommodation in the south may no longer be functional; they may simply not work in the north. A number of observers have commented on the dislocation of the Negro family system and the damage to personality structure in northern cities.[77] There is no way of life there that fully succeeds in counteracting their categorical status, and neither do Negroes in the north accept social inferiority as accommodatingly as in the south. Under such circumstances, Negroes may suffer the worst of two worlds: their subordination in the larger society and the dysfunctions of the minority community. It is not surprising then that even the spurious stability of the south may disappear with migration.

The Northern Ghetto

Even in the north, however, Negroes are not merely atomized individuals excluded from full participation in the larger society. They also live in

[77] Banton, *op. cit.*, p. 161.

communities, albeit communities that lack adequate social organization to fulfill all institutional functions. Nevertheless, communities do exist, and mobile Negroes must not only gain entrance into the larger society, they must somehow escape their own community.[78] It is not easy to do since the Negro community takes the form of a black ghetto that grows increasingly concentrated. While other ethnic enclaves have tended to dissolve in time, Negroes have become more segregated in physically deteriorated areas yielding high rates of social pathology as does any slum. Such residential segregation reinforces the social and cultural isolation of Negroes, who have no choice but to associate exclusively with each other in formal as well as informal relations.[79] Negroes are forced to live in the overcrowded conditions of the urban ghettos regardless of their income and ability to pay for better housing.

> The modern American ghetto is a Black Belt from which the occupants can escape only if they move into another well-defined Negro community. It is not, as the ghetto of old, an area which houses a people concerned with perpetuation of a peculiar (and different) culture. It is no longer composed of black people almost all of whom are too poor to afford decent shelter. . . . The ghetto has all income and social classes. . . .[80]

Compounding the strains of such an existence are the peculiar ambiguities of the racial situation. Southern patterns of adjustment break down under the impact of new uncertainties in the north. There is less rigidity in intergroup relations, but Negroes are frequently at a loss to know to just what extent (and where) there is some flexibility, if not freedom, in their minority status.[81] Traditional accommodations were achieved at great psychic cost; their dissolution may be even more destructive to the personality—at least in the short run. And there is no core of cultural strength and communal integration to help Negroes to cope with a changed situation that is itself unclear. Continued segregation has been a product of categorical discrimination rather than a social expression of meaningful tradition. It is not enough to be bound together by an arbitrary racial distinction imposed by an alien dominant group, a distinction whose historical significance has not been confirmed by contemporary choice.

[78] Lewis M. Killian and Charles Grigg, *Racial Crisis in America* (Englewood Cliffs, N.J.: Prentice-Hall, Spectrum Books, 1964), p. 125.

[79] Marden and Meyer, *op. cit.*, pp. 257, 265–66; John Sirjamaki, *The Sociology of Cities* (New York: Random House, 1964), pp. 245–46.

[80] Robert C. Weaver, *The Negro Ghetto* (New York: Harcourt, Brace & Co., 1948), p. 7.

[81] Marden and Meyer, *op. cit.*, pp. 270–71.

For this reason, as we have already suggested, some Negroes strive to invent a culture for themselves. The process is not without difficulties, perhaps insuperable.

> An impoverished, frustrated, angry collectivity invents a poor culture. Built on isolation and resentment, it is more likely to be an attack on the established way of life than a creative new one—a contraculture that denies the old values without having anything to put in their place.[82]

To some extent lower-class Negroes have created an institutional structure in response to their victimized existence, a social reaction to severe deprivation. There is primarily a social network, some extended kin and "the 'street system' of buddies and broads which tie (although tenuously and unpredictably) the 'members' to each other. . . ." There are also all the forms of entertainment and escape, which sometimes serve as the means by which the participants "instruct, explain, and accept themselves."[83] It remains, however, their common suffering that draws them together, a suffering that derives from their shared powerlessness to determine their own life chances; they have virtually no say in shaping the conditions under which they live. Their socially imposed situation throws together disparate individuals and different classes for whom shared suffering is not a sufficient source of communal cohesion. There are often bitter conflicts and grave contradictions within the Negro community,[84] a community in which no one chooses to live as such.

In its isolation, Negro life has been dominated by the need to adjust to whites and to take them into account at every turn. At no time is a black man in any position to take anything for granted. In a sense, the Negro in the northern city is even more isolated than the Negro in a small southern town. The former lives in a completely Negro world in his black ghetto; he has only the most stylized and impersonal contact with whites in his economic relations, and that is without significant communication. There is, of course, greater contact with the mass media in the north so that Negroes have more awareness of the dominant culture, if no more access to it. This doubtless serves only to increase social frustration. Migration from the south brings some relief from the more direct and humiliating forms of white domination, and by contrast new arrivals feel relatively satisfied with their changed situation in the north. Those born in the north experience greater relative deprivation as they measure their

[82] Yinger, *op. cit.*, pp. 88–89, 92–93.
[83] Rainwater, *op. cit.*, p. 178.
[84] Redding, *op. cit.*, pp. 37–38.

conditions against the standards of the dominant group. This Negro "does not consider his lot to be relatively good, because he has not known worse." And he is sensitive to the subtler forms of discrimination he encounters there.[85]

In New York City, one half of the nonwhites over twenty years of age in 1960 were from the south. Although there is a smaller proportion of Negroes there than in other northern cities, there has been a great increase in their numbers. These newcomers arrive without marketable skills or transferable institutions;[86] their previous way of life is not always an effective source of survival under different conditions. The essential characteristic of their life, however, does not change with migration, the coercive element underlying it.[87]

> The Negro way of life, no matter what its content and emphases may be, is essentially a forced way of life. The color or race line is the most important single factor making for a Negro world distinct from the local white world. Consciousness of color or race is an all-pervading influence. All aspects of life tend to be race-ridden.[88]

The existence of black ghettos protects the dominant group from social contact with Negroes, but it does not diminish the impact of categorical status for the residents. The consequences may even be exacerbated.

Most Negroes migrate from the south to "better their condition." They seek not only employment, but an environment where there is at least less overt and obvious exclusion. Yet they do not leave behind their subordination. Even in the north, they "live in a state of intense and perpetual awareness that they are a black minority in a white man's world." The very fact of the ghetto is a reminder, and so is the limited employment, if any, available to them. They encounter discrimination daily, and such experiences, past and present, are part of their personality structure; there is thus no escape from race consciousness.[89] Intellectuals who have escaped from the ghetto have depicted the sterility of its isolation. Driven to so enclosed a life by forces beyond their control, Negroes have incorporated,

---

[85] Leonard Broom and Norval D. Glenn, *Transformation of the Negro American* (New York: Harper & Row, 1965), pp. 22, 36, 175.

[86] Nathan Glazer and Daniel P. Moynihan, *Beyond the Melting Pot* (Cambridge, Mass.: The M.I.T. Press & Harvard University Press, 1963), pp. 25–26.

[87] For the most recent and comprehensive summary of the conditions and consequences of the Negro situation, see Alphonso Pinkney, *Black Americans* (Englewood Cliffs, N.J.: Prentice-Hall, 1969).

[88] Lewis, *Blackways, op. cit.,* p. 28.

[89] Drake and Cayton, *op. cit.,* pp. 385, 390.

and in an exaggerated form at that, the worst of American life, "conspicuous consumption, pursuit of the products of a mass culture, devotion to frivolous trivialities, and a plethora of escapist religion."[90]

Physical distance is not necessary when there is social distance rigidly secured by a caste-like situation (there are, for example, racially mixed residential areas in a number of southern cities); intimacy becomes threatening, however, when it implies equal status. Although there is now residential segregation in the south as Negroes assume some symbols of mobility, the black ghetto is a social invention of the north. Three out of four Negroes live in cities, and one out of two of these lives in a northern city. For all its numbers, the ghetto is not a viable community. It has been described in stark detail by Kenneth Clark, who underscores the fact that it cannot support its people. Even its small businesses are marginal ones providing personal services. Property is for the most part owned by persons who live outside the community and take their profits home. Even the numbers racket in Harlem is controlled by whites. Those who are employed are likely to work at menial jobs with minimal wages. Thirty-seven percent of the Negro males in New York are in unskilled and service jobs; the unemployment rate is twice as high as that of whites and rising faster. Consequently resources within the ghetto are insufficient to maintain its population, let alone to bring about self-development.[91]

In studying Bronzeville in Chicago, Drake and Cayton also found that Negroes are not only excluded from the commercial life of the city, they exercise no economic control even within their own community. "While Negro enterprises constituted almost half of all the businesses in Negro neighborhoods, they received less than a tenth of all the money spent by Negroes within these areas." Negro businessmen are simply unable to compete with whites; they can't meet the price or provide equivalent service. They have difficulty in procuring capital and credit and securing choice locations. Negroes lack not only training and experience in business, they lack sufficient patronage to allow them to amass capital and make improvements. They stress racial solidarity to attract customers, but there is no ethnic tradition for economic cooperation.[92]

Although the church has not got the same significance as it has in the south, it remains the single most important institution in the north. Negroes compensate for their daily subservience in their churches (or on

[90] *Ibid.,* p. x.
[91] Clark, *op. cit.,* pp. 22, 27, 29, 35–37.
[92] Drake and Cayton, *op. cit.,* pp. 437–38.

the streetcorners); there they are free from the emotional restraints imposed by inferior status. The church has more than a cathartic role, however; it has the potential power of popular support within the community. Nevertheless, its strength is often dissipated, according to Clark, in a pre-occupation with trivia and a struggle for status. It also has that degree of organization necessary for sustained protest because of its institutional autonomy. In every other institution, Negroes are dependent on whites for financial control. In the church, they manage their own affairs, in part because it is the most segregated of institutions.[93] Its role as a "race institution" is emphasized in its competition with secular institutions. Although the church is free of white domination, it is not entirely free of charges of cynicism by Negroes. Unlike other leaders, ministers are answerable only to their congregations, but they may have much for which they must answer.

> During the Depression the charge that the church was a "racket" was encountered everywhere in Bronzeville. This typically Chicago reaction expressed a doubt of motives that did not necessarily mean refusal to cooperate with the church but did indicate disapproval of the emphasis placed upon money by the preacher.[94]

There are many of the lower class, however, who remain outside of the church, removed from its influence. Their resentment is such that they are impervious to its sacred symbols and indifferent to its secular activities. They express themselves pointedly in their apathy and aggression, and their "primary mode of escape is through 'having a good time.' "[95] For those who do belong to a church, membership does not necessarily vitiate militancy. A nationwide study of metropolitan Negroes finds that it is true that the greater the religiosity, the lower the percentage of militants. And those who belong to fundamentalist sects are the least likely to be militant. Among militants, however, a majority scored "very religious" or "somewhat religious." Religious concern and racial protest are thus not mutually exclusive, at least not when the religiosity has a temporal orientation. Members of predominantly white denominations are least likely to be otherworldly in their concerns, and therefore most likely to be militant.[96]

---

[93] Clark, *op. cit.,* pp. 175, 177, 183.
[94] Drake and Cayton, *op. cit.,* pp. 398–419.
[95] *Ibid.,* p. xxii.
[96] Gary T. Marx, "Religion: Opiate or Inspiration of Civil Rights Militancy Among Negroes?" *American Sociological Review,* Vol. 32, No. 1 (February 1967), pp. 67, 69, 70–71.

The findings suggest the irony that it is the most segregated sectarian churches that most support the status quo.

The Cornell studies directed by Robin Williams deal mostly with working- and lower-class communities in smaller towns, but the sociological patterns are essentially the same. Again, a diversity of social types are thrown together in a single isolated world, bound by the sheer fact of being black in a white world. Here they can practice avoidance of the exclusion they encounter elsewhere. There is, however, little middle-class leadership in these communities and much more apathy among their inarticulate and uneducated members. The employment situation varies from community to community, but it is never good. Elmira is perhaps typical, with a high proportion of Negroes in unskilled or semiskilled industrial jobs or in service occupations. There is an ambiguous pattern of discrimination in public accommodations that results in uncertainty for Negroes and reinforces their avoidance response to the extent that they overestimate the amount of discrimination that actually exists. Although Negroes are economically dependent on the general community, they are socially confined to their own community. They live, therefore, in semi-isolation, all the while aware of dominant cultural patterns. They keep up with Negroes elsewhere, with whom they feel a sense of common identity, by reading the Negro press. And they go to other cities frequently to visit their communities of origin.[97]

As a dependent segment of the larger society, each of these communities lacks a full complement of the institutions necessary for collective existence. In Kent, for example, some institutions are shared with the general community, and some are segregated branches of dominant institutions; few exist exclusively for Negroes. As a result, many institutional patterns have a makeshift quality. They are pragmatic adjustments to social restrictions and therefore frequently ad hoc in character. Such patterns do not have within them the potential for structuring change; they are "geared to adjust to the demands of life now and not to carving out or initiating that which is new or different."[98] Rohrer and Edmonson suggest that the institutions of the New Orleans Negro community can be characterized by their recent organization, and that organization is not always effective.

> Many Negro institutions and organizations have not developed naturally as means of satisfying the indigenous needs of Negroes as such, but for the

[97] Williams, *op. cit.*, pp. 224–25, 229, 237–39.
[98] Lewis, *Blackways, op. cit.*, pp. 82–83, 292, 312.

most part have borrowed their structure, ritual, and form from white society. However, the institutional and organizational forms that were effective in white society frequently proved to be relatively ineffectual in satisfying the peculiar needs of the socially and economically submerged Negro masses.[99]

Although the dominant culture gives a kind of enforced unity to Negro institutions, it is also disrupting and demoralizing for the participants. White patterns serve as the standard for accepted behavior from which Negroes see themselves as deviating when they cannot conform to conventional norms.[100]

There is, however, an elaboration of sociability within the Negro community that compensates for the exclusion of its members from participation in the larger society. A plethora of social clubs and voluntary associations permit Negroes to avoid dominant rejection and thereby to assuage their self-esteem. Their extensive social activity constitutes a large part of their status seeking within the confines of a segregated community. There is even an elite who have set themselves apart as Negro "society." Extremely conscious of their inferior status in American society, they maintain an exclusive social life of their own, emulating, in so far as possible, the behavior of upper-class whites.[101]

> For many Negroes, it appears that "social" life became identified with the condition of freedom. "Social" life among the masses of Negroes was a free and spontaneous expression of their desire to escape from the restraints of work and routine. But for those who set themselves apart as Negro "society," "social" life became a more formalized activity.[102]

Negroes have a relatively larger number of associations than whites and are more likely to belong to them. This is true in spite of the fact that Negroes are predominantly lower class, and organizational membership occurs in greater frequency in the middle and upper class in the dominant group. It is in this respect that Gunnar Myrdal described them as "exaggerated Americans." In one study conducted in Lincoln, Nebraska in 1960, adult Negroes were found to belong to more formal voluntary associations than their white counterparts at all levels, especially in the lower class. Negroes were also more likely to be affiliated with religious organizations.

[99] Rohrer and Edmonson, *op. cit.,* p. 29.

[100] Lewis, *Blackways, op. cit.,* p. 29.

[101] E. Franklin Frazier, *Black Bourgeoisie* (New York: Free Press, 1957), p. 204.

[102] *Ibid.,* pp. 203–4.

Most of the voluntary associations are nonutilitarian with expressive functions for the immediate gratification of their members.[103] In still another study, lower-class Negroes in Detroit were more likely to belong to organizations than lower-class whites in Chicago. Although there is some positive relationship between organizational membership and socioeconomic status among Negroes, it is not as pronounced as among whites. Voluntary associations appear to be the focus of the social life of the Negro community, whereas they may have only nominal significance for the dominant group.[104]

In fact, no minority group is more socially segregated than Negroes. Lenski found in his Detroit sample of 1030 Negroes that 98 percent were married to members of their own race and had Negroes as close relatives.[105] This social endogamy obtains in Chicago's Bronzeville as well as in every other black ghetto in the country. There is an extensive network of clique and associational structures involving members of the community in intimate relationships exclusively within the in-group.

Middle-class life is based on the trivia of club activity; it is a source of social stability, along with the secure income that affords it.[106] The clubs of New Orleans Negroes are primarily recreational, whatever their stated goals. They are mostly small and ephemeral groups with an average membership of fifteen. Because they are social in orientation, they are stratified by class to a high degree. The social clubs of middle-class Negroes, like the church groups of the lower class, are largely for women. There are, for example, bridge and garden clubs as well as sororities, all of which also give dances and fashion shows. In addition, there are lodges, fraternities, and athletic clubs for men.[107]

[103] Nicholas Babchuk and Ralph V. Thompson, "The Voluntary Associations of Negroes," *American Sociological Review,* Vol. 27, No. 5 (October 1962), pp. 652–53.

[104] Anthony M. Orum, "A Reappraisal of the Social and Political Participation of Negroes," *American Journal of Sociology,* Vol. 72, No. 1 (July 1966), pp. 35, 37, 45.

[105] Gerhard Lenski, *The Religious Factor* (Garden City, N.Y.: Doubleday, 1961), p. 36.

[106] Drake and Cayton, *op. cit.,* pp. xiii, xxii.

[107] Rohrer and Edmonson, *op. cit.,* p. 45.

Black Styles of Life

The Negro community, like any minority community, is a stratified one. The internal status differences have an even more serious significance than in other minorities, and they are often more socially divisive. Negroes are not only more cut off from the larger society, they are also more concentrated in segregated areas. Higher-status groups in the Negro community are concerned with differentiating themselves from lower-status groups, and these distinctions are carefully maintained. Members of the middle class are particularly resentful of the dominant group's categorical perception that lumps together all Negroes as if they were an undifferentiated mass. They have little access to areas of second settlement, and physical proximity may bring them into association with a lower class with which they do not want to be confused. Because of the importance of its internal stratification system, there is more than usual diversity in style of life within the community. And that diversity has more than usual significance; it reflects the lack of a common cultural core. The greater social segmentation that results undermines communal cohesion.

Although there has been some change in the occupational distribution of Negroes, it has scarcely been enough to normalize it. Two-thirds of them are still lower-class, unskilled workers with irregular, if any, employment and precarious incomes. Recent findings of the Census Bureau indicate that the number of nonwhite families living in poverty has been reduced in the past decade from 49.5 percent to 30.7 percent in 1967, but these three out of ten families continue to be without sufficient income for subsistence. (Only 8.4 percent of white families remain similarly impoverished.) Although nonwhite family income is rising faster than white income, it has not yet reached two-thirds the white level.[108] There has been some increase in the number of skilled workers who, along with clerical and service workers, make up a middle class whose respectability is in large part contingent upon familial stability. Members of the upper class are mostly professionals and semiprofessionals.

The Negro community is thus not a middle-class one, even though there has been some increase in the mobility of its members. And the gap between the middle and upper classes and the lower class is a wide one, perhaps wider than ever. The problems of disorganization among the

[108] Peter Kihss, "Study Finds Nonwhites Earn More," *The New York Times,* May 3, 1969, p. 37.

latter are so great that the higher status groups are inadequate to deal with them. They are too busy maintaining their own social adaptations, which, in turn, constitute their fine line of distinction from the lower class.[109] Since some of the traditional functions of the minority community are not fulfilled for Negroes, individual mobility is rendered all the more difficult. Such mobility may be an anomaly in a racial situation that requires a massive breakthrough to permit the building of a solidly based middle class. So extensive a communal change cannot be accomplished in the established terms of the ethnic precedent.

One review of sixteen stratification studies of criteria of prestige among Negroes finds education emphasized most frequently; occupation and income are second and third in importance respectively. Although income gains emphasis in the north, economic differentiation is still less significant than educational differentiation. The higher evaluation of education among Negroes than among whites may be due to its greater scarcity value and its greater utility in the acquisition of other bases of prestige. Education is more unequally distributed among Negroes and brings a greater gain in occupation, although the Negro college graduate continues to have a lower occupational status than the white graduate.[110] Perhaps also there is historical basis for the significance of education among Negroes. Most slaves were forbidden to learn reading and writing, which appeared to them to be a precious tool with obvious advantages. Education was the prerogative of the master class and thus endowed with a prestige it still retains.[111]

Especially significant as an indication of status among Negroes are the behavior patterns associated with the dominant group. These center on sexual and marital mores and family life.[112] With most incomes comparatively low, what a person does with his money also becomes an important index of status. It is through the expenditure of income that both educational achievement and future aspirations find expression.

> Most Negroes seem to adopt a pattern of conspicuous behavior and conspicuous consumption. Maintaining a "front" and "showing off" become very important substitutes for getting ahead in the economic sense.[113]

[109] Glazer and Moynihan, *op. cit.*, pp. 37, 52–53.
[110] Norval D. Glenn, "Negro Prestige Criteria: A Case Study in the Bases of Prestige," *American Journal of Sociology*, Vol. 68, No. 6 (May 1963), pp. 647–50, 652.
[111] Powdermaker, *After Freedom, op. cit.*, p. 299.
[112] *Ibid.*, p. 61.
[113] Drake and Cayton, *op. cit.*, pp. 389, 517.

Associated with these criteria of prestige is skin color. At least until recently fair skin has been a status symbol that operated in marital selection to enhance eligibility.[114]

"Having a good time" is more than a source of status; it serves as an escape from the tensions of contact with whites. Social pleasure is part of the adjustment to separate and subordinate status as well as a relief from the routine of work. There is a sharp distinction between those who do and those who do not value decorous public behavior, but everyone makes the most of leisuretime. Members of the lower class live in a social world apart from both whites and other Negroes, and they thus have less use for decorum.[115] Work, as such, also has no value for them. There is no premium on incentive since they are unable to alter their status. This accounts for the random idling behavior that characterizes many of them, the anodynes that ease the frustrations of their double subordination. The attitude toward social security benefits is part of this general reaction to the lower-class situation: the benefits are something that is due the recipients, a salve which there is little shame in accepting.[116]

Their several distinct social worlds constitute the respective psychological reality of members of the Negro community. The mother-centered household is one such significant world in the lower class. Its solidarity is expressed by a high degree of cooperation among females, with men regarded as inimical, exploitative as well as exploitable.[117] Unable to provide stable economic support for the household, men exercise little control within it. Women are often bitter that they still have to take love on male terms, and that men may trade love for a living. The tensions of such relationships frequently erupt in violence, and the liaison usually dissolves after a short duration.[118] It is the women of this world who are most likely to belong to the churches and clubs of the lower class.

The gang, by contrast, is centered around exclusively masculine interests; its ideology is mutually exclusive with that of the matriarchy. Manhood is defined in terms of independence, secretiveness, aggressiveness,

---

[114] Howard E. Freeman, David Armor, J. Michael Ross, Thomas F. Pettigrew, "Color Gradation and Attitudes Among Middle-Income Negroes," *American Sociological Review,* Vol. 31, No. 3 (June 1966), p. 365.

[115] *Ibid.,* pp. 387, 519, 523.

[116] *Ibid.,* p. 718; Lewis, *Blackways, op. cit.,* pp. 124, 127–28.

[117] Daniel Thompson, "The Formation of Social Attitudes" in Bernard E. Segal, ed., *Racial and Ethnic Relations* (New York: Thomas Y. Crowell, 1966), pp. 99, 103.

[118] Drake and Cayton, *op. cit.,* pp. 583–85.

and sexual prowess. All ties are temporary and loose, and there is no basis for establishing family stability. The men scorn middle-class standards and hate authority. They are touchy with whites, resentful of being treated like inferiors or "women"; the power of the dominant group is a challenge to their masculinity, and gang members find ways of expressing their hatred accordingly.[119] "More than most social worlds, perhaps, the streetcorner world takes its shape and color from the structure and character of the face-to-face relationships of the people who live in it." Friendships, which tend to be romanticized, are a source of security as well as self-esteem. They are sustained by an exchange of money, goods, services, and emotional support.[120]

These friendships, however, do not stand up well under the stress of crisis. The dearth of psychological and material resources undermines the whole structure of personal relationships. Self-interest is too pressing, and each one must ultimately look to himself alone. The friendships necessarily lack depth for there is finally nothing cooperative about survival. The relationships are easily dissolved under pressure, and the pressures are many.[121] For those who are effectively removed from the sources of economic power, definable groups have limited survival value. People cultivate a variety of others in anticipation of tapping some of their material surplus when there is any. These networks exist only from the reference point of the person manipulating others at a specific time for specific purposes. They thus support the short-run exploitation of resources.[122]

"Living on the edge of both economic and psychological subsistence, the streetcorner man is obliged to expend all his resources on maintaining himself from moment to moment." He is all too aware of the hopelessness of his future, and his self-indulgence in the present reflects his sense of despair. The streetcorner man "travels light," in effect, free of excess emotional baggage. Because he is always aware of the probability of trouble, he is in a constant state of readiness to leave. Such an awareness prevents him from sinking roots into the world in which he lives. Deep and enduring ties to family and friends would limit his freedom of move-

---

[119] Thompson, *op. cit.*, pp. 104–5.
[120] Liebow, *op. cit.*, pp. 161, 174–76.
[121] *Ibid.*, pp. 180, 206–7, 216.
[122] Norman E. Whitten, Jr., and John Szwed, "Introduction: Negroes in the New World, Anthropologists Look at Afro-Americans," *Trans-Action*, Vol. 5, No. 8 (July–August 1968), pp. 51, 54.

ment, thus compromising his one source of security when trouble does come. The social world of the streetcorner is thus neither self-contained nor self-sustaining. It is not impervious to the values and sentiments of the larger society, but a sanctuary from failure in dominant terms. There is a shadow system of values constructed out of public fictions that accommodate its members to their failure, "permitting them to be men once again provided they do not look too closely at one another's credentials."[123]

Attempting to conceal his failure from himself and others, the streetcorner man must necessarily assign little priority to matters of employment. Jobs occupy a low position in his scale of values. Jobs, for those who have them, are menial ones that do not pay enough to support a family.[124]

> *"For his part, the streetcorner man puts no lower value on the job than does the larger society around him.* He knows the social value of the job by the amount of money the employer is willing to pay him for doing it."[125]

Both employer and employee are contemptuous of such work, and there is, of course, no commitment to the job. The experience of employment is so empty that the men do not even talk about it among themselves. All jobs are alike, and if a man knows that someone is working, he knows all he needs to know. Yet he sees middle-class occupations as a source of self-respect and social prestige, and he values them. He would also like to be a person in his own right, acknowledged by others for the attainment of such a job, but he has no expectation of doing so. "To think about his [own] job is to see himself as others see him, to remind him of just where he stands in this society."[126]

Unlike the situation in the south, the church has little influence among the lower-class members of the northern ghettos. Mostly women belong, and even for them church membership may only be a substitute for club membership. It does not offer enough to satisfy either the emotional needs or the social aspirations of the younger generation either. Men especially are cynical about the church and the material motives of the clergy.

> Bronzeville is in revolt against Heaven, and the rebellion centers in the lower class. It is reflected in continuous vitriolic attacks upon preachers and church members. It is a part of the general secularization of life in the urban, industrial society. . . . It takes the form of a protest against the alleged cupidity and hypocrisy of church functionaries and devotees.[127]

[123] Liebow, *op. cit.,* pp. 65–66, 68–71, 209, 213–14.
[124] *Ibid.,* pp. 34–35, 39–40, 222.
[125] *Ibid.,* p. 57.
[126] *Ibid.,* pp. 56, 58, 60–61, 63.
[127] Drake and Cayton, *op. cit.,* pp. 615, 617, 629, 650.

Religion is no longer the focus of lower-class life. Most Negroes in the lower class organize their behavior around having a good time, utilizing the cheaper forms of commercial recreation; local bars are favorite gathering places. "Broadly speaking, the social structure of the lower class is less organized, less stable, and less coordinated than that of the middle class."[128]

By contrast to life on the streetcorner, the middle class is characterized by a complex web of voluntary associations that gives it a certain cohesiveness and formal structure. These organizations symbolize the aspirations of their members and permit the display of other status symbols. The middle class is made up of joiners who stress proper social connections. In their insecure position, they suffer the tensions of striving. They must strike some balance, with limited incomes, between conspicuous consumption to maintain status and the achievement of long-range goals.[129] There is also considerable resentment accompanying their respectability. Members of the middle class resent those who do not adhere to strict moral standards. Since they regard themselves as superior to the masses, they resent being classified with them by whites. They also resent segregation, which impedes the achievement of able and ambitious men.[130] The value they place on decorum is, in part, a function of their desire for the good opinion of the dominant group.

"The black bourgeoisie is constituted of those Negroes who derive their incomes principally from the services which they render as white-collar workers." Those in business, and they are not many, are likely to provide personal services for Negroes, which white establishments refuse to do.[131] Higher-status Negroes are more likely to be professionals serving other Negroes than businessmen, for whom there is an insufficient economic base within the community. What the members of the middle class have in common is a stable income; their wives may also work in semiprofessional or clerical jobs. One study of professionals finds that a high proportion of their fathers (59.2 percent) were also white-collar workers, suggesting little vertical mobility between the generations.[132] Another study reveals that high-status Negroes have the same values as middle-class whites, and they desire to associate with whites. Their identification with

[128] Rohrer and Edmonson, *op. cit.,* p. 54.

[129] Drake and Cayton, *op. cit.,* pp. 662, 668–69.

[130] Thompson, *op. cit.,* pp. 99–100.

[131] Frazier, *Black Bourgeoisie, op. cit.,* pp. 43, 55.

[132] G. Franklin Edwards, *The Negro Professional Class* (New York: Free Press, 1959), pp. 19, 49.

other Negroes is weak, and their ambivalence increases with their status.[133]

Middle-class Negroes often appear to have dedicated their lives to becoming walking refutations of racial stereotypes. Having accepted the values of the dominant group, they also seek to share in the status symbols of personal success. The interracial church outside the ghetto, for example, may be a social instrument for upwardly mobile and upper-middle-class Negroes.[134] The upper class guards its status jealously, perhaps because there is so little to distinguish it from the middle class. It comprises no more than 5 percent of the Negro community, and most of its members are only middle class by the standards of the larger society. Skin color has considerable importance among those of high status. Fair-skinned Negroes, especially women, tend to form cliques based on skin color, and there is a premium on fair skin in marital mobility.[135]

Upper-class Negroes are almost completely absorbed in the social ritual and struggle for status. There are few persons of wealth in the black ghetto. Those who don't move out withdraw from participation in the community. There is no tradition of support for community services, and there are too few wealthy Negroes in any case to sustain communal programs with private funds. There are only three or four Negro families of inherited wealth in the country. The others are too insecure to assume civic responsibility and philanthropic leadership, although they often depend on the ghetto for their income; they are busy protecting their economic interests. Those who have made their money in such illicit activities as the numbers racket tend to maintain their residential roots in the ghetto, but they are not accepted socially by the rest of the upper class.[136]

Even more than most minority communities, the black ghetto is a narrow world with a parochial outlook, and its intellectuals have always chafed at its provincialism. Those with the ability to deal with broader problems lose influence within the ghetto, which demands focus on its particular problems. Talents that can succeed in the larger society cannot be controlled by the ghetto and are rarely permitted to be useful within it. Individuals of certain levels of interest and competence are thus excluded from effectiveness and even regarded as deserters. The ghetto has no role for them to play since they are unwilling to meet the demands of its re-

[133] Donald L. Noel, "Group Identification Among Negroes: An Empirical Analysis," *The Journal of Social Issues*, Vol. 20, No. 2 (April 1964), p. 102.

[134] Clark, *op. cit.*, pp. 58, 60, 177.

[135] Drake and Cayton, *op. cit.*, pp. 498, 514–15.

[136] Clark, *op. cit.*, pp. 174, 189–90.

stricted vision. The confinement of the ghetto requires either that one exploit it or rebel against it, and such a choice is inconsistent with intellectual standards.[137]

Violence and Community

There can be no concept of community in a group whose members hold each other in contempt, and there can be no tradition of mutual aid where there is a prevalence of self-hatred. Without an independent sense of social honor, interaction within a minority group only reflects the negative images of the dominant group. Each minority member then has no alternative but to see the other in the alien terms of the larger society. Under such circumstances, community constitutes a social looking glass that destroys as it distorts, thereby reinforcing the power of the dominant group. There is no psychological refuge in this kind of community; one sees oneself in the other, and one sees him as the dominant group does.

In addition, a minority group that lacks the alternative values of an ethnic culture lacks the institutional resources for creating a community. The minority groups that emigrated to this country had that advantage over the deculturated groups. They didn't bring capital, but they brought with them a culture, which proved to be critical in their survival, whatever their marketable skill or lack of it. When (and if) a community that lacks adequate institutional resources becomes organized, it is oriented toward conflict with the dominant group. A contraculture is more likely to develop than a subculture. A minority contraculture is not the product of an ethnic history and its cultural traditions, but of hopeless frustration and consequent conflict. It originates in the deprived situation of complete powerlessness, and its values are reaction-formations, "inverted norms that express the resentment of an oppressed group whose members have caught the image of human dignity but are deprived of the means for achieving it in their own lives."[138] The values of a minority contraculture, such as they are, are usually an inversion of the dominant culture that does not free its members from susceptibility to the derogation of the larger society. There can be no social detachment when there is only a mirror-image of

[137] *Ibid.,* pp. 193–94.
[138] Yinger, *op. cit.,* p. 122.

the dominant culture that does not offer alternative values and personal autonomy.

There is no independence for the minority when there is such involvement with the dominant culture, however negative, but there is the increasing possibility of violence. The very fact that communal organization emerges makes it a probability. With psychological resources that are as insufficient as the social resources, there may be individual acts of vengeance and massive eruptions of rioting. When a community begins to be organized, violence is more effectively directed at the dominant group. Violence, too, becomes organized and thus less self-destructive; in turn, it reinforces the community, serving as a source of social cohesion at the same time that it satisfies the shattered psyches of the members. For the diverse and divided minority, direct confrontation may succeed in crystallizing a sense of community. Any consequent violence is all the more dangerous for not being random.

Riots are most likely to occur when social institutions function inadequately, and minority grievances cannot be resolved under existing intergroup arrangements. Lack of faith in the larger society exacerbates the minority response, heightening the potential for violence.[139] Newspapers report the accumulation of weapons among some Negroes, for instance, as indication of preparation for urban guerrilla warfare. There are now predictions of intentional insurrection rather than spontaneous rioting. Such violence is part of the sense of community and collectivism of a new breed of black activists, who do not measure social progress in terms of the individual Negroes who are mobile, but in terms of the masses who are not. There are no longer psychological defenses or social supports for a passive adaptation to their minority situation. Young Negroes, in particular, refuse to be abused as they have been in the past. Many have formed groups to protect themselves and their communities from police brutality, among other things. They see police as violent and are now ready to retaliate. Police violence does indeed precede or supersede ghetto violence, and young blacks now strike back with increasing intensity.[140]

The protective organizations that are arming in black ghettos are de-

---

[139] Stanley J. Lieberson and Arnold R. Silverman, "The Precipitants and Underlying Conditions of Race Riots," *American Sociological Review,* Vol. 30, No. 6 (December 1965), p. 897.

[140] Thomas A. Johnson, "Worse Racial Strife Than Riots Feared by Analysts," *The New York Times,* October 22, 1968, pp. 1, 33.

termined that their communities will no longer be disrespected, particularly by police, nor their members be treated as if they were less than human. It is a calculated risk; they are not unaware of the repressive response—and the fact that they must ultimately lose to greater force. For some the risk is worth it; it is preferable to not fighting at all. In the politics of despair, death may be the sole source of dignity, and existence in the ghetto no life at all. There is thus a decline in disorganized self-destructiveness with the diminution of mob rioting. The danger of directed violence, however, increases as the more organized community mobilizes what resources it has for conflict. It is through such means that they hope to gain what they need to build a better community.

The prospects for real change in the racial situation appear grim. Social segregation and categorical status combine to make the Negro literally as well as metaphorically invisible. This invisibility protects members of the dominant group from a sense of individual responsibility for the Negro's plight. In so far as conscience operates at all, in or out of the American dilemma, it does so in a personalized manner. Although the disparity remains between the American creed and the social reality, there is little to externalize any guilt the dominant group may feel and to bring it into active focus. The dominant group sees no evil, therefore it knows no evil; it thus believes that it has done no wrong. Since few members of the dominant group (or any other group for that matter) know any Negroes, they have no personal involvement in the racial situation and can shrug it off as someone else's problem. And it is someone else's problem as far as they are concerned—until there is violence. Then there is a repressive reaction; it is defined as a matter of property and the presumed protection thereof.

Although there may now be some willingness, at least among upper-middle-class whites, to let Negroes help themselves, there is no willingness to do anything for them. There is too little understanding that individual mobility may not be possible for Negroes until there is a massive breakthrough for the whole group because their situation is so different from that of religious minorities. The assumption is that other ethnic groups improved themselves, Negroes should do so also. White responses lag decades behind black demands, and whites are now prepared to accept only the individual mobility that they resisted in the past. The dominant group is not prepared to enact sweeping social change and to incur its costs. This gives additional impetus to the ideology of separateness that is

currently held by black nationalists. The hope is that separatism will increase the probability of mobility hitherto limited as much by lack of
qualification as by lack of opportunity.

> But there *is* the reality of the white backlash. It is the newest version of
> the American dilemma. There has come to exist a new and popular ac-
> ceptance of equality of opportunity for qualified Negroes. . . . The white
> backlash consists of a reluctance to accept those *intermediate* steps that are
> necessary to make equality a reality for the many Negroes who are in no
> way prepared to live according to white middle-class standards.[141]

It is the demand for the social resources with which to establish separate
communities that engenders conflict. Negroes may be able to create a
cultural raison d'être for such communities, but they lack a sociological
starting point for their establishment. The dominant group, on the other
hand, accepts the hypothetical, and even the actual, existence of black
separatism, but it will not support it materially. It refuses to provide the
resources necessary for rendering Negro communities self-sufficient and
socially adequate. Perhaps the greatest resistance comes from those earlier
ethnic groups that did take care of themselves. As lower-middle-class
minorities, these groups are the most threatened by Negro demands. In
the social context of the struggle for status, these are the groups who are
the least secure about their own success.

Perhaps it is a contradiction in sociological, if not in human, terms to
expect the dominant group to supply the wherewithal that permits the
minority group to become independent of it. If the minority group opts to
remain separate socially, it is expected to maintain itself. The alternative
presumably is to integrate, that is, if the minority group qualifies itself,
and if the dominant group accepts it. The institutional structure of American society usually makes integration a more likely possibility than separatism, when there is no longer any distinctive ethnic culture. Since
integration presupposes acculturation to dominant norms, it does not require any acceptance of social differences on the part of the larger society.
But the masses of Negroes are not educationally and economically prepared for upward mobility and individual integration. They do not have
available to them the traditional means of earlier ethnic groups. There is
thus all the greater possibility of direct confrontation and violent conflict
between blacks and whites. Although neither blacks nor whites constitute
homogeneous social entities, they react to each other as if they are, par-

[141] Lewis M. Killian, *The Impossible Revolution?* (New York: Random House,
1968), p. 132.

ticularly in the crisis of conflict. Their history of mutual categorization denies the heterogeneity of the respective groups, and they define the racial situation in literal terms of black and white.

The situation is exacerbated by the fact that Negroes do not always understand it themselves, although they experience it daily and feel it deeply. They bear the scars of slavery without having known it personally. It is no longer even a living memory, but past history, yet they must continue to endure its consequences. It simply compounds the injustices imposed upon Negroes that theirs is a heritage that is not a heritage. They have reason enough for their suffering in the present without the reason of the past, which is not their reason; it was their ancestors, and not they, who were slaves. Still they pay the price, as if the costs had not been high enough already. The deculturation imposed by slavery has intensified the impact of the categorical treatment accorded subordinate status. Negroes thus not only do not have the reason of the past for their plight, they have no raison d'être in the present. Without cultural justification, social separateness is difficult to sustain. And in so far as Negroes do not understand the consequences of their situation, they are not able to cope with them. It also makes it all the more difficult to create a community.

Chapter 11

Religious and Racial Contrasts in Community

MINORITY groups are characterized by their categorically lowered life chances. Their identifying characteristics, whether physical or cultural, serve only as a source of social visibility. It is the relative powerlessness of minority groups that defines their disadvantaged situation, underlying their exclusion from participation in the institutions of the larger society. Whatever the resulting degree of deprivation, both real and relative, it is their desire for dominant values that is critical, for such aspiration engenders social conflict. The power of the dominant group is manifested in its monopoly of values. The institutional control it exercises is enforced by the practice of discrimination (and presumably explained by prejudice). Since the dominant group regards minorities as socially unequal, they are considered ineligible for inclusion in the larger society; such integration would threaten its vested interests.

The struggle for status, interpreted so astutely by Robert Park, is the source of the minority problem, a problem that occurs between groups conscious of their differences by virtue of the contact that has taken place. A differential power distribution permits one group to put another into a subordinate position—and to keep it in its place. Any attempt on the part of the minority to rise from what is regarded as its rightful place is more than resented, it is resisted by the dominant group. The resolution of such conflict is found in the patterns of accommodation that are embedded in the reciprocal expectations of the social order.[1] These expectations are as much imposed upon the minority group as accepted by it; when traditional accommodations break down, there is always coercion to sanction subordination.

[1] Robert E. Park, "The Nature of Race Relations," in *Race and Culture* (New York: Free Press, 1950), pp. 81–83, 98.

The Necessity of Community

The consequences of the minority situation, both social and psychological, would be entirely destructive without the existence of community. The communities that members of minority groups are impelled to establish counteract the stigma of categorical status that would otherwise incur only self-hatred. Minority members cope with these consequences within the context of their respective communities. Their disadvantaged situation creates a sense of shared social fate that supports their communal solidarity. They are subject to the discrimination of the dominant group because of the ascribed status of their ethnic birth. The resulting mutual orientation of minority members reinforces their resistance to dominant derogation. The patterns of response to their relative deprivation are institutionalized in their communities, which emerge in reaction to the closure of the dominant group that they experience. In this respect, the minority community constitutes an accommodation to the underlying conflict of the categorical condition.

The institutions of the minority community make possible a separate way of life and thus some access to values, whether distinctive or acculturated. These institutions are protected by the minority's independent practice of closure. Its ideology of self-exclusion, once sacred and now secular, maintains the minority's sense of social honor. It is this self-exclusion that mitigates the effects of social exclusion. The family is particularly significant in the social structure of the minority community since this community is premised on ethnic birth, an involuntary and inescapable categorical status that is negatively evaluated in the larger society; such status takes social precedence over any individual achievement and hence serves, if only by default, as a source of communal cohesion. The network of informal interpersonal relations within the minority community is characteristically supported by a variety of voluntary associations, many of which are affiliated with the religious institution.

The formal organization of the community acquires a vested interest in perpetuating itself, and this institutionalization requires some special identity to justify the separate existence of the minority group. Its life chances are enhanced in so far as it can provide values independent of (if not different from) those of the dominant group. The minority community is not often completely isolated from the surrounding society; it is usually dependent on it economically and eventually integrated into it politically. Yet it offers a way of life that provides minority members some of the social alternatives and personal autonomy denied them by the dominant group. The individual responses that are incorporated into the communal patterns become the source of socialization into living with the minority situation.

The literal visibility of color means that the racial experience in American society is qualitatively different from that of the religious experience. Hence the communities that emerge out of these experiences are not entirely comparable, even by contrast. The very incomparability suggests the serious, and perhaps irresoluble, differences between them. The structural consequences of the racial situation are such that the resulting communities are unable to fulfill the necessary functions for their minority members. By way of summarizing, we will contrast the institutional and ideological resources of the religious communities with the inadequately organized communities of racial groups. It is the religious community that is thus far prototypical; the racial communities, being less organized, manifest more variation among their respective structures.

Goal Achievement

Insofar as the minority group is institutionalized, it is no longer only a network of interpersonal relations, but a community. There are still the primary groups of peers made up of family and friends, but there is more —there is a formal structure that permits the pursuit of goals, however limited by lack of opportunity in the larger society. The possibility of social rationality may well be the most significant function of the minority community, for it is this function, if fulfilled, that most effectively counteracts the discrimination of the dominant group. The community that provides institutionalized means to desired ends offers more than social compensation for the relative deprivation of minority members, it offers an effective alternative. In the matter of mobility, there are role models to reinforce individual motivations. And even more important, there is the mutual recognition of achievement in shared terms.

The early immigrants were forced to adjust to the economic necessity of their alien circumstances. That adjustment in itself modified their ethnic traditions, but it also laid the groundwork for later achievement. They worked as unskilled laborers in an industrial economy, relinquishing

the occupational pursuits of their rural past. The second and third generations of these nationality groups eventually entered into the lower-middle-
and middle-class occupations that serve as the economic basis of the contemporary religious community. As its members escape from the slums,
the community is relocated in better urban neighborhoods. But ethnic
specialization continues to accompany social segregation among religious
minorities as restrictive employment remains a prevalent practice of the
dominant group, reinforcing its social exclusiveness. Members of these
communities are therefore most likely to be self-employed in small business or independent professions, or they are employed in civil service,
which discriminates less than private corporations.

The religious community that emerges out of ethnic birth is characterized by economic differentiation. Its internal stratification in turn leads
to some variation in styles of life, evidenced in a proliferation of class-
linked organizations. For all the kinds of clubs and cliques, it is essentially
a middle-class community, most cohesive as a minority group in the lower
middle class. As long as there remains relatively little occupational variety,
level of income is a more significant source of status within the religious
community. Money, and what it can buy, is what makes a difference socially. There may still be some conflicting economic and ethnic considerations at the point where dominant and minority stratification systems
overlap. There are sometimes contradictory behavior patterns involved in
their respective life styles, but these usually represent differences in taste
rather than value; it is the underlying principle that is problematic. Those
of higher status begin to aspire for the good opinion of the dominant
group, for which they are considered snobbish. They cannot afford to risk
their status in the minority community, however, since it remains their
primary source of social acceptance.

The structure of any minority community is a function of its position
in the larger society. Its stratification is a reflection of its access to dominant values. Thus when minority members are successful, the community
that incorporates their mobility is more effective in countering the prejudice and discrimination of the dominant group. By reducing the degree of
deprivation, it diminishes the cause for derogation. The racial community,
by contrast, lacks the structure provided by adequate institutional resources; it therefore has insufficient capacity to cope with the consequences
of the minority situation. The physical visibility of color is compounded
by the self-perpetuation of modern poverty. There is no economic basis
for the racial community to maintain itself and to permit its members to

solve their problems. It is therefore difficult, if not impossible, for them to engage in self-help and mutual aid.

The functions of community remain relatively unfulfilled among racial groups due to the paucity of resources. There are not enough values available within the community to make up an independent way of life, and its members are denied all access to dominant values. This deprivation is all the more frustrating to those who, by virtue of acculturation or deculturation, accept the desirability of dominant values. It accounts in part for the high rates of personal disorganization and social pathology. Those with educational or economic achievement tend to leave the community, and even to lose their identity, if they can. If they cannot, they isolate themselves socially, withdrawing from participation in the community. The potential for leadership is thereby lost. Only now does there begin to be a middle class that might provide the basis for building a more sufficient community that can support itself.

The racial community is thus a lower-class one whose economic situation renders it institutionally inadequate. The unemployment and underemployment of its members have severe consequences for its communal structure. There is therefore less likely to be the culturally defined way of life of earlier ethnic groups. There are rather only the pragmatic (and not always functional) adaptations to the material circumstances of poverty; accepted expectations, derived from dominant norms, simply cannot be enacted in such a community. Hence members of the racial community suffer more than members of religious communities from the disruption of behavior characteristic of the minority experience. They cannot achieve goals, if indeed they still aspire to any, since there are no available means leading to them. This is the point at which apathy sets in, when no legitimate expectations are allowed the members of a minority group. And then they resent the success of the few who are mobile.

Collective Action

To the extent that goals can be achieved within the minority community members have a capacity for collective action. Social solidarity that derives from a sense of shared destiny leads to a concerted effort to improve the minority situation, thereby minimizing the destructive responses of individuals. The effectiveness of such action inheres in its organization; the informal tradition of mutual aid is reinforced by the formal associations of the community that has acquired adequate resources. Welfare activities, for example, are carried out by indigenous organizations in the religious community, organizations that represent an acculturated transformation of ethnic associations. They support the in-group sentiments of the members that in turn support the institutional structure.

As the religious community grows more socially differentiated, there are, of course, more internal conflicts. Although there are divisive strains, organizational unity continues to prevail. Voluntary associations reinforce shared communal interests in part by reasserting the priority of categorical status within the minority group as well as in the larger society. The leadership of the community becomes more professionalized and thereby acquires a vested interest in the minority situation on which its status rests. Still, its professionalism enhances the communal capacity for organized action. Collective effort has improved the essential aspects of the categorical condition without attempting to break down social barriers. Members of the religious community also want to maintain distance in intergroup relations, protecting their sense of exclusiveness with their own practice of closure.

The racial community is critically different in this respect. In its impoverishment there is little organization beyond the extended family, and its members can't afford to be of much assistance to each other. Because of its lack of resources, the family itself may be unstable. There is little tradition for formal organization and hence few voluntary associations that are indigenous in nature. As a result, there is not only less mutual aid than in the religious community, there is also less group identity and greater reliance on outside agencies. The settlement of commuting groups may be so tentative that they feel little need to try to improve their minority situation in the United States. The deculturated groups also experience particular difficulty in social organization, albeit for other reasons. Their members are not only isolated from the larger society, they are often isolated from each other. There is thus little source of social unity within these groups to serve as a basis for communal cohesion.

Negroes have the most severe problem in community, and therefore institutional functions are inadequately fulfilled, if at all. Their voluntary associations are primarily social in orientation, and their defense organizations are likely to be subsidized by the dominant group. Militant nationalism now offers a renewed source of social identity and community organization that helps to counteract the coercion of the past. Its stress on self-improvement even fulfills some of the traditional functions of the minority community. Insofar as there is the beginning of militancy among other racial groups, it will help to structure their communities, which in turn will help to improve their respective situations. This process, of course, reverses the past pattern of the ethnic experience in which collective action emerged out of an established community. Another new source of social organization for racial minorities is the externally enacted institutions of the federal government.

Social Intimacy

The increased capacity for goal achievement is thus the most significant sociological function of the minority community, a function that is more adequately fulfilled the greater the sufficiency of the social structure. The community also has, however, social psychological functions for its members. Their shared meanings and values are institutionalized, thereby providing a meaningful basis for mutually oriented behavior. The concomitant ideological function of these underlying values is to justify the minority situation in intelligible terms to those who must live with it.

With each other, members of minority groups find the ease of familiarity, both social and cultural. As social peers they are able to enjoy appropriate modes of interaction and maintain their primary relations within the context of the in-group. There can be intimate communication among them because of their shared situation and mutual identification. And their selective association in turn reinforces their selective perception so that they continue to see the world and their position in it in the same way. The social support they find in their individualized acceptance of each other counters the categorical rejection they experience with the dominant group.

The source of this intimacy in the religious community derives from the ghettos of the immigrants. It was the ghetto that was the original ethnic community. As such, it constituted an adaptation to alien status formally institutionalized around the church or synagogue, which embodied and transmitted the distinctive values that became central to ethnic identity. The cultural insulation that characterized the ghetto was protected by social isolation and physical segregation and defended by a sacred ideology. Its closure enforced endogamy as well as ethnicity, thereby contributing to the strength of the family and the cohesion of the community.

The informal sociability of the immigrants followed the patterns they had known in their village life in the old country. There were also voluntary associations organized around the need for mutual aid. The native language was always used within the confines of the ghetto.

The distinctive culture and ethnic institutions of the immigrants were the source of community that ultimately structured the minority situation of religious groups. Consequently, the major religious communities are structurally similar regardless of their national origins. By the second and third generation, the community is acculturated, if still segregated. Access to dominant values through its minority institutions is made possible by the economic advancement of its members. Their marginality is resolved through the loss of cultural uniqueness and the mutual recognition of their achieved status. Institutions and organizations are appropriately adapted to a dominant style of life, modifications brought about by entry into lower- and middle-class occupations.

Kinship ties continue to undergird the cohesion of the religious community, which is further strengthened by the primary relations of the peer group. These social bonds remain essentially endogamous in nature. They are supported by a network of voluntary associations and formal organizations, all of which encourage sociability, whatever their stated goals. The attachment to the community is such that it seems defensive at times. The racial community is not always able to offer its members such social comfort. Those groups that still retain some cultural distinctiveness can maintain at least a semblance of a way of life. Deculturated groups, however, have been left few social resources.

The racial groups in American society are all isolated, usually ecologically and certainly socially. For the Spanish-speaking groups, this isolation is reinforced by the continued use of their native language. There is, of course, some protection in such isolation, but so also is there greater deprivation. The family, the essence of the ethnic community, may be too strained to serve even as a significant source of sociability among racial groups. Lacking sufficient resources, it may be disorganized to the point of dissolution. In fact, the processes of deculturation undergone by Indians and Negroes systematically attempted to destroy the family (and all too often succeeded) lest it offer a wellspring of social strength. The primary relations of peers may also be threatened by the exigencies of survival. The reciprocal obligations of friendship can be burdensome in the chronic crisis of the racial situation; there is always trouble, and one must be prepared to face it alone. Nor is there much tradition for the institutionalized sociability of ethnic associations.

Personal Identity

The minority community that is capable of fulfilling its institutional functions creates for its members a social reality free of dominant images. Such a communal context permits them a sense of wholeness and worth as human beings, a sense otherwise undermined by categorical treatment in the larger society. Minority members who see each other as persons thereby maintain their sense of dignity. They are also better able to achieve personal identity. The positive social images that are reflected among themselves encourage the self-esteem that is prerequisite to personality development.

There may also be found among minority members a compensatory sense of superiority counteracting the social inferiority imposed upon them. Reciprocal stereotypes of the dominant group reflect the lingering (and not necessarily unfounded) ethnocentrism of those who are heir to an ethnic culture. Although such reactive categorization restores the pride of a minority, it also reinforces social distance in intergroup relations. The stylized response to the dominant group established by communal precedent obviates painful affect, but so also does it eliminate any intergroup possibility but the ritualized one. This is characteristic of the religious group, whose very communal security mitigates against meaningful interaction with the dominant group.

The original ethnic community embodied alternative values to the dominant culture. It could therefore serve as an independent source of social honor. Because the immigrants believed in their own worth and that of their way of life, the destructive consequences of dominant derogation were diminished. They had values, so they were able to value themselves. Yet the religious community remains an accommodation to intergroup conflict that threatens neither the power nor the prestige of the dominant group. It asks for nothing from the larger society, not even social recognition of its economic achievement, so that the dominant group's monopoly of status is maintained.

These same values that were a source of social security for the immigrants created cultural conflict for ensuing generations; their mobility was accompanied by marginality. By the second and third generation, acculturation brings about a decline in cultural distinctiveness, and ethnic identity is transformed into a religious one. But the religious institution changes in form to maintain its importance in identity. It is itself acculturated

to the dominant pattern, with no more scope or significance than the secular institutions with which it competes. No longer crucial in defining a way
of life, the church and synagogue are still central to communal sociability.
They become, in effect, community centers encouraging (if no longer in-
suring) endogamy as minority status is increasingly based on religion
rather than ethnicity.

The racial community suffers critically by contrast. Although the
Spanish-speaking groups retain some ethnic heritage that sustains their
racial pride, the deculturated groups, by definition, have no such resource.
The compulsory adoption of dominant values inhered in the systematic
processes of deculturation, and the resulting demoralization has been compounded by legal subordination. Finally, Indians and Negroes become convinced of their own inferiority. Without distinctive values, they have
neither social alternatives nor personal autonomy. They lack effective
choice and thus lose self-esteem. Subject to extreme coercion, deculturated
groups have not been able to exercise any control whatsoever over their
own life chances. And since they have no independent source of social
honor, self-hatred is all but inevitable.

It is not possible to provide protective socialization without independent
values to defend against dominant derogation. There is no way of explaining the minority situation to each new generation as external to itself.
Since deculturation precipitates an acceptance of dominant values, the
social inferiority imposed by them is necessarily internalized. In a recent
journalist's report of the approximately 6,000 Blackfoot Indians on reservations, the suicide rate was found to be 100 per 100,000, or ten times the
rate for Americans as a whole. Suicide is most common among adolescents,
whereas in the larger society it increases with age. As pride is lost, Indians
turn to liquor. There is a consequent disintegration of the family, with a
high rate of marital dissolution. Children are increasingly alienated as they
begin to experience a sense of shame and self-hatred. They can find no
escape from the dominant group's judgment that the Indian is inferior,
and they begin to believe the stereotypes about them. Such youngsters
know nothing but frustration in their lives. "Hope is a word that has
little meaning."[2]

---

[2] Steven V. Roberts, "Hope Has Little Meaning for Blackfoot Indians," *The
New York Times,* May 6, 1969, p. 49.

Limitations of Enclosure

The functions of the minority community are not without concomitant dysfunctions for its members. Its enclosure is sheltering, of course, but it may also be limiting. Minority members may not explore the changing reality of the larger society as a result. Unaware of new opportunities, they may fail to qualify themselves for further participation in dominant institutions. The stress placed on categorical status by the minority community itself can be stifling. In counteracting categorical status, the community gives it as much priority as the larger society does, thereby reducing the social options available within the minority context. Sometimes there is too little individual variation in the group because of its emphasis on unity, especially in its conflict with the dominant group.

The mutual expectations of the minority community are premised on the shared birth of its members. This social presupposition may be threatened by intellectual detachment, and hence there is considerable communal ambivalence about its most creative individuals. Members of the minority community are insecure about their status since it is, after all, a negatively evaluated one in the larger society. Any alternative perspective to their own might undermine their ideological defenses and arouse an awareness of their standing in respect to the dominant group. They demand therefore an unquestioning commitment to the community in return for their social acceptance.

The self-limiting qualities of the minority group impel the young to rebel against communal restrictions. It is their exploration of social alternatives that provides the dynamics of intergenerational conflict, and consequent change. The ideologies of the community become more vulnerable as its members become acculturated. The decline in ethnicity may mean that minority institutions lose their membership to participation in the larger society. With the third generation in the religious community this process begins, and the resulting integration suggests the potential for assimilation.

The status values of the dominant group are incorporated into the religious community with the third and succeeding generations. Members of the younger generation capitalize on the class values already achieved by their elders to gain access to increasing college education and salaried employment. Their move to the suburbs breaks down some of the social enclosure of the established community. The consequences are manifested in taste patterns that reflect a changing style of life. Closer interaction with the dominant group brings about social similarities not acquired in the marketplace in which an earlier generation had been acculturated. As younger members of the religious community become more like the dominant group, there is less justification for a separate existence. And insofar as there is less social exclusion in the larger society, there are more mixed organizational affiliations among them, and even a greater number of intergroup friendships.

For all this newly acquired sophistication, there are still economic and emotional ties to the religious community reinforced by essentially endogamous primary relations. Exclusion does continue, and family and friends remain largely within the bounds of the in-group. New organizational occupations, however, are leading to social acceptance in the larger society. Some younger members of religious minorities are being incorporated into the status communities of the dominant group, and it is through their occupations that they cross ethnic boundaries. Membership in the religious institution constitutes their one formal affiliation—and acknowledgment of minority identity. This identity has been effectively narrowed to a religious definition that is institutionally transmitted only by the church or synagogue. Its one source of informal support is the intimate interpersonal relationships of the in-group.

Such primary relations, however endogamous, may not be sufficient to sustain the religious community. Occupation is becoming a determinant of one's way of life that transcends ethnic birth and enclosure. There is an increasing rate of intermarriage among religious minorities as their economic specialization and social segregation disappear, leaving only an attenuated religious affiliation. Racial groups have by no means advanced to this point; their situation is so different that they may never do so. Even the dysfunctions of the racial community offer a striking contrast to those of the religious community.

Nothing is more dysfunctional for members of racial minorities than the incorporation of their categorical status into the structure of their own communities. When this occurs, as it is most likely to in deculturated groups, it fosters an acceptance of the status quo, mitigating against the possibility of enacting change in the minority situation. With little social stability and less personal security, individuation may be inadequate. Such leadership as there is lacks initiative; the vested interests of communal institutions are self-interested. Insofar as there is social diversity, it is divisive in the absence of a common cultural core. And there are insufficient institutional resources to ease these strains. Even among the Spanish-speaking, the church plays no significant role in their communal structure; among Negroes, its social consequences are basically conservative. Worse still, the family is burdened to the breaking point.

The ultimate dysfunction of the racial community is its potential for violence. The destructive responses, ranging from apathy to aggression, cannot be channeled by communal institutions in a state of structural insufficiency. These responses become all the more dangerous when the community becomes organized around conflict with the dominant group. These responses reflect the critical differences between religious and racial communities. The difference in their degree of relative and real deprivation has made a qualitative difference in their respective situations. Their time span for anticipated change is significantly affected, and that has even more significant consequences for the state of mind of their members.

Members of religious minorities have always been able to maintain a modicum of hope because they could anticipate at least some change in their situation at a foreseeable point in the future. If not for themselves, then for their children, there would be the mobility that would bring material comfort. Members of racial minorities, by contrast, see no possibility for change in their own lifetime or that of their children. Change postponed indefinitely has no meaningful reality and hence offers no grounds for hope. There are no future prospects with a concrete existence in the present; the daily lives of racial minorities are therefore inundated with despair, a despair that may on occasion be overcome only by violence. The new militant nationalism among Negroes, for example, disavows dominant values to proclaim physical force, declaring as a virtue what should not be a necessity.

There are those who claim that we are all minorities today, at least sociologically speaking. It is not so, not even as a metaphor. The assertion reflects the sense of powerlessness that pervades modern society. All of its members experience the frustration of being unable to participate effectively in the bureaucratic structures that shape their lives. Suspecting that they have lost control over their own life chances, some members of the dominant group have acquired a minority mentality. They now seek a sense of community to ease their feelings of fragmentation and isolation. In so doing, they romanticize the traditional community. The tensions of their alienation have led to a search for social sharing in which they idealize minorities as role models.

Although there are certainly experiences in American society that are analogous to those of the minority situation, there are none that are entirely comparable. Such an identification with minorities is thus spurious in its essence. Unlike any form of class situation in the United States, the minority situation is based on an accident of birth that socially defines a negatively evaluated categorical status. The sense of powerlessness of some members of the dominant group is doubtless valid, but it is not a function of an ascribed characteristic. It is therefore neither involuntary nor inescapable; it may be only a partial phenomenon for them, peripheral in its impact on their actual behavior. Minority members are always affected by their status, necessarily impeded in all their actions. The dominant group does, after all, maintain its basic power over them, whatever weakness some of its members may experience.

Because of this unavoidable and unalterable fact of their social existence, minorities also have need of myths. They live in communities that make possible, within the respective limits of their structural capacity, an institutionalized way of life, but they do not thereby exercise control over their life chances. Ultimately subject to dominant power, minority members are deprived of a certain psychic satisfaction, in addition to everything else. As long as they are treated like outsiders, they will make myths, creating their own gods in compensation for their suffering. Sometimes the minority myth is one of power, power exceeding the dimensions of natural possibility. The claim to the superhuman, however, is as much a denial of humanity as being considered subhuman. Yet minority members who have known humiliation are not always content to be mere mortals. Nevertheless, for all the functions of myth-making, and they are many for the demeaned minority, the only effective counter to categorical treatment is the declaration of humanity through the assertion of individuality.

Bibliography

*Allport, Gordon W., *The Nature of Prejudice*. Garden City, N.Y.: Doubleday Anchor Books, 1958.

Arensberg, Conrad M., and Solon T. Kimball, "Community Study: Retrospect and Prospect." *American Journal of Sociology,* Vol. 73, No. 6 (May 1968), pp. 691–705.

———, *Culture and Community.* New York: Harcourt, Brace & World, 1965.

Ayalti, Hanan, J., *Yiddish Proverbs.* New York: Schocken Books, 1963.

Babchuk, Nicholas, and Ralph V. Thompson, "The Voluntary Associations of Negroes." *American Sociological Review,* Vol. 27, No. 5 (October 1962), pp. 647–55.

Baldwin, James, *Notes of a Native Son.* Boston: Beacon Press, 1955.

Banton, Michael, *Race Relations.* New York: Basic Books, 1967.

Barclay, Allan G., and D. R. Cusumano, "Testing Masculinity in Boys Without Fathers." *Trans-Action,* Vol. 5, No. 2 (December 1967), pp. 33–35.

*Berger, Peter L., *Invitation to Sociology.* Garden City, N.Y.: Doubleday Anchor Books, 1963.

*Bernard, Jessie, *Marriage and Family Among Negroes.* Englewood Cliffs, N.J.: Prentice-Hall, A Spectrum Book, 1966.

Berry, Brewton, *Race and Ethnic Relations.* Boston: Houghton Mifflin Co., 1965.

*Billingsley, Andrew, *Black Families in White America.* Englewood Cliffs, N.J.: Prentice-Hall, A Spectrum Book, 1968.

Breton, Raymond, "Institutional Completeness of Ethnic Communities and the Personal Relations of Immigrants." *American Journal of Sociology,* Vol. 70, No. 2 (September 1964), pp. 193–205.

Broom, Leonard, and John I. Kitsuse, *The Managed Casualty.* Berkeley: University of California Press, 1956.

———, and Norval D. Glenn, *Transformation of the Negro American.* New York: Harper & Row, 1965.

———, and Eshrel Shevky, "Mexicans in the United States: A Problem in Social Differentiation." *Sociology and Social Research,* Vol. 36, No. 3 (January–February 1952), pp. 150–58.

Burma, John H., *Spanish-Speaking Groups in the United States.* Durham, N.C.: Duke University Press, 1954.

*Caudill, William, and George De Vos, "Achievement, Culture, and Personality: The Case of the Japanese American." In *Racial and Ethnic Relations,* edited by Bernard E. Segal. New York: Thomas Y. Crowell, 1966, pp. 77–89.

*Cayton, Horace R., "The Psychology of the Negro Under Discrimination." In *Minority Problems,* edited by Arnold M. Rose and Caroline B. Rose. New York: Harper & Row, 1965, pp. 210–19.

*Indicates paperback edition.

*Clark, Kenneth B., *Dark Ghetto: Dilemmas of Social Power.* New York: Harper & Row, Harper Torchbooks, 1965.

*Cleaver, Eldridge, *Soul on Ice.* New York: Dell, A Delta Book, 1968.

Coles, Robert, *Children of Crisis.* Boston: Little, Brown & Co., 1964.

Davie, Maurice R., *Negroes in American Society.* New York: McGraw-Hill, 1949.

*Dollard, John, *Caste and Class in a Southern Town.* Garden City, N.Y.: Doubleday Anchor Books, 1957. Originally published in 1937.

*Drake, St. Clair, and Horace R. Cayton, *Black Metropolis: A Study of Negro Life in a Northern City.* 2 vols. New York: Harper & Row, Harper Torchbooks, 1962. Originally published in 1945.

Duncan, Beverly, and Otis Dudley Duncan, "Minorities and the Process of Stratification." *American Sociological Review,* Vol. 33, No. 3 (June 1968), pp. 356–64.

Edwards, G. Franklin, *The Negro Professional Class.* New York: Free Press, 1959.

Elkins, Stanley M., *Slavery.* Chicago: University of Chicago Press, 1959.

Ellison, Ralph, *Shadow and Act.* New York: Random House, 1953.

Erikson, Erik H., *Identity: Youth and Crisis.* New York: W. W. Norton, 1968.

*Essien-Udom, E. U., *Black Nationalism.* New York: Dell, 1962.

Fanon, Frantz, *Black Skin, White Masks.* New York: Grove Press, 1967.

Fichter, Joseph H., S.J., *Social Relations in the Urban Parish.* Chicago: University of Chicago Press, 1954.

———, "The Marginal Catholic: An Institutional Approach." *Social Forces,* Vol. 32, No. 2 (December 1953), pp. 167–73.

*Fitzpatrick, Joseph P., "The Adjustment of Puerto Ricans to New York City." In *Minorities in a Changing World,* edited by Milton L. Barron. New York: Alfred A. Knopf, 1967, pp. 277–88.

Fong, Stanley F. M., "Assimilation of Chinese in America: Changes in Orientation and Social Perception." *American Journal of Sociology,* Vol. 71, No. 3 (November 1965), pp. 265–73.

Francis, E. K., "The Nature of the Ethnic Group." *American Journal of Sociology,* Vol. 52, No. 5 (March 1947), pp. 393–400.

Frazier, E. Franklin, "The Ambivalence of Negro Intellectuals." In *Negro Protest Thought in the Twentieth Century,* edited by Francis L. Broderick and August Meier. Indianapolis, Ind.: Bobbs-Merrill, 1965, pp. 97–102. This essay originally was written in 1927.

———, *Black Bourgeoisie.* New York: Free Press, 1957.

———, *Negro Youth at the Crossways.* Washington, D.C.: American Council on Education, 1940.

———, "The Negro Family in Chicago." In *Contributions to Urban Sociology,* edited by Ernest W. Burgess and Donald J. Bogue. Chicago: University of Chicago Press, 1964, pp. 404–18.

———, "The Negro's Vested Interest in Segregation." In *Race Prejudice and Discrimination,* edited by Arnold M. Rose. New York: Alfred A. Knopf, 1953, pp. 332–39.

Freeman, Howard E., et al., "Color Gradation and Attitudes Among Middle-Income Negroes." *American Sociological Review,* Vol. 31, No. 3 (June 1966), pp. 365–74.

Gans, Herbert J., *The Urban Villagers*. New York: Free Press, 1962.

Glazer, Nathan, "Negroes and Jews: The New Challenge to Pluralism." *Commentary*, Vol. 38, No. 6 (December 1964), pp. 29–34.

*———, "The Peoples of America." In *Minorities in a Changing World*, edited by Milton L. Barron. New York: Alfred A. Knopf, 1967, pp. 139–49.

———, "The Puerto Ricans." *Commentary*, Vol. 36, No. 1 (July 1963), pp. 1–9.

———, and Daniel P. Moynihan, *Beyond the Melting Pot*. Cambridge, Mass.: The M.I.T. and Harvard University Press, 1963.

Glenn, Norval D., "Negro Prestige Criteria: A Case Study in the Bases of Prestige." *American Journal of Sociology*, Vol. 68, No. 6 (May 1963), pp. 645–57.

———, and Ruth Hyland, "Religious Preference and Worldly Success: Some Evidence from National Surveys." *American Sociological Review*, Vol. 32, No. 1 (February 1967), pp. 73–85.

*Goffman, Erving, *Stigma: Notes on the Management of Spoiled Identity*. Englewood Cliffs, N.J.: Prentice-Hall, A Spectrum Book, 1963.

Goldstein, Sidney, and Calvin Goldscheider, *Jewish Americans: Three Generations in a Jewish Community*. Englewood Cliffs, N.J.: Prentice-Hall, 1968.

*Gordon, Milton M., *Assimilation in American Life*. New York: Oxford University Press, 1964.

———, "Assimilation in America: Theory and Reality." *Daedalus*, Spring, 1961, pp. 263–85.

Greeley, Andrew M., "Influence of the 'Religious Factor' on Career Plans and Occupational Values of College Graduates." *American Journal of Sociology*, Vol. 68, No. 6 (May 1963), pp. 658–71.

Grier, William H., and Price M. Cobbs, *Black Rage*. New York: Basic Books, 1968.

*Hagan, William T., *American Indians*. Chicago: University of Chicago Press, 1961.

Handlin, Oscar, "Historical Perspectives on the American Ethnic Group." *Daedalus*, Spring, 1961, pp. 220–32.

———, *The Newcomers*. Cambridge, Mass.: Harvard University Press, 1959.

———, *The Uprooted*. Boston: Little, Brown & Co., 1951.

Hannerz, Ulf, "What Negroes Mean by 'Soul.' " *Trans-Action*, Vol. 5, No. 8 (July-August 1968), pp. 57–61.

*Hapgood, Hutchins, *The Spirit of the Ghetto*. New York: Schocken Books, 1902, 1966. Preface and notes by Harry Golden.

Heller, Celia Stopnicka, "Class as an Explanation of Ethnic Differences in Mobility Aspirations." *International Migration Review*, Vol. 2 (Fall, 1967), pp. 31–39.

*———, *Mexican American Youth: Forgotten Youth at the Crossroads*. New York: Random House, Studies in Sociology, 1966.

Herberg, Will, *Protestant–Catholic–Jew*. Garden City, N.Y.: Doubleday, 1956.

Hill, Mozell C., "A Comparative Analysis of the Social Organization of the All-Negro Society in Oklahoma." *Social Forces*, Vol. 25, No. 1 (October 1946), pp. 70–77.

Horton, John, "Order and Conflict Theories of Social Problems as Competing Ideologies." *American Journal of Sociology*, Vol. 71, No. 6 (May 1966), pp. 701–13.

Hughes, Everett C., and Helen M. Hughes, *Where Peoples Meet.* New York: Free Press, 1952. See especially Chapter 7, "Status and Identity," pp. 100–15.

Jackson, Elton F., "Status Consistency and Symptoms of Stress." *American Sociological Review,* Vol. 27, No. 4 (August 1962), pp. 469–80.

Johnson, Charles S., *Growing Up in the Black Belt.* Washington, D.C.: American Council on Education, 1941.

*Joseph, Stephen M., ed., *The Me Nobody Knows: Children's Voices from the Ghetto.* New York: Avon Books, Discus Books, 1969.

*Kardiner, Abram, and Lionel Ovesey, *The Mark of Oppression.* Cleveland, Ohio: World Publishing Co., Meridian Books, 1962. Originally published in 1951.

Kelly, William H., "The Economic Basis of Indian Life." *The Annals of the American Academy of Political and Social Science,* Vol. 311 (May 1957), pp. 71–79.

*Killian, Lewis M., *The Impossible Revolution?* New York: Random House, Studies in Sociology, 1968.

*———, and Charles Grigg, *Racial Crisis in America.* Englewood Cliffs, N.J.: Prentice-Hall, A Spectrum Book, 1964.

*Kitagawa, Daisuke, "The American Indian." In *Minority Problems,* edited by Arnold M. Rose and Caroline B. Rose. New York: Harper & Row, 1965, pp. 26–32.

Kramer, Judith R., and Seymour Leventman, *Children of the Gilded Ghetto.* New Haven, Conn.: Yale University Press, 1961.

Lenski, Gerhard, *The Religious Factor.* Garden City, N.Y.: Doubleday, 1961.

*Leo, John, "The American Catholic Is Changing." In *Minorities in a Changing World,* edited by Milton L. Barron. New York: Alfred A. Knopf, 1967, pp. 305–14.

Lewin, Kurt, "Self-Hatred Among Jews." In *Race Prejudice and Discrimination,* edited by Arnold M. Rose. New York: Alfred A. Knopf, 1953, pp. 321–32.

*Lewis, Hylan, "Agenda Paper No. V: The Family: Resources for Change—Planning Sessions for the White House Conference 'To Fulfill These Rights,' November 16–18, 1965." In *The Moynihan Report and the Politics of Controversy,* by Lee Rainwater and William L. Yancey. Cambridge, Mass.: The M.I.T. Press, 1967, pp. 314–43.

*———, *Blackways of Kent.* New Haven, Conn.: College and University Press, 1964. Originally published in 1955.

*———, "Culture, Class, and Family Life Among Low-Income Urban Negroes." in *Employment, Race, and Poverty,* edited by Arthur M. Ross and Herbert Hill. New York: Harcourt, Brace & World, A Harbinger Book, 1967, pp. 149–72.

*———, *Culture, Class, and Poverty.* Washington, D.C.: CROSS-TELL, 1967.

*Lewis, Oscar, *La Vida.* New York: Random House, Vintage Books, 1968.

Lieberson, Stanley J., "A Societal Theory of Race and Ethnic Relations." *American Sociological Review,* Vol. 26, No. 6 (December 1961), pp. 902–10.

———, "The Old-New Distinction and Immigrants in Australia." *American Sociological Review,* Vol. 28, No. 4 (August 1963), pp. 550–65.

———, and Arnold R. Silverman, "The Precipitants and Underlying Conditions of Race Riots." *American Sociological Review,* Vol. 30, No. 6 (December 1965), p. 897.

*Liebow, Elliott, *Tally's Corner.* Boston: Little, Brown & Co. 1967.

*Lincoln, C. Eric, *The Black Muslims in America.* Boston: Beacon Press, 1961.

Lopata, Helena Znaniecki, "The Function of Voluntary Associations in an Ethnic Community: 'Polonia.' " In *Contributions to Urban Sociology,* edited by Ernest W. Burgess and Donald J. Bogue. Chicago: University of Chicago Press, 1964, pp. 203–23.

MacIver, Robert M., *Community.* 3rd ed. New York: Macmillan, 1931.

*McNickle, D'Arcy, *The Indian Tribes of the United States.* London: Oxford University Press, 1962.

McWilliams, Carey, *Brothers Under the Skin.* Rev. ed. Boston: Little, Brown & Co., 1951.

*Madsen, William, *Mexican-Americans of South Texas.* New York: Holt, Rinehart & Winston, 1964.

*Malcolm X, with the assistance of Alex Haley, *The Autobiography of Malcolm X.* New York: Grove Press, 1964.

Manasse, Ernest M., "Max Weber on Race." *Social Research,* Vol. 14 (June 1947), pp. 191–221.

Marden, Charles F., and Gladys Meyer, *Minorities in American Society.* 2nd ed. New York: American Book Co., 1962.

Martindale, Don, *American Social Structure.* New York: Appleton-Century-Crofts, 1960.

———, *Community, Character and Civilization.* New York: Free Press, 1963.

Marx, Gary T., "Religion: Opiate or Inspiration of Civil Rights Militancy Among Negroes?" *American Sociological Review,* Vol. 32, No. 1 (February 1967), pp. 64–72.

———, *North from Mexico.* Philadelphia: Lippincott Co., 1949.

Memmi, Albert, "Does the Jew Exist?" *Commentary,* Vol. 42, No. 5 (November 1966), pp. 73–76.

Merton, Robert K., "The Self-Fulfilling Prophecy." In *Social Theory and Social Structure.* Rev. ed. New York: Free Press, 1957, pp. 421–36.

Mills, C. Wright, Clarence Senior, and Rose K. Golden, *The Puerto Rican Journey.* New York: Harper & Row, 1950.

Mittelbach, Frank G., and Joan H. Moore, "Ethnic Endogamy—The Case of Mexican Americans." *American Journal of Sociology,* Vol. 74, No. 1 (July 1968), pp. 50–62.

Moynihan, Daniel P., "The Irish of New York." *Commentary,* Vol. 36, No. 2 (August 1963), pp. 93–107.

Myrdal, Gunnar, with the assistance of Richard Sterner and Arnold Rose, *An American Dilemma.* New York: Harper & Bros. 1944.

Nabokov, Peter, "The Peyote Road." *The New York Times Magazine* (March 9, 1969), pp. 30–31, 129 ff.

Nisbet, Robert A., *The Sociological Tradition.* New York: Basic Books, 1966.

Noel, Donald L., "Group Identification Among Negroes: An Empirical Analysis." *The Journal of Social Issues,* Vol. 20, No. 2 (April 1964), pp. 71–84.

Novak, Michael, "American Catholicism after the Council." *Commentary,* Vol. 40, No. 2 (August 1965), pp. 50–58.

Orum, Anthony M., "A Reappraisal of the Social and Political Participation of

Negroes." *American Journal of Sociology,* Vol. 72, No. 1 (July 1966), pp. 32–46.

Padilla, Elena, *Up from Puerto Rico.* New York: Columbia University Press, 1958.

Park, Robert E., *Human Communities.* New York: Free Press, 1952.

———, "The Nature of Race Relations." In *Race and Culture.* New York: Free Press, 1950, pp. 81–116.

Pettigrew, Thomas F., *A Profile of the Negro American.* Princeton, N.J.: Van Nostrand, 1964.

———, "Negro American Personality: Why Isn't More Known?" *The Journal of Social Issues,* Vol. 20, No. 2 (April 1964), pp. 4–23.

*Pinkney, Alphonso, *Black Americans.* Englewood Cliffs, N.J.: Prentice-Hall, 1969.

Poll, Solomon, *The Hasidic Community of Williamsburg.* New York: Free Press, 1962.

*Porter, John, *The Vertical Mosaic.* Toronto: University of Toronto Press, 1965.

Poussaint, Alvin F., "A Negro Psychiatrist Explains the Negro Psyche." *The New York Times Magazine* (August 20, 1967), pp. 52–53 ff.

*Powdermaker, Hortense, *After Freedom.* New York: Atheneum, 1968. Originally published in 1939.

*———, *Stranger and Friend: The Way of an Anthropologist.* New York: W. W. Norton, 1967, pp. 129–205.

Rainwater, Lee, "Crucible of Identity: The Negro Lower-Class Family." *Daedalus,* Winter, 1966, pp. 172–216.

Rand, Christopher, *The Puerto Ricans.* New York: Oxford University Press, 1958.

Ransford, H. Edward, "Isolation, Powerlessness, and Violence: A Study of Attitudes and Participation in the Watts Riot." *American Journal of Sociology.* Vol. 73, No. 5 (March 1968), pp. 581–91.

*Redding, J. Saunders, *On Being Negro in America.* Indianapolis, Ind.: Bobbs-Merrill, Charter Books, 1962. Originally published in 1951.

Ringer, Benjamin B., *The Edge of Friendliness: A Study of Jewish-Gentile Relations.* New York: Basic Books, 1967.

*Rohrer, John H., and Munro S. Edmonson, *The Eighth Generation Grows Up.* New York: Harper & Row, Harper Torchbooks, 1960.

*Rose, Peter I., *They and We.* New York: Random House, 1964.

Rosenberg, Morris, "The Dissonant Religious Context and Emotional Disturbance." *American Journal of Sociology,* Vol. 68, No. 1 (July 1962), pp. 1–10.

Rosenthal, Erich, "Acculturation Without Assimilation? The Jewish Community of Chicago, Illinois." *American Journal of Sociology,* Vol. 66, No. 3 (November 1960), pp. 275–88.

*Sartre, Jean-Paul, *Anti-Semite and Jew.* Translated by George J. Becker. New York: Grove Press, Black Cat Books, 1962. Originally published in 1948.

Seligman, Ben B., *Permanent Poverty: An American Syndrome.* Chicago: Quadrangle Books, 1968.

Shibutani, Tamotsu, and Kian M. Kwan, *Ethnic Stratification.* With contributions by Robert H. Billigmeier. New York: Macmillan, 1965.

*Silberman, Charles E., *Crisis in Black and White.* New York: Random House, Vintage Books, 1965.

*Simmons, Ozzie G., "The Mutual Images and Expectations of Anglo-Americans and Mexican-Americans." In *Minorities in a Changing World,* edited by Milton L. Barron. New York: Alfred A. Knopf, 1967, pp. 289–304.

Simpson, George E., and J. Milton Yinger, *Racial and Cultural Minorities.* 3rd. ed. New York: Harper & Row, 1965.

Sirjamaki, John, *The Sociology of the Cities.* New York: Random House, 1964.

Siu, Paul C. P., "The Isolation of the Chinese Laundryman." In *Contributions to Urban Sociology,* edited by Ernest W. Burgess and Donald J. Bogue. Chicago: University of Chicago Press, 1964, pp. 429–42.

Sklare, Marshall, and Joseph Greenblum, *Jewish Identity on the Suburban Frontier: A Study of Group Survival in the Open Society.* New York: Basic Books, 1967.

Stein, Maurice R. *The Eclipse of Community.* Princeton, N.J.: Princeton University Press, 1960.

Steiner, Stan, *The New Indians.* New York: Harper & Row, 1968.

Stonequist, Everett V., *The Marginal Man.* New York: Charles Scribner's Sons, 1937.

————, "The Marginal Man: A Study in Personality and Culture Conflict." In *Contributions to Urban Sociology,* edited by Ernest W. Burgess and Donald J. Bogue. Chicago: University of Chicago Press, 1964, pp. 327–45.

Strodtbeck, Fred L., "Family Interaction, Values, and Achievement." In *Talent and Society,* edited by David C. McClelland, Alfred L. Baldwin, Urie Bronfenbrenner, and Fred L. Strodtbeck. Princeton, N.J.: Van Nostrand, 1958, pp. 135–94.

Sutherland, Robert L., *Color, Class, and Personality.* Washington, D.C.: American Council on Education, 1942.

*Thomas, Piri, *Down These Mean Streets.* New York: New American Library, Signet Books, 1968.

Thomas, William I., and Florian Znaniecki, *The Polish Peasant in Europe and America.* Chicago: University of Chicago Press, 1918.

Thompson, Daniel, "The Formation of Social Attitudes." In *Racial and Ethnic Relations,* edited by Bernard E. Segal. New York: Thomas Y. Crowell, 1966, pp. 97–110.

Tuck, Ruth D., *Not With the Fist.* New York: Harcourt, Brace & Co. 1946.

Van den Berghe, Pierre L., *Race and Racism.* New York: John Wiley & Sons, 1967.

Vogt, Evon Z., "The Acculturation of American Indians." *The Annals of the American Academy of Political and Social Science,* Vol. 311 (May 1957), pp. 137–46.

Wakefield, Dan, *Island in the City.* Boston: Houghton Mifflin Co., 1959.

Ware, Carolyn F., "Ethnic Communities." *Encyclopedia of the Social Sciences,* Vol. 5, pp. 607–13.

Warner, W. Lloyd, and Leo Srole, *The Social Systems of American Ethnic Groups.* Yankee City Series, Vol. 3. New Haven, Conn.: Yale University Press, 1945.

Weaver, Robert C., *The Negro Ghetto.* New York: Harcourt, Brace & Co., 1948.

Weber, Max, *Ancient Judaism.* Translated and edited by Hans H. Gerth and Don Martindale. New York: Free Press, 1952.

*————, *Basic Concepts in Sociology.* Translated by H. P. Secher. New York: The Citadel Press, 1963.

*————, "Class, Status, Party." In *From Max Weber: Essays in Sociology,* translated by Hans H. Gerth and C. Wright Mills. New York: Oxford University Press, Galaxy Books, 1958, pp. 180–195.

Wellman, David, "The *Wrong* Way to Find Jobs for Negroes." *Trans-Action,* Vol. 5, No. 5 (April 1968), pp. 9–18.

Whitten, Norman E., Jr., and John Szwed, "Introduction: Negroes in the New World, Anthropologists Look at Afro-Americans." *Trans-Action,* Vol. 5, No. 8 (July–August 1968), pp. 49–56.

Whyte, William Foote, *Street Corner Society.* Chicago: University of Chicago Press, 1955. Originally published in 1943.

Wilensky, Harold L., and Jack Ladinsky, "From Religious Community to Occupational Group: Structural Assimilation Among Professors, Lawyers, and Engineers." *American Sociological Review,* Vol. 32, No. 4 (August 1967), pp. 541–61.

Williams, Robin M., Jr., *Strangers Next Door.* Englewood Cliffs, N.J.: Prentice-Hall, 1964.

Winch, Robert F., Scott Greer, and Rae Lesser Blumberg, "Ethnicity and Extended Familism in an Upper-Middle-Class Suburb." *American Sociological Review,* Vol. 32, No. 2 (April 1967), pp. 265–72.

*Wirth, Louis, "Culture Conflict and Misconduct." In *On Cities and Social Life,* edited by Albert J. Reiss, Jr. Chicago: University of Chicago Press, Phoenix Books, 1964, pp. 229–43.

*————, "The Ghetto." In *On Cities and Social Life,* edited by Albert J. Reiss, Jr. Chicago: University of Chicago Press, Phoenix Books, 1964, pp. 84–98.

*————, *The Ghetto.* Chicago: University of Chicago Press, Phoenix Books, 1958. Originally published in 1928.

*————, "The Problems of Minority Groups." In *On Cities and Social Life,* edited by Albert J. Reiss, Jr. Chicago: University of Chicago Press, Phoenix Books, 1964, pp. 244–69.

*Wissler, Clark, *Indians of the United States.* Revisions by Lucy W. Kluckhohn. Garden City, N.Y.: Doubleday Anchor Books, 1967 ed.

*Wood, Arthur Evans, *Hamtramck.* New Haven, Conn.: College and University Press, 1962.

*Yinger, J. Milton, *A Minority Group in American Society.* New York: McGraw-Hill, 1965.

————, "Social Forces Involved in Group Identification or Withdrawal." *Daedalus,* Spring, 1961, pp. 247–62.

*Yuan, D. Y. "Voluntary Segregation: A Study of New York Chinatown." In *Minorities in a Changing World,* edited by Milton L. Barron. New York: Alfred A. Knopf, 1967, pp. 263–76.

Zola, Irving Kenneth, "Culture and Symptoms—An Analysis of Patients' Presenting Complaints." *American Sociological Review,* Vol. 31, No. 5 (October 1966), pp. 615–30.

Zorbaugh, Harvey W., *The Gold Coast and the Slum.* Chicago: University of Chicago Press, 1929.

INDEX

Index